PQ   69-6561
2123   Russell
R8   Voltaire, Dryen &
1966   Heroic tragedy

Date Due			
		JUL	2000
		JUN	2004
JUL	X X 2015		
		JUN 09	

VOLTAIRE, DRYDEN
& HEROIC TRAGEDY

VOLTAIRE, DRYDEN & HEROIC TRAGEDY

BY TRUSTEN WHEELER RUSSELL

AMS PRESS, INC.
NEW YORK
1966

Copyright 1946, Columbia University Press
New York

Reprinted 1966
with permission of Columbia University Press

AMS PRESS, INC.
New York, N.Y. 10003

Manufactured in the United States of America

To the memory of my brother

JOSEPH PARKER RUSSELL

PREFACE

THE LIMITS of this study, at first simply an inquiry into the relations of Voltaire with Dryden, have gradually been extended as the effect of epic theory upon Voltaire's critical writings and plays became apparent. Dryden's conception of heroic tragedy has already been studied in numerous books and articles, and it has been generally recognized that his ideal was derived from a definite body of French critical dogma. In my own investigation I became convinced that the impact of French epic doctrine was direct and powerful and certainly significant in the case of Voltaire himself and that it would be worth while to re-examine his dramatic theory and practice in the light of this immediate influence. I have therefore attempted to build a background of dramatic criticism between 1650 and 1750 and then place Voltaire's critical comments and his plays against it. It also became evident that Voltaire thought of English tragedy and particularly of Dryden as possessing the epic qualities which he felt were lacking in the current French theater. Specific instances of Voltaire's direct knowledge of Dryden have been brought together and reviewed in a transition chapter. The analogy between Voltaire and Dryden has proved constantly useful, for Dryden was clear and precise in defining and defending his literary aim, while Voltaire apparently felt no need of justification since the gospel of epic tragedy had been preached by several generations of French critics.

Voltaire, not only in the *Henriade* and in his tragedies but in his life and writings in general, consciously sought to fulfill the neoclassic ideal of the epic poet, a fact that is relevant to this study although not my chief concern. According to this conception the poet should be legislator, philosopher, monarch of all the sciences, and a kind of preceptor to the state. Despite the pedantry and pomp of some of its seventeenth-century expositors there is something noble and civilized, something, perhaps, essentially French in this ideal. That Voltaire embodied it so worthily is, I think, one of his claims to greatness.

The edition of Voltaire's works quoted is that of Moland (52 volumes, Garnier, Paris, 1877–85). References are to "Œuvres," volume and page. For Dryden I have used the Scott-Saintsbury edition (18 volumes, London, 1882–93) except for the plays, for which I have gone to the Nonesuch

Press edition (London, 1931–32), edited by Montague Summers. The former is referred to as "Works" and the latter as "Nonesuch ed." In quotations the original spelling and punctuation have been followed. Dates of plays refer to first performances.

Most of my research was done at the Columbia University Library, the New York Public Library, and the Widener Library; my sincere thanks are due for their courteous assistance.

I am grateful for helpful criticism to members of the French and English faculties of Columbia University who read this work in manuscript. It is a particular pleasure to acknowledge my indebtedness to Professor Norman L. Torrey for many constructive suggestions while the work was in progress. Professor Jeanne Varney made a number of most valuable suggestions in regard to the chapter on Voltaire's style. I desire to express my thanks also to Professor Thomas W. Swedenberg, of the University of California at Los Angeles for permitting me to consult his work, before its publication, on the neoclassic theory of the epic in England.

This study owes very much to my late brother Joseph Parker Russell, whose broad humanism has been an inspiration and whose resources of insight and encouragement were always so generously at my command.

TRUSTEN WHEELER RUSSELL

New York
January 15, 1946

CONTENTS

CHAPTER I   INTRODUCTION

VOLTAIRE's program for renewing French tragedy was essentially that of Rapin, Le Bossu, and Dacier, whose critical treatises, published during the last quarter of the seventeenth century, were decisive influences in determining the critical climate of France and England for three generations. These critics maintained that since tragedy was essentially an epic poem in dramatic form, it should, like the epic poem, teach a moral lesson useful to the state, portray noble heroes to serve as examples of conduct, and be expressed in a metaphorical and elevated epic style. They did not originate this theory of the affinity between epic poem and tragedy, for it was inherent in neoclassic criticism; they simply gave it new emphasis and precision. In England similar views were held, and the Restoration and Augustan ages produced a kind of heroic tragedy, best represented by the plays of Dryden and by such formal Augustan tragedies as Addison's *Cato,* which was similar in many respects, particularly with regard to critical conception, to that of Voltaire. I have undertaken to present the evidence of this heroic conception of tragedy, to trace its source in neoclassic theory, and to show its importance for understanding Voltaire's approach to the theater and his relations with the English stage.

For the neoclassic community of critics which dominated western Europe from 1650 to 1750, the didactic epic was the crowning glory of a nation's literature, the goal of all worthy poets, and tragedy was considered the representation in the theater of the mood and atmosphere of the epic poem. The epic poet was conceived to be a kind of official philosopher, whose role surpassed in importance even that of statesmen and military leaders. It was before such a background of extravagant homage to the epic genre that French poets of 1650–70 composed no less than forty epic poems. It was before this background that Milton conceived *Paradise Lost,* Dryden planned to write an *Arthuriad,* and Pope translated the *Iliad.*

There is evident in the writings of French critics of the final quarter of the seventeenth century a feeling of disappointment that France had somehow failed to find a great epic poet among the men of letters who graced the court of Louis XIV, a poet who could properly speak for the glorious age and commemorate it in enduring verse as Virgil had done for the age of Augustus. A kind of critical *enquête* was conducted into the failure of France to realize its supreme literary ambition, and the resulting deduction of French critics was apparently well expressed in Malézieu's celebrated remark that "les Français n'ont pas la tête épique." It was due partly to this feeling of frustration that critics in general and Dacier in particular tended to emphasize tragedy, a field in which they felt that France had more nearly approached perfection. It was generally conceded that the English possessed the seriousness and vigor, in both epic and tragic poetry, which the French lacked, although it was clearly perceived that the English were wholly without taste and were ignorant of or neglected the rules. In Milton, French critics recognized elements of outstanding epic genius, and in English tragedy they found a unique capacity for great and stirring subjects. Also the metaphorical style of English poetry, they acknowledged, reflected the robust character of the people and made Racine seem effeminate by comparison. Their conclusion was that a kind of tragedy surpassing that of both ancients and moderns would be created if English vigor could be combined with French taste and correctness. This formula came to be accepted, verbally at least, by many leading critics of the day, including Voltaire.

Voltaire's program for the reform of the French theater was to give epic elevation to tragedy by infusing a moral lesson, by portraying grandiose events, and by heightening the style. These objectives formed the essential basis of Dacier's conception of tragedy, and Dacier was of primary importance among early influences upon Voltaire. In turning to English drama Voltaire was influenced by the views of Rapin, Saint-Evremond, Muralt, DuBos, and numerous lesser critics who emphasized the superior capacity of the English for heroic poetry. Moreover, it was neoclassic Restoration and Augustan tragedy, epic in style and theory and dominated by operatic spectacle and political and religious propaganda which Voltaire saw when he visited England in 1726–28. Shakespeare was played only in expurgated and adapted versions, the genuine Shakespearean revival not coming until well after 1740, when restorations began to be made. Swift, for example, mentions Shakespeare only once in his writings, and Addison, in his *An Account of the Greatest English Poets,* makes no mention of him. When the

actor Quin, toward the middle of the century, heard Garrick read from
a restored version of *Macbeth,* he asked what play it was. Even Garrick
cut the grave diggers' scene from *Hamlet,* to Voltaire's satisfaction, and
Dryden and Davenant's opera version of *The Tempest* continued to be
preferred until early in the nineteenth century.

Voltaire found in the English Restoration and Augustan theaters not
only a conception of formal tragedy cast in the same artificial mold as his
own but also a philosophical content suited to his didactic purpose. Henri
Peyre, in his *Le Classicisme français* [1] points out that the neoclassic
period in England corresponds to two different periods in French literary
history. English neoclassicism was contemporary with the philosophical
and political speculations of Hobbes, Locke, and Mandeville and became permeated with the new ideas characteristic of the Enlightenment.
Neoclassic doctrine held that a poet, before composing a heroic poem,
should look about him and decide what lesson was most needed by his
nation. With the religious broils of the time constantly threatening a
renewal of civil war, there was no doubt in the minds of Hobbes,
Davenant, or Dryden that religious fanaticism was the chief evil of the
day, and they seized upon the new doctrines to bolster their arguments
against bigotry and to support their claims for a benevolent absolutism
in government. France, in contrast, had its period of neoclassicism under
Louis XIV, when liberalism in thought was officially frowned upon.
In France, consequently, the Enlightenment found little expression in
print until after the death of that monarch in 1715. It is not surprising
to have Voltaire say again and again that what struck him most in English literature was the ability of English poets to argue philosophical
and political questions in elevated verse.

In fine, the record indicates, I think, that the theory of heroic tragedy
inherent in neoclassic criticism and given new authority and precision
in the last quarter of the seventeenth century by the treatises of Rapin,
Le Bossu, and Dacier provides the background against which not only
Restoration and formal Augustan tragedy in England but the tragedies
of Voltaire as well must be placed. By examining Voltaire's acquaintance
with Dryden and the similarity not only of their conception of tragedy
but also of their philosophical point of view I have emphasized that it
was primarily the English theater of 1660–1725 which Voltaire had in

[1] Peyre, *Le Classicisme français,* p. 197.

mind in his own innovations, not the Elizabethan stage. To the extent that Shakespeare was played in London during the first half of the seventeenth century, his plays must be considered part of the background of Voltaire's views on the English theater, and there can be little doubt that Voltaire borrowed some exterior incidents from Shakespeare's plays, as he did from a heterogeneous group of London productions. In speaking of Dryden I have stressed the Dryden of the *Essay of Heroique Plays* rather than the Dryden of the *Preface to the Fables,* because I believe that Voltaire never comprehended the underlying respect of Dryden for Shakespeare, but took him at his word when, at the height of his favor at the Stuart court, he declared that Shakespeare had written when English poetry was in its infancy and men were dull and conversation was low.

The heroic quality of Voltaire's conception of tragedy has been recognized in a general way in recent Voltairian criticism. Emile Faguet, in commenting upon Voltaire's idea of the proper subject matter for tragedy, said that Voltaire thought that tragedy ought to be "un poème historique, ou même épique, mis sur la scène." Similarly André Bellessort, in his *Essai sur Voltaire,* in 1925, has the following to say in respect to the essential nature of tragedy as Voltaire saw it:

C'était bien ainsi qu'il concevait la tragédie: la plus touchante des prédications, l'exaltation de la vertu, le spectacle effrayant du danger des passions, un appel à l'humanité dans un langage qui ne ressemble pas à celui du peuple et dont la pompe doit avoir quelque chose de sublime, devant une assemblée des plus belles personnes et des plus grands personnages.[2]

Here, without saying "heroic" and without reference to critical doctrines, Bellessort has given a definition of tragedy substantially as Dacier gave it: a moral lesson in elevated style portraying "grandeur d'âme" for the admiration and imitation of the nobility. Raymond Naves, in his *Le Goût de Voltaire* (1938), defines epic in terms of style and says that for the eighteenth century it was "la présentation cérémonieuse, fiereté du ton, style sentencieux et magnifique" and that it was exemplified in Voltaire's tragedies. Naves writes:

Le génie épique de Voltaire est incontestable, mais ce n'est sûrement pas dans la *Henriade* qu'il apparaît le mieux, car il revêt beaucoup plus aisément la forme oratoire que la forme narrative. C'est lui qui anime à peu près toutes

[2] Bellessort, *Essai sur Voltaire,* p. 82.

ses tragédies, particulièrement les tragédies historiques qui, nous l'avons vu, correspondent le mieux à son goût. Alimenté par certaines ressources du théâtre anglais, il répand d'abord autour de ces pièces une atmosphère de combat, ou d'émeute, un cliquetis d'armes, des échos de fanfares et de clameurs populaires, extrêmement propices au développement de la psychologie héroïque. Puis il se répand dans la trame des scènes, il colore l'éloquence et renforce la versification.[3]

To provide perspective for a discussion of Voltaire's relations with the English theater it is essential to review the course of critical opinion in this regard. That there was a relation between Voltaire's *Alzire* and Dryden's *The Indian Emperour* was evidently the belief 'of the Abbé Dubourg as early as 1743, for in translating Dryden's play he changed the name of the Indian Queen to "Alsyre." To the Abbé Yart, ten years later, the resemblance of *Alzire* to *The Indian Emperour* was the most obvious manifestation of Voltaire's interest in the English theater.

Two early nineteenth-century critics, Villemain and Demogeot, emphasized Voltaire's interest in Restoration and Augustan tragedy. Villemain said that *La Mort de César* and *Brutus* reflected the influence of Addison's *Cato* rather than of Shakespeare's Roman plays and that Voltaire had even borrowed from Addison's play "quelques beaux traits." Of Dryden, Villemain said that Voltaire "dans son théâtre, a beaucoup profité de ce brillant poète. Il y a des ressemblances assez marquées entre la pompe de son *Alzire,* de sa *Sémiramis,* et ces belles tirades rimées de Dryden, surchargées d'images élégantes, mais un peu communes." Demogeot, in his history of French literature, remarked similarly that Voltaire took Dryden "plus d'une fois pour modèle" and that "comme chez notre brillant compatriote, on rencontre dans les tragédies de Dryden la tirade à effet, la sentence ambitieuse, l'image éclatante, mais anti-dramatique."

After the middle of the nineteenth century Voltaire's numerous references to Shakespeare are taken more at their face value, and critics accept the name of Shakespeare as a satisfactory symbol for the English theater in respect to any possible influence upon Voltaire. Voltaire's *Brutus* and *La Mort de César* are commonly linked with *Julius Caesar,* *Zaïre* with *Othello, Eriphyle* and *Sémiramis* with *Hamlet,* and *Mahomet* with *Macbeth.* Albert Lacroix, in his *De l'influence de Shakespeare dans la littérature française,* 1856, assumes that Voltaire's stage innovations, in

---

[3] Naves, *Le Goût de Voltaire,* p. 475.

so far as they represent English influence, were inspired by Shakespeare. Henri Lion, in his *Les Tragédies de Voltaire,* 1895, takes a similar point of view. He thinks, for instance, that Voltaire should have mentioned his obligation to Shakespeare's *Othello* in his preface to *Zaïre.*[4]

Texte, in his *Rousseau et les origines du cosmopolitisme littéraire,* 1895, says that Voltaire's references to English literature are for the most part second hand and can be traced in critical comments of previous English and French writers. But Texte accepts the view that Shakespeare is the chief influence in regard to Voltaire's relations with the English theater. The same is true of the studies of Jusserand and Lounsbury. Jusserand, in his *Shakespeare en France,* published in 1899, mentions the resemblance between Voltaire's Roman plays and *Julius Caesar,* between *Zaïre* and *Othello, Eriphyle* and *Hamlet.* Lounsbury in his *Shakespeare and Voltaire,* in 1902, asserts that no dramatist ever owed to another a more distinctive obligation than Voltaire did to Shakespeare,[5] and he scolds Voltaire for not admitting that in *Zaïre* he was adapting *Othello.* He finds the "calumnies" against Shakespeare in the preface to *Sémiramis* an attempt by Voltaire to conceal his debt to *Hamlet.*

But in all these studies it is also recognized that there is a gulf which separates the dramatic conceptions of Voltaire and Shakespeare. Lion says that the manner in which Voltaire uses suggestions from Shakespeare reveals his total lack of comprehension of Shakespeare. Texte and Jusserand agree that Voltaire's borrowings are wholly exterior and indicate his superficial understanding of the plays he went to. Lounsbury declares that, although Voltaire's Roman plays were probably inspired by Shakespeare, it is extremely difficult to trace any real influence, and he concludes that Voltaire, due to innate lack of insight into man's spiritual nature, did not comprehend the true nature of Shakespeare. Texte, Jusserand, and Lounsbury all agree, also, that Voltaire's blindness in regard to Shakespeare was characteristic of the literary age, not only in France but in England as well, and that Voltaire's opinions of Shakespeare were an accurate reflection of the ideas of Bolingbroke, Chesterfield, and other contemporary Englishmen with whom Voltaire talked.

Lanson, in his *Histoire de la littérature française,* 1894, and Faguet, in

---

[4] Lion, *Les Tragédies et les théories dramatiques de Voltaire,* p. 73.
[5] Lounsbury, *Shakespeare and Voltaire,* p. 119.

several studies brought out in 1900, lend strength to the view that Voltaire's dramatic conceptions were more in harmony with the English theater of 1660–1725 than with Shakespeare. Lanson says that the Restoration and the reign of Queen Anne were the periods when English and French critical ideas drew near enough together to allow an interpenetration of influence. Dryden gave to Voltaire "l'idée d'un drame plus violent; Addison, par son *Caton,* l'instruisit à moraliser la tragédie, à y poser nettement la thèse philosophique."

Faguet, in university lectures published in the *Revue des cours et conférences,* concurs in Lanson's opinion that *Brutus* and *La Mort de César* were experiments in imitation of English Augustan tragedy. Faguet repeats that Voltaire's judgments of Shakespeare were the opinions of the English critics of the period and were based on neoclassic critical conceptions. But Faguet says also that Voltaire's chief debt to English drama was the idea of putting heroes from his own country's history on the stage, and that it was Shakespeare's historical tragedies which gave him the idea.

Edouard Sonet, in his *Voltaire et l'influence anglaise,* published in 1926, revived to a certain extent the question of Voltaire's debt to Dryden. He points out that neoclassic critics of England generally preferred Dryden to Shakespeare and that Voltaire accepted their viewpoint. Sonet says that Voltaire's opinions of Shakespeare reflected his reading of Dryden's dramatic criticism and that Voltaire's dramatic style was, to a certain extent, influenced by Dryden's.

Voltaire emprunta à Dryden [writes Sonet] une certaine élégance, un certain luxe de langage, certains détails brillants [but Sonet adds that] tout ce que le théâtre anglais lui fournit d'idées nouvelles, il le doit à Shakespeare. Cela ne l'empêcha pas de placer Dryden au-dessus de tous les écrivains qui l'avaient précédé.[6]

F. C. Green, in *Minuet,* published in 1935, emphasizes the abyss which separates Voltaire's conception of tragedy from that of Shakespeare. Professor Green says that, while some of Voltaire's plays indicate definite attempts to imitate Shakespeare, these attempts only show how impossible it was for Voltaire to understand what Shakespeare meant by a tragic dilemma. *Zaïre,* he says, is far from revealing Shakespearean influence, but is rather proof of the impossibility of any real *rapprochement,*

---

[6] Sonet, *Voltaire et l'influence anglaise,* p. 42.

let alone fusion of French and English types of tragedy. He does think, however, that Voltaire was referring to Shakespeare when, in the preface of *Zaïre,* he said that he had obtained from the English the idea of representing his nation's history upon the stage. Professor Green's conclusion is that English influence was limited to nonessentials and that Voltaire never understood Shakespeare's art.

In 1929 Norman L. Torrey, in an article in *Modern Philology,*[7] emphasized that there is no mention of Shakespeare in the *English Notebook,* in which Voltaire wrote down observations on English literature and quotations from English writers while he was in England and which he used in later years as a kind of commonplace book. Dryden, Professor Torrey notes, is mentioned frequently, however, and lines from Dryden which Voltaire wrote down in the notebook he later paraphrased in an important passage in *Zaïre.* There were four or five other notebooks by Voltaire, bound together among the papers in the Voltaire library in Leningrad, and some of the entries in these notebooks apparently date back to the time of Voltaire's visit to England. A photostatic reproduction of these notebooks, which Voltaire's secretary Wagnière called the *Sottisier,* is in the Library of Congress. Again there is no mention of Shakespeare, but there are numerous quotations from Dryden. The Dryden citations actually outnumber those from any other English author, not excluding Pope.

If Voltaire found nothing to put down regarding Shakespeare in the notebooks which contain his most intimate early impressions of the English theater, it would seem strange that Shakespeare should become a figure of pre-eminent importance in Voltaire's ideas upon English drama. It is true that Voltaire mentions Shakespeare in his critical writings far more often than he does any other English dramatist, but his comments are commonly those made by other critics and there are indications that it was not until later in the century, under the pressure of growing French interest in Shakespeare, that Voltaire read *Hamlet, Julius Caesar,* and *Othello* with care, and then they were read with a view to defeating those who were leading a movement in favor of imitating Shakespeare. Voltaire's references to Dryden, on the other

[7] Torrey, "Voltaire's English Notebook," *Modern Philology,* XXVI, No. 3 (February, 1929), 307–25.

hand, although far fewer, reveal the keen interest in details of style that is typical of Voltaire's best criticism.

A study of all the instances which Voltaire's collected works contain showing his interest in Dryden reveals that he had him in mind throughout his long career and evidently found in him a kindred spirit whose high sense of the epic poet's mission was his own and whose trenchant verses on political and religious questions were useful models. Moreover, comparison of the critical writings and plays of Voltaire and Dryden reveals a common conception of the epical nature of tragedy. Dryden, by his own assertion, wrote "heroic" tragedy, and he defined it as an epic poem in little. Essentially, Dryden's heroic tragedy is heroic romance material raised to epic dignity by grandeur of style. It has not occurred to critics to see in some of Voltaire's most typical plays, *Zaïre, Alzire, Adélaide du Guesclin,* and *Tancrède,* a similarly "heroic" type of play; but examination of the critical background of Voltaire's product reveals that in theory as well as in practice his conception was close to that of Dryden. This parallel conception of tragedy is a blow at the theories of Shakespearean influence, for it indicates that even Voltaire's idea of putting his nation's history on the stage is much closer to Dryden's heroic tragedies than to Shakespeare's historical tragedies, for Voltaire, like Dryden, did no more than dramatize the feats of the chivalric heroes of the French romances.

In summary, an examination of Voltaire's criticism and plays against the background of neoclassicism reveals that Voltaire was close to the heroic conception of tragedy held by neoclassic critics, that his introduction into tragedy of a moral lesson was based essentially upon the epic doctrine of the poet's social function, that even his message of antifanaticism and political conservatism was in accord with epic tradition reaching back to Virgil, that in regard to English drama his ties were with the Restoration and Augustan theaters, not with Shakespeare, and that, finally, in such plays as *Zaïre, Alzire,* and *Tancrède* he was actually very close to the heroic formula of Dryden, whose example, the evidence indicates, was particularly useful.

CHAPTER II   THE CRITICAL BACK-GROUND OF HEROIC TRAGEDY

Neoclassic critics evolved two great conceptions which dominated their thinking: the five-act tragedy, limited and concentrated by the rules of the three unities, and the didactic epic. Emphasis was on the epic poem as the genre most capable of rendering an author and his nation immortal, and the epic, it is clear, was thought to include tragedy within its compass. The function of the epic was conceived to be the glorification of the established government, the education of the prince and nobles and the inspiring of respect and restraint in the people. Tragedy, differing chiefly in exterior form, was considered to have the same highly didactic and political aim. The identification of tragedy with epic was made on the basis of the *Poetics* of Aristotle, it being recalled that Aristotle had said that the two kinds were similar and that a critic who could judge one could judge the other.[1] Neoclassic critics generally forgot that Aristotle's chief concern was with tragedy; they did not see that his approach was aesthetic rather than ethical and that the *Poetics* had been written partly to refute Plato, on the basis that art is moral, but that morality is not its purpose.

The theory of epic didacticism was derived ultimately from Plato, and the attempts of early critics to justify poetry on the grounds of social utility. Greek critics said that Ulysses was meant to be a pattern of all virtues and that Homer's representation of the gods, to which objections had been made, was purely allegorical.[2] Plutarch, in his essay "How a Young Man Ought to Hear Poems," held that an epic poem should serve as a storehouse of examples for imitation.[3] Roman critics agreed that the epic poem should offer images of virtue and vice with delightful teaching as the goal. Horace defended poetry as ethical and civilizing,[4]

---

[1] Butcher, *Aristotle's Theory of Poetry and Fine Art*, London, 1911, p. 23. Aristotle often draws analogies and makes distinctions between the epic poem and tragedy, particularly in chapters xviii, xxiii, xxiv, xxvi. An analysis of the comments of Aristotle on the relations of epic and tragedy is contained in Throop, "Epic and Dramatic," *Washington University Studies*, V (October, 1917), 1–32.

[2] Butcher, *Aristotle's Theory of Poetry and Fine Art*, pp. 215 ff.

[3] *Ibid.*, p. 217; see also Tillyard, *The Miltonic Setting*, p. 145.

[4] Spingarn, *A History of Literary Criticism in the Renaissance*, p. 11. See also Bray, *La Formation de la doctrine classique en France*, p. 61.

and Virgil, in composing the *Aeneid,* meant to justify the empire and provide a pattern of mild rule to Octavius.[5]

Italian critics inherited the problem of justifying poetry. Petrarch, in the preface to *De viris illustribus,* says that he chose two sorts of themes, one showing what was to be followed, the second, what avoided. This, in embryo, is the Renaissance notion of epic and tragedy.[6] Scaliger, accepting the epic poem as the norm by which all poetry should be judged,[7] deified Virgil as the greatest of philosophers as well as the greatest of poets and held that the *Aeneid* was a school of manners. Tasso, believing that epic and tragedy alike presented examples of conduct to be imitated or avoided, said that epic poetry portrays deeds of valor, courtesy, generosity, and piety for the purpose of arousing admiration and delight, while tragedy excites chiefly pity and terror by showing the misfortunes which result from evil conduct.[8] An epic hero, according to Tasso, should provide a perfect pattern for imitation; a tragic hero should be neither perfectly good nor altogether bad. Minturno approached the drama through the epic.[9] Departing from Aristotle's conception of the tragic hero, he believed that the business of tragedy as well as of the epic poem was to move to admiration for great men, and he saw no reason why tragedy, like the epic poem, could not portray perfect heroes.[10]

The pre-eminence of the epic was a doctrine central to French critical theory during the sixteenth and seventeenth centuries. Pelletier maintained that the author of a heroic poem most deserved the title "poet." [11] Vauquelin la Fresnaye accepted the epic poem as the leading genre and said that its purpose was the inculcation of virtue.[12] The Pléiade made its supreme objective the creation of a great national epic and hoped that France would have its Virgil in Ronsard.[13] In the seventeenth century

---

[5] Tillyard, *The Miltonic Setting,* p. 144.   [6] *Ibid.,* p. 151.

[7] Spingarn, *A History of Literary Criticism in the Renaissance,* p. 111.

[8] Parsons, "The English Heroic Play," *The Modern Language Review,* XXXIII, No. 1 (January, 1938), 2. See also Dowlin, *Sir William Davenant's Gondibert,* p. 30: "In fact, his treatise can with justice be called an attempt to apply Aristotle's treatment of tragedy to the epic."

[9] See Spingarn, *A History of Literary Criticism in the Renaissance,* p. 110: "Minturno's definition of epic is merely a modification of Aristotle's definition of tragedy."

[10] *Ibid.,* p. 84.   [11] *Ibid.,* p. 211.

[12] Duchesne, *Histoire des poëmes épiques français du XVIIe siècle,* p. 41. See also Spingarn, *A History of Literary Criticism in the Renaissance,* p. 212.

[13] Duchesne, *op. cit.,* p. 29; see also Spingarn, *A History of Literary Criticism in the Renaissance,* p. 211.

the desire to achieve fame as an epic poet became a literary obsession; more than one hundred heroic poems, according to Toinet's list, were brought out, if translations are included.[14] The epic fever reached its high point in the two decades 1650–70, when about forty were published, among them the major works of Chapelain, Desmarets, Lemoyne, and Scudéry.

In France, as in Italy, the theory of tragedy was closely related to that of the epic, epic didacticism permeating dramatic criticism and the rules of tragedy being applied to the epic. Chapelain made no fundamental distinction between epic and tragedy in the preface to his translation of Marini's *Adonis,* where he says:

L'Action illustre selon Aristote, ou se représente ou se raconte. Quand on la représente, la tragedie s'en forme, lorsqu'on la raconte, l'épopée.[15]

Rapin's opinion, in his *Comparaison d'Homère et de Virgile* (1667) is similar.

L'Epopée, dit Aristote, est une imitation, ou une peinture d'une action illustre: Elle a cela de commun avec la Tragedie: il y a toutefois cette difference, que celle-cy imite par la representation, & l'autre par la narration, Ainsi sa matiere est une action heroïque, sa forme est la Fable, sa fin est d'instruire les Princes & les Grands.[16]

This is the gospel of heroic tragedy as it will be expressed or implied in the writings of Le Bossu, Dacier, Dryden, Voltaire, and neoclassic critics in general. Segrais, in defending the unity of time in the *Aeneid,* likewise identified tragedy with the epic.

Je diray seulement, aprés Aristote, que la principale difference de la Tragedie & de l'Epopée, consiste en ce que la Tragedie se doit passer en deux Soleils, & que l'autre n'a point de temps limité.[17]

In general the tragedian was bound by the epic requirement of teaching by example, and the epic poet was expected to observe the dramatic unities. Scudéry mentions with pride that the action of *Ibrahim* is limited to a single year.[18] Le Bossu, in his celebrated treatise on the epic,

---

[14] Toinet, *Quelques recherches autour des poèmes héroïques-épiques français du dix-septième siècle,* p. i; also bibliography.

[15] Dowlin, *Sir William Davenant's Gondibert,* p. 76.

[16] Rapin, "La Comparaison d'Homère et de Virgile," in *Les Œuvres du P. Rapin,* I, 101.

[17] Jean Regnaud de Segrais, "Preface," in *Traduction de l'Eneïde de Virgile,* Paris, 1668, p. 48.

[18] Dowlin, *Sir William Davenant's Gondibert,* p. 37.

suggests that six months would best conform to Aristotle's precept.[19] Others favored a single season or the length of a summer campaign.[20] Saint-Amant went to the extreme of making *Moïse sauvé* conform exactly to the unity of place,[21] as did La Calprenède his *Cléopâtre*.[22] Nicolas Courtin, in composing his heroic poem *Charlemagne Pénitent* observed the one-year rule and divided the poem into five cantos to correspond to the five acts of tragedy.[23]

Aristotle's theory of pity and terror as the end of tragedy was either neglected or interpreted to mean the fear aroused by the punishment of the wicked. This was the conception of La Mesnardière, who said that tragedy was addressed to princes and tyrants that they might witness the punishment of wicked kings and the reward of good ones.[24] Vossius, Mambrun, and Le Moyne held similar opinions.[25]

Corneille and Racine were outside the narrow orbit of neoclassic formalists. Corneille not only accepted the unities with reservations, but maintained that the benefit of tragedy was due chiefly to the truthful portrayal of character.[26] The famous quarrel with d'Aubignac was about this very issue. D'Aubignac charged that *Sophonisbe* failed to meet the requirements of art and morality, since it represented a king as wicked. Plainly going to epic doctrine, D'Aubignac argued that "il faut enseigner des choses qui maintiennent la société publique, qui servent à retenir les peuples dans leurs devoirs, et qui montrent toujours les souverains comme des objets de vénération, environnés des vertus comme de la gloire, et soutenus de la main de Dieu, qui ne les défend pas moins des grands crimes que des grands malheurs." [27] Racine, refusing, like Corneille, to be bound by the narrow limits of neoclassic dogma, thought of men,

---

[19] Bray, *La Formation de la doctrine classique en France*, p. 287.
[20] *Ibid.*   [21] *Ibid.*
[22] *Ibid.*, p. 38.   [23] Courtin, *Charlemagne pénitent*, "Preface."
[24] Bray, *La Formation de la doctrine classique en France*, p. 68.
[25] *Ibid.*, p. 69.
[26] See Peyre, *Le Classicisme français*, pp. 108–9. Peyre writes: "Chez Racine, on le sait, la morale reste aussi étrangère à ces tragédies de passion, de folie, de meurtre, et de suicide qu'elle l'est aux drames de Shakespeare, et sans doute davantage. Reste Corneille. Les intentions morales ont été si souvent célébrées chez lui que nous pouvons en effet croire les lire dans ses tragédies. Il est pourtant certaine préface de *Médée*, moins souvent citée que les discours théoriques du poète, mais fort révélatrice à cet égard. Le grand Corneille y proclame que son unique but est de plaire, et de plaire 'comme dans la portraiture,' par la vérité seule."
[27] Bray, *La Formation de la doctrine classique en France*, p. 72; see also Bray, *La Tragédie Cornélienne devant la critique classique*, p. 53.

not of political utility. His tragedies are heightened by a classic economy of structure and a restrained intensity of expression inspired by his intimate knowledge of Greek drama. Their antique heroic atmosphere is not more than a kind of envelope containing the tragic essence. Although it is probably true, as neoclassic critics charged, that he went to the heroic romances for some of his plots, he did not, like his successors, borrow their superficial psychology.

The full weight of the theory of epic didacticism was brought to bear upon tragedy in the last quarter of the seventeenth century. During this period, when Louis XIV was becoming devout under the influence of Mme de Maintenon and the Jesuits, a reform movement, headed by Rapin, Le Bossu, and Dacier, was launched against the heroic romances. The purpose of heroic poetry, critics asserted, was to provide a moral lesson by precept and example. The proper subject matter was great men and great events, and style should be properly elevated. French poets, influenced by the heroic romances, had fallen away from this ideal and were entertaining the public with sentimental situations lifted from these inferior products. Even learning had declined, and the language itself had become enervated, had lost its variety, its vigor, its harmony, until it was no longer capable of sustaining the tone proper to heroic poetry. The heroes of Racine and Corneille, though they bore Greek names, were actually French courtiers, and the imitators of Racine, in particular, were borrowing his faults rather than his perfections.

Controversy over the romances, which continued throughout the first half of the eighteenth century, had been characteristic of neoclassic criticism since the Renaissance. Scaliger had defended Heliodorus's *An Aethiopian History* as a true epic.[28] Tasso had sought to justify the romances of Boiardo and Ariosto as epic poems and had invoked Plato and Thomas Aquinas to support his contention that love was a "noble habit of the will," and hence an acceptable subject for heroic poetry.[29] Many French critics also attempted to justify the heroic romance as a legitimate epic. Chapelain, in the preface to the *Adonis,* maintained that Marini had written an epic poem;[30] Scudéry, in the preface to

---

[28] Spingarn, *A History of Literary Criticism in the Renaissance,* p. 36.

[29] Parsons, "The English Heroic Play," *The Modern Language Review,* XXXIII, No. 1 (January, 1938), 2–3.

[30] Dowlin, *Sir William Davenant's Gondibert,* pp. 21 ff.

his sister's *Ibrahim,* made an epic of it by proving its moral purpose and showing how it followed the epic rules for unity of action.[31] Bishop Huet, in an introductory essay to *Zayde* (1670) of Segrais, made the most celebrated defense of the romance.[32] He distinguished between epic and romance with respect to subject and style, saying that the epic deals chiefly with politics and war and only incidentally with love, while the romance deals chiefly with love and only incidentally with politics and war, and that in style it is pitched in a lower key, to which prose is suitable.[33] But its purpose, like that of epic poetry is to show "la vertu couronnée, & le vice chatié," and its pleasing fiction is only a sugar coating for the moral hidden beneath the surface.[34] Yet Huet admits the deplorable effect of the romances on serious learning and regrets that women read nothing else and that men, to please, have come to look upon a serious knowledge of ancient history and literature as pedantry.[35] Boileau mildly frowned upon the influence of the romances in the *Art poétique,* warning dramatists not to "Peindre Caton galant, et Brutus dameret"; [36] in *Les Héros de roman* he satirized the tendency of the romances to make love the end of everything and protested that Cyrus, Brutus, and Pharamond were not Parisian galants.

Three works of great authority crystallized the hostility of critics toward the romances and fixed the theory of epic didacticism upon tragedy. The first of these, published in 1674 and translated and brought out in London the same year by the celebrated Thomas Rymer, was Rapin's *Réflexions sur la poétique d'Aristote.*[37] Rapin declares that the epic poem "is that which is the greatest and most *Noble in Poesie."* [38] Its purpose is "to serve for a pattern and instruction to the *Grandees,* and to be a *publick* example of virtue." [39] Its subject matter should be the enterprises of war, treaties of peace, embassies, negotiations, voyages, councils, and revolutions, the various images of all that happens in the lives of great men.[40] Its style should be elevated and majestic to conform to the high and serious character of its purpose and subject.[41] The

---

[31] *Ibid.,* p. 23.
[32] Huet, "De l'origine des romans," in Jean Renaud de Segrais, *Zayde, histoire espagnole,* I, 1–c.
[33] *Ibid.,* pp. v–vi.   [34] *Ibid.,* p. iii.   [35] *Ibid.,* p. xciv.
[36] Boileau, *Œuvres complètes,* I, 340.
[37] Rapin, *Reflections on Aristotle's Treatise of Poesie.*
[38] *Ibid.,* p. 72.   [39] *Ibid.,* p. 76.   [40] *Ibid.,* p. 79.   [41] *Ibid.,* p. 43.

French, blinded by Ariosto and Marini, who hid what was irregular in their works by glittering faults and false beauties, have strayed from this lofty conception.[42]

Applying the same standards to tragedy as to epic poetry, Rapin writes that tragedy is a *"publick Lecture,* without comparison more *instructive* than Philosophy." [43] The Ancients would have found it mean and senseless to have love-sick heroes whining about frivolous kindnesses, when they might be made admirable by great and noble thoughts. French tragedians, he charges, have been too greatly influenced by the popular taste for the Italian and Spanish romances. Even so, he hesitates to inveigh too sharply against the Parisian theater because of the great favor it receives from the public.[44]

As for the French tongue, it has been robbed of the boldness in expression necessary to sustain a sublime style and has become unfitted for great subjects by the effeminate taste of the age and an exaggerated regard for purity of form. A passage from Rapin, echoed later in the writings of Dryden, Voltaire, and many eighteenth-century critics in France and England, is as follows:

Of late some have fallen into another extremity, by a too scrupulous care of *purity of language:* they have begun to take from *Poesie* all its *nerves,* and all its *majesty,* by a too *timerous* reservedness, and *false modesty,* which some thought to make the *Character* of the *French* Tongue, by robbing it of all those *wise and judicious boldnesses* that *Poesie* demands: they would retrench, without reason, the use of *Metaphors,* and of all those *Figures* that give life and *lustre* to the *expressions:* and study to confine all the excellency of this admirable Art within the bounds of a *pure* and correct Discourse, without exposing it to the danger of any high and *bold flight.*[45]

Recalling that Aristotle advised the use of metaphors and comparisons, he recommends a return to the example of the Greek theater and to the figurative language of Homer and Virgil.[46] It is not enough that language be apt and clear, it must be lofty and splendid; the expressions must be noble and magnificent, the colors lively, the draughts bold, and the terms should come roundly from the mouth and fill the ears.

In an unprecedented reference for the period Rapin mentions the English drama, implying that the French might well profit by English

[42] *Ibid.,* pp. 73–74, pp. 99–100.   [43] *Ibid.,* p. 103.
[44] *Ibid.,* p. 112.   [45] *Ibid.,* p. 50.
[46] *Ibid.,* p. 45.

as well as by Greek examples.[47] Where he obtained his knowledge of the English theater in 1674 is not known. Mark Van Doren suggests that he may have learned English in order to read Dryden.[48] He may also have read some of Saint-Evremond's judgments of English drama, which were circulated in manuscript even before they began to appear in printed form in 1668 in the constantly augmented editions of the *Œuvres mêlées*.

The English, Rapin notes, manifest a genius for serious poetry comparable to that of the ancients.[49] They surpass the French in sublimity of thought and hardiness of expression, but fall short of the French in sureness of taste and correctness of form. They are a barbaric people, who delight in bloodshed, even in their sports, and their genius for tragedy is probably due to their cruel natures.[50] The English language reflects the hardy temperament of the race, being fitted eminently for great expressions.

The movement toward a more moral and elevated theater was given powerful impetus by a second authoritative exposition of the theory of epic didacticism: Le Bossu's *Traité du poëme épique* which appeared in 1675. It obtained widespread recognition in England as well as in France, and the doctrine of poetry as allegory will be generally linked with the name of Le Bossu. Rigault says of Le Bossu's reputation in France:

La critique française du XVIIe siècle explique Homère par Aristote, et Aristote par le P. Le Bossu, qu'admirent à l'envi les plus beaux esprits du temps; l'idée qui prédomine, c'est que l'épopée est un apologue et Homère un Esope de génie.[51]

In England Le Bossu was the most frequently quoted of all French

---

[47] *Ibid.*, p. 122.   [48] Van Doren, *The Poetry of John Dryden*, p. 292.

[49] Rapin, *Reflections on Aristotle's Treatise of Poesie*, pp. 111, 122.

[50] Dryden knew Rapin's *Réflexions* and was probably answering this charge in the "Epilogue" to *Aureng-Zebe* (1675), Nonesuch ed., IV, 162, in the following lines:

"Bold Brittons, at a brave Bear-garden Fray,
Are rouz'd: and, clatt'ring Sticks, cry, *Play, play, play.*
Mean time, your filthy Forreigner will stare,
And mutter to himself, *Ha gens Barbare!*
And, Gad, 'tis well he mutters; well for him;
Our Butchers else would tear him limb from limb.
'Tis true, the time may come, your Sons may be
Infected with this French civility;
But this in After-ages will be done:
Our poet writes a hundred years too soon."

[51] Rigault, "Histoire de la querelle des anciens et des modernes," in *Œuvres complètes*, I, 387.

critics, not excluding Boileau.[52] His celebrated definition of the epic poem, accepted as final throughout neoclassic Europe, is as follows:

> L'Epopée est un discours inventé avec art, pour former les mœurs par des instructions déguisées sous les allégories d'une action importante, qui est racontée en Vers d'une maniere vrai-semblable, divertissante & merveilleuse.[53]

According to Le Bossu the poet must first choose some piece of instruction applicable to his times, then devise a fable to illustrate it, and finally, if possible, find a historical action appropriate to the fable.[54] It is the hidden allegory which distinguishes the great epic poems of Homer and Virgil from plain morality writ in verse and from plain history versified, such as Lucan's *Pharsalia*. Homer saw danger threatening the states of Greece as a result of a misunderstanding among the princes, and he designed the *Iliad* to warn of his peril.[55] Virgil even more perfectly realized the office of poet.[56] In view of the change from commonwealth to empire, Virgil wished to provide an example of mild and tolerant rule to Octavius and of respect and restraint to the citizens. He therefore made the dominant qualities of Aeneas humanity and piety and took care to show that great revolutions in government are brought about by the gods, who are sure to punish those who resist. Le Bossu recognizes that admiration is the passion most proper to epic poetry and that pity and terror are most suited to tragedy,[57] but he draws upon epic and tragedy alike to illustrate his discussion and says that they differ chiefly in exterior form.[58] His mechanical scheme of discussing successively the moral, subject, form, manners, machines, sentiments, and expressions was widely imitated by critics of England and France for a century.

Specifically to complement Le Bossu's treatise and to demonstrate that tragedy, like the epic poem, was pure allegory, the learned André Dacier made his widely acclaimed translation of Aristotle's *Poetics* in 1692.[59] In a lengthy introductory essay he says that poetry originated when Greek poets, who were the philosophers and theologians of their

---

[52] Clark, *Boileau and the French Classical Critics in England (1660–1830)*, p. 243.

[53] Le Bossu, *Traité du poëme épique*, p. 14.   [54] *Ibid.*, p. 37.

[55] *Ibid.*, pp. 43 ff.   [56] *Ibid.*, pp. 65 ff.   [57] *Ibid.*, p. 347.   [58] *Ibid.*, pp. 273 ff.

[59] Dacier, *La Poëtique d'Aristote*. Bray in *La Formation de la doctrine classique en France*, p. 49, commenting on the lack of acquaintance with Aristotle, notes that there was only one other translation of the *Poetics* into French in the sixteenth and seventeenth centuries and only one edition in Greek.

time, sought a remedy for the disorders of the public festivals.[60] Instead of trying to stamp out the taste for these spectacles, which had degenerated into debauchery, they devised new ones which hid a moral fable and gave the people "des instructions déguisées sous l'apast du plaisir, comme les Medecins déguisent par quelque douceur les remedes qu'ils donnent à leurs malades."[61] Epic poetry, perfected by Homer, had been found useful for its influence on men's habits, but was not "assez vif" to correct their passions. They recognized that a kind of poem was needed "qui en imitant par l'action, fît sur l'esprit un effet plus prompt & plus sensible: c'est ce qui donna lieu à la Tragedie."[62] Spectators who were lazy or stupid and had need of "une instruction grossiere, & qui tombe sous les sens" were thus amused in a useful manner.[63]

Dacier argues with serene logic that since the rules for poetry were formulated by Aristotle, no poet can possibly succeed without obeying them. The first rule is that poetry, whether epic or dramatic, should be a fable invented in the way in which Aesop invented his fables.[64] "Selon les regles d'Aristote une Tragedie est l'imitation d'une action aliegorique & universelle, qui convient à tout le monde & qui par le moyen de la compassion & de la terreur modere & corrige nos passions."[65] Some modern plays, thought to be tragedies, are imitations of particular actions invented only to divert the spectators. They are not only not the same art as tragedy, but they are not art at all. "En un mot" concludes Dacier in regard to such a work, "ce n'est pas une fable, & par consequent ce n'est nullement une Tragedie, puisque la Tragedie ne peut subsister sans fable."[66]

The chief purpose of tragedy is to portray the punishment which overtakes all wrongdoers.[67] The best sort of tragedy is that which portrays the punishment of those committing involuntary faults and guilty only of imprudence.

Elle nous apprend à nous tenir sur nos gardes, & à purger & moderer les passions qui ont été la seule cause de la perte de ces malheureux.[68]

If everyone followed the teaching of the Bible there would be no need for tragedy.[69] Even the pagans recognized that

---

[60] Dacier, *La Poëtique d'Aristote*, "Préface," pp. iiii ff.
[61] *Ibid.*, p. v.   [62] *Ibid.*   [63] *Ibid.*, p. xiii.   [64] *Ibid.*, p. viii.
[65] *Ibid.*   [66] *Ibid.*, p. ix.   [67] *Ibid.*, p. xiii.   [68] *Ibid.*
[69] *Ibid.*, p. xii.

si les peuples eussent pû être toûjours nourris des solides veritez de la Philosophie, jamais les Philosophes n'auroient eu recours aux fables pour leur donner des instructions.

Dacier concludes:

Si, aprés cela on condamne la Tragedie, il faudra aussi condamner l'usage des fables, que les hommes les plus saints ont employées, & dont Dieu même n'a pas dedaigné de se servir, car la Tragedie n'est qu'une fable, puisqu'elle a été inventée comme la fable, pour former les mœurs par des instructions déguisées sous l'allegorie d'une action. Il faudra aussi condamner l'Histoire; car l'Histoire est bien moins grave, & moins morale que la fable, en ce qu'elle est particuliere, au lieu que la Fable est generale & universelle & par consequent plus utile.[70]

To the fable thesis of Rapin, Le Bossu, and Dacier and to their unfavorable criticism of the French stage strength was added by the writings of Mme Anne Lefèvre Dacier, a celebrated Greek scholar as was her husband. In the preface to her translation of the *Iliad* in 1699, for instance, she contrasts again the high seriousness, the elevated subject matter, and the majestic style of Greek poetry with the frivolous preoccupation with gallantry and the effeminate style of French poetry. Le Bossu, she writes, was the first to penetrate through the allegorical fiction to the true significance of the *Iliad*.[71] She was compelled to use prose to translate the *Iliad,* because the French language had been robbed of its force by false standards of purity and by rigid rules for versification.[72] She urges the French to imitate the inversions, metaphors, images, and magnificent epithets of Greek poetry.

From the foregoing account it is clear that the ethical theory of epic poetry, central to neoclassic doctrine, was considered to apply to tragedy as well as to the epic poem.[73] With this didactic criterion critics of the last quarter of the seventeenth century charged that the French theater

[70] *Ibid.*, p. xiii.
[71] Anne Lefèvre Dacier, *L'Iliade d'Homère traduite en françois avec de remarques,* I, vii ff.
[72] *Ibid.*, pp. xxix ff.
[73] Francisque Sarcey (cited in Clark, Barrett Harper, *European Theories of the Drama,* p. 390), quotes Molière's assertion that "There is no other Rule of the theatre than that of pleasing the public," and then comments: "We have laughed at this over-statement; we have not taken it at all seriously; and less than sixty years ago our fathers saw what difficulty those who were then called the Romanticists experienced in freeing themselves from the fetters of the code of tragedy laid down by Bossu, put into verse by Boileau, commented upon and reënforced by all the critics of the eighteenth century, with Voltaire at their head and after him La Harpe and Marmontel."

lacked seriousness and majesty and that the French language had lost the strength required for heroic poetry. Deploring the influence of the heroic romances critics censured Racine for his preoccupation with love and the effeminate simplicity of his style and urged poets to return to the example of the Greeks. Rapin not only held up the example of the Greeks but also thought that the English theater, by its seriousness, its grandeur of subject matter, and its bold and figurative style, also offered a useful model, despite the lack of taste and of knowledge of the rules which the English displayed.

CHAPTER III FRENCH CRITICAL OPINION, 1700-1750

THE EPIC conception, which made of tragedy a branch of moral philosophy, went unchallenged in France during the first half of the eighteenth century. Believing that Racine had lowered the tone of the theater by his emphasis on gallant love, critics joined in an attempt to raise tragedy to the dignity of epic poetry by requiring high moral seriousness and elevation of subject matter. Opinion was less uniform in regard to style, sentiment in favor of a more elevated style often being qualified by fear of too epic a tone. Voltaire's deliberate attempt to attain an epic style in his plays met with some favor, but opposition was present from the first, and it became much stronger after 1750.

Less learned men than their predecessors, critics of the period showed less veneration for the ancients. They recognized, for instance, that pity and terror, the most powerful of all emotions, had been necessary to hold the attention of audiences in the great theaters of Greece and Rome, but more refined emotions, they believed, such as admiration and heroic love, were better suited to the theaters of Paris. Discussions as to what Aristotle meant by "purgation through pity and terror" lacked significance, although few critics had the frankness of Saint-Evremond, who said that no one understood what Aristotle meant. The epic theories of the age were embodied in Fénelon's allegorical prose epic *Télémaque,* considered the best epic since Homer and Virgil. *Athalie* was thought to be the most nearly perfect of modern tragedies.

Interest in the English theater is more and more apparent in the criticism of the period, and there was a growing tendency to substitute imitation of the English for imitation of the ancients. It was acknowledged that the English possessed a superior genius for elevated poetry and their language a superior capacity for sublime expression. The genius of the English, it was thought, was due to their serious and melancholy nature and their tumultuous history.[1] Many critics recom-

---

[1] In the *Mercure de France* of December, 1742, pp. 2647–48, the Abbé Yart protested that subjects for tragedy were available in French history as well as in Spanish, Italian, or English history. He wrote: "Leur Histoire n'est pas beaucoup plus féconde que la nôtre en Evenemens tragiques; nous avons eû, comme eux, de Grands Hommes, des

mended that the figurative style of English poetry, with its metaphors and comparisons, should be imitated and that the English custom of enriching language by new words and the revival of old ones should be employed in rejuvenating the French language.

Since the English theater plays such an important role in dramatic criticism during the period, an attempt will be made in the present chapter to follow the course of the growing current of interest in English drama, as well as to trace the influence of the epical conception of tragedy propounded by Rapin, Le Bossu, and Dacier. As English tragedy will often be viewed as embodying the epic qualities which French critics will seek to introduce into the French theater, the relation between the two currents is close.

The heroic tragedies of Dryden, with their comparatively slight regard for the unities, their turbulent plots, their ghosts, battles, drums, trumpets, and guns, well represented to French critics the barbarity they were prepared to find on the English stage, while the declamatory tirades, reminiscent of Corneille, the familiar heroic romance situations, and the learned prefaces, replete with the critical terms of D'Aubignac, Corneille, Rapin, and Le Bossu, were elements which brought his plays within the realm of understanding. Moreover, Dryden's criticism of French drama as effeminate and frivolous, his jingoistic vaunting of the superiority of English poetry, stung French writers and inspired replies for a hundred years.

French critics of the period knew little about English literature prior to the Restoration, for they went chiefly to Rapin, Saint-Evremond, and early commentators such as Muralt among French sources, and to Dryden, Rymer, Langbaine, and Collier among English commentators. Shakespeare was little more than a gigantic shadow dimly perceived through the references made by these critics.[2] Rymer derided Shakespeare and praised Dryden; Langbaine and Collier charged Dryden with plagiarism and immorality, and their attacks were particularly relished by French men of letters, who wished to emphasize that the kernel of English genius had to be separated from a vast amount of chaff. When

---

Révolutions & des Guerres de toutes les especes; en un mot, il y a eû dans les vertus & dans les vices des François d'assés grands contrastes pour en faire des coups de Théâtre."

[2] Croce, in *Ariosto, Shakespeare and Corneille*, pp. 321–22, observes that France has never understood Shakespeare well and that in the period of Voltaire the English "both in speech and literature, were almost as indifferent to Shakespeare as were the French."

Rowe, Gildon, Addison, and Steele were translated there was still found in these later critics much talk of Dryden, whose influence continued.

The relatively calm and classic air of formal Augustan tragedy seems to have aroused less interest than Restoration tragedy, perhaps because of its very conformity to French rules. Addison's *Cato* was called the best of English tragedies, but its cold artificiality was recognized. Also, France was about two generations behind England politically and philosophically, and the Restoration stage, with its skepticism, its heavy content of political and religious argument, spoke to the age of Voltaire with particular pertinence. When Voltaire imitated Addison and injected republican ideas into *Brutus* and *La Mort de César,* Frenchmen evidenced only an abstract interest, but when he followed Dryden and introduced anticlerical sentiments and propaganda for tolerance into *Zaïre* and *Alzire,* there was a lively response.

Saint-Evremond was a contemporary of Rapin, but the elegant and worldly air of his writings brings him closer to the eighteenth century than to his own generation. In his critical essays, which were widely circulated in manuscript before they were collected and published,[3] he accepts Rapin's conception of tragedy as a school of manners, but argues that the glorious deeds of illustrious heroes, offered for admiration and imitation, are of more value than the terrifying punishment of wicked actions portrayed in the Greek theater.[4] The Greeks were a primitive people and delighted in showing the barbarous cruelty of the gods and the futility of the human will. A refined and Christian society delights in noble achievements.

What should be sought above all else in tragedy is "une grandeur d'âme bien exprimée, qui excite en nous une tendre admiration. Il y a dans cette sorte d'admiration quelque ravissement pour l'esprit; le courage y est élevé, l'âme est touchée." [5] Declaring that illustrious actions painted with as much historical accuracy as possible are the proper subject matter for tragedy, Saint-Evremond criticizes Racine's *Alexandre* for its emphasis upon gallantry rather than upon heroic deeds.[6] Racine's

---

[3] The first French edition of the *Œuvres mêlées* was published in 1668; the first English translation, in 1685. For an account of French and English editions see Daniels, *Saint-Evremond en Angleterre,* pp. 155 ff.

[4] Saint-Evremond, "De la tragédie ancienne et moderne," in *Saint-Evremond, critique littéraire,* pp. 111 ff.   [5] *Ibid.,* p. 118.

[6] *Ibid.,* "Dissertation sur la tragédie de Racine intitulée *Alexandre le Grand,*" pp. 137 ff., 142 ff.

characters are French courtiers rather than Greek warriors. Love may be portrayed, but it should be the heroic love of Corneille's tragedies, the spur of heroic action.[7] As for style, it should be majestic and worthy of great poetry.[8] The poet should use noble and rare comparisons and metaphors, though there is some danger of giving too epic a tone. The French have too delicate a taste and too great a tendency toward abstraction and would do better to imitate the force of Corneille's style than the simplicity of Racine's.[9] Some English tragedies, if pruned of their crudities, would be very fine, but the English have no conception of the rules, and their plays are confused jumbles of terrible events.[10]

Dryden's conception of tragedy is close to the theory of Saint-Evremond, and his dramatic criticism often shows his familiarity with Saint-Evremond's essays.[11] There is no way of proving, however, that Dryden met and talked with Saint-Evremond, as Rigault presumed.[12] Voltaire's ideal of tragedy, as exemplified in Zaïre, is also close to the conception of Saint-Evremond, and Voltaire's dramatic criticism likewise reflects an intimate acquaintance with his essays.[13]

One of the most important single sources of information about the English and the English theater during the first half of the new century was Muralt's Lettres sur les Anglois. Written in England in 1694,[14] they proved so popular that their Swiss author, after his return to France, composed his Lettres sur les François, between 1694 and 1698.[15] Texte

---

[7] Ibid., pp. 145 ff.　　　　[8] Ibid., "Sur les tragédies," pp. 129 ff.

[9] Ibid.　　　　[10] Ibid., pp. 133–34.

[11] Daniels, Saint-Evremond en Angleterre, pp. 99 ff. Daniels also states (p. 102) that probably Saint-Evremond was acquainted with Dryden's essays through conversations with Buckingham. Havens in The Abbé Prévost and English Literature, p. 14, says that Dryden's interest in the theory of the influence of climate upon literature was awakened by reading Saint-Evremond.

[12] Rigault, "Histoire de la querelle des anciens et des modernes," in Œuvres complètes, I, 302.

[13] Demogeot, in his Histoire de la littérature française, p. 465, calls Saint-Evremond the "maître de Voltaire." Cf. Saintsbury, George, Miscellaneous Essays, p. 215: "Voltaire was undoubtedly his scholar and all the lesser lights of the eighteenth century have to acknowledge the same obligation at first or second hand." Voltaire, in regard to Saint-Evremond's charge of frivolity against the French theater, remarks (Œuvres, XXIV, 218) that "il faut avouer que Saint-Evremond a mis le doigt dans la plaie secrète du théâtre français," and that while Saint-Evremond lacked genius, he had "beaucoup d'esprit et de goût."

[14] Muralt, Lettres sur les Anglois et les François et sur les voiages, pp. 45 ff. J. B. Rousseau commented on the letters in 1715 and one of them was published in Les Nouvelles Littéraires de la Haye in May, 1718. The first printed edition was dated 1725 and reviewed in journals of that year.

[15] Ibid., "Introduction," p. 45.

thought it probable that Voltaire had the letters with him in the Bastille when he was planning his trip to England and that he took them to guide his early English studies.[16] In an early edition of his own letters on England, Voltaire speaks of Muralt as "le sage & ingénieux Mr de Muralt," praise which he suppressed in later editions, as he frequently suppressed reference to sources which had been very useful to him.[17] Like Muralt, for instance, Voltaire thought that the numerous religions permitted to exist in England resulted in a lack of hypocrisy, which contrasted with the state of affairs in France.[18] Rousseau imitated the letters in his *Lettre sur les spectacles* and in passages of other works in which he compares the seriousness of English writers with the frivolity of the French.[19] Le Blanc used Muralt's work extensively in his *Lettres d'un François.*[20]

The English are portrayed by Muralt as people of violent and melancholy disposition [21] whose history is marked by tragic catastrophies.[22] They are so proud and resolute that they prefer self-destruction to the defeat of their ambitions, so ferocious that when aroused reason has no influence on them. They have a habit of remaining silent unless they have something important to say and are poor courtiers, because they prefer to tell the truth than to flatter their superiors. Their language is strong and capable of expressing the violent passions of their nature,[23] and they have a genius for tragedy superior to that of the French.[24] Of the English theater he remarks: "Si les Anglois pouvoient se resoudre à y être plus simples, & à étudier davantage le Langage de la Nature, ils excelleroient sans doute dans le Tragique par dessus tous les Peuples de l'Europe." [25]

The only play which he mentions specifically is Dryden and Lee's

---

[16] Texte, "Béat Louis de Muralt et les origines du cosmopolitisme littéraire au XVIIIe siècle," *Revue d'histoire littéraire de la France,* I (1894), 16. Texte also observes (p. 26) that while it was only with the publication of Voltaire's *Lettres anglaises* that "l'anglomanie devient une puissance," yet before the time of Voltaire and of Prévost, Muralt had given "le coup de cloche" and that Muralt himself "résume avec éclat toute une propagande obscure, mais patiente et merveilleusement tenace, que depuis la révocation de l'édit de Nantes, les réfugiés d'Angleterre et de Hollande avaient commencée sur nos frontières."

[17] *Ibid.,* p. 16.

[18] Voltaire, *Lettres philosophiques,* ed. by Lanson, II, 112.

[19] Texte, "Béat Louis de Muralt et les origines du cosmopolitisme littéraire au XVIIIe siècle," *Revue d'histoire littéraire de la France,* I (1894), 16–17.

[20] *Ibid.,* p. 19.   [21] Muralt, *Lettres sur les Anglois,* pp. 132 ff.

[22] *Ibid.,* p. 123.   [23] *Ibid.*   [24] *Ibid.*

[25] *Ibid.*

Oedipe, which he offers as an example of the brutality of the English stage—Oedipe appearing before the spectators with his eyes torn out.[26] He is vexed with Dryden for his attacks upon the French theater: "Le plus fameux d'entre leurs Poëtes Tragiques d'aujourd'hui traite *Corneille* à peu près comme *Schadvel* traite *Moliere,* c'est-a-dire qu'il le pille & fait des Préfaces pour en dire du mal."[27] He refers to Shakespeare as "un de leurs meilleurs aciens Poëtes" who put the nation's turbulent history into his tragedies.[28]

Fénelon, in his *Lettres sur les occupations de l'Académie,* which he addressed in 1714 to André Dacier, permanent secretary, also sets forth a didactic theory of poetry close to that of Rapin.

D'ailleurs, la poésie a donné au monde les premières lois: c'est elle qui a adouci les hommes farouches et sauvages, qui les a rassemblés des forêts ou ils étoient épars et errants, qui les a policés, qui a réglé les mœurs, qui a formé les familles et les nations, qui a fait sentir les douceurs de la société, qui a rappelé l'usage de la raison, cultivé la vertu, et inventé les beaux-arts; c'est elle qui a élevé les courages pour la guerre, et qui les a modérés pour la paix.[29]

Despite the fact that his prose epic, *Télémaque,* was hailed by the age as the finest example of the epic in modern times, Fénelon says that the French do not have the genius required for epic poetry and limits his remarks chiefly to tragedy.[30] Like Saint-Evremond, he believes that the French should return to the moral seriousness of the Greek theater, substituting, however, Christian conceptions for the barbaric notions of the Greeks.[31] Current French tragedy, instead of being a moral spectacle, resembles the heroic romances, even Corneille and Racine having yielded to the popular taste for gallantry.[32] Fénelon repeats that tragedy should deal with great historical events and should not resemble comedy, which is limited to the "mœurs des hommes dans une condition privée."[33] If Racine had composed his "Oedipe," which was to have had no love in it, he would have won the favor of Church and public alike.[34] Turning to English literature in his discussion of style, Fénelon remarks that the French, who have too great a pride in the purity of their

---

[26] *Ibid.*   [27] *Ibid.,* p. 124.   [28] *Ibid.,* p. 123.
[29] Fénelon, "Lettre sur les occupations de l'Académie," in *Œuvres,* III, 228.
[30] *Ibid.,* p. 218.   [31] *Ibid.,* p. 246.   [32] *Ibid.,* p. 236.
[33] *Ibid.,* p. 235.   [34] *Ibid.,* p. 237.

tongue, should do as the English do: enrich their language with words borrowed from foreign languages.[35] Anticipating Voltaire's objections to the rigidity of the French rules for versification, he says that the greatest poets are forced to write weak lines and flat verses to meet the necessity of rhyme.[36] Heroic poetry is particularly handicapped in attaining the variety and majesty required.

Texte thinks that Fénelon obtained from Andrew Michel Ramsay the idea of a limited monarchy portrayed in Book V of *Télémaque,* a conception later adopted by Voltaire in his *Lettres philosophiques.*[37] Ramsay, a Scotchman converted to Catholicism by Fénelon, composed a treatise on epic poetry which was prefixed to the first authorized edition of *Télémaque.*[38] He makes the customary neoclassic explanation of the allegorical basis of epic poetry and says that *Télémaque* is superior to all other epic poems, because its moral is superior.[39] Homer and Virgil were concerned with the particular needs of their own peoples, but Fénelon had for his aim "le bonheur du genre-humain." The moral of *Télémaque* is in the tradition of the later ancients, of Plato, Socrates, and Cicero.[40]

Ramsay says that tragedy has the same moral aim as the epic poem, but it portrays the punishment of the wicked rather than the reward of the virtuous.

Il y a deux manières d'instruire les hommes pour les rendre bons. La première, en leur montrant la difformité du vice, & ses suites funestes; c'est le dessein principal de la *Tragédie.* La seconde, en leur découvrant la beauté de la vertu, & sa fin heureuse; c'est le caractère propre à *l'Epopée,* ou poëme épique. Les passions qui appartiennent à l'une, sont la terreur & la pitié; celles qui conviennent à l'autre, sont l'admiration & l'amour. Dans l'une, les acteurs parlent; dans l'autre, le poëte fait la narration.[41]

This distinction is not rigid, for parts of the *Iliad* are in the manner

---

[35] *Ibid.,* pp. 220–21.   [36] *Ibid.,* p. 237.

[37] Texte, *Jean-Jacques Rousseau et les origines du cosmopolitisme littéraire,* p. 25. Texte writes: "Déjà Fénelon, instruit de la constitution anglaise par l'Ecossais Ramsay, rêve d'un gouvernement qui laisse les rois 'tout-puissants pour le bien et impuissants pour le mal.' " Texte adds that "la formule a été reprise textuellement par Voltaire: *Lettres anglaises,* viii." Voltaire says (*Œuvres,* XIV, 71) that Ramsay wrote to him in regard to Fénelon as follows: "S'il était né en Angleterre, il aurait développé son génie et donné l'essor sans crainte à ses principes, que personne n'a connus."

[38] Andrew Michel Ramsay, "Discours de la poësie épique," prefixed to Fénelon, *Les Aventures de Télémaque,* pp. i–ii.

[39] *Ibid.,* pp. xxii–xxiii.   [40] *Ibid.,* p. xxi.   [41] *Ibid.,* p. ii.

of tragedy. For example, the fury of Achilles is not a suitable subject for admiration and imitation, for it brings misfortune upon Greece.

Ramsay justifies the use of prose in the same way that Mme Dacier had justified it.[42] The majesty of expression proper to epic poetry is not attainable in French verse. In England, Milton liberated verse from the constraint of rhyme; some day the French will also achieve the noble liberty of verse without rhyme.

In the few years between Fénelon's *Lettre sur les occupations de l'Académie* and Du Bos's *Réflexions critiques sur la poésie et la peinture,* published in 1719, interest in English literature rapidly gathered momentum in France. Muralt's *Lettres sur les Anglois* were widely circulated in manuscript and cited in literary journals.[43] The *Spectator* was translated in 1714 [44] and went through at least eight editions before 1728.[45] In 1715 Collier's *Short View of the Immorality and Profaneness of the English Stage* was translated, and it immediately found many readers.[46] In 1717 the most extensive reference to English literature yet to appear in any French journal, an article of some fifty pages, was printed in the *Journal littéraire,* of the Hague, and there were increasingly numerous references in the *Mercure de France* [47] and other magazines.

The "Dissertation sur la poësie angloise" which appeared in 1717 in the *Journal littéraire,* of the Hague,[48] was of outstanding importance in turning the attention of French writers toward the English theater. The article favored the opinion, fast becoming prevalent, that France and England were pre-eminent in literature and that their qualities were complementary. The article declares that, despite neglect of the rules, English genius "a brillé dans tous les genres d'écrire tant en prose qu'en vers" [49] and that the French are wrong to disdain English literature. Probably the English are justified, the article continues,[50] to charge that the French language, as a result of the exaggerated purity of French

---

[42] *Ibid.,* pp. xxviii–xxx.

[43] See the comment of Charles Gould in "Introduction," p. 45, to his edition of Muralt, *Lettres sur les Anglois et les François et sur les voiages.*

[44] Jusserand, *Shakespeare en France sous l'ancien régime,* p. 133.

[45] Telleen, *Milton dans la littérature française,* Paris, 1904, p. 23.

[46] Jusserand, *op. cit.*

[47] For an account of early references to English literature in French journals see *ibid.,* pp. 145 ff.; also Lovering, *L'Activité intellectuelle de l'Angleterre d'après l'ancien "Mercure de France,"* pp. 15 ff.

[48] "Dissertation sur la poësie angloise," *Journal littéraire,* IX (1717), 157–216.

[49] *Ibid.,* p. 159.   [50] *Ibid.,* p. 160.

taste, has become inferior to the English language as a poetic medium. The English tongue is richer, because the English adopt foreign words and phrases, invent new terms, and employ the most hardy metaphors.[51] "Point de belle Poësie sans la hardiesse" advises the writer of the article in recommending imitation of the English.[52] The failure of the French in the field of epic poetry is in part due to the overrefinement of the French language. *Télémaque,* however, equals anything the ancients or the moderns have produced, and Fénelon's prose is superior to the blank verse in which Milton wrote *Paradise Lost.*[53]

In speaking of English drama, the article mentions chiefly Dryden and Shakespeare. Dryden, "un des plus estimez dans le genre," dares to call the tragedies of Corneille "whipped-cream tragedies," [54] but one has only to compare Dryden's *Oedipe* with that of Corneille to see that the best part of Dryden's play was pillaged from that of Corneille, whole scenes having been copied word for word.[55] With respect to Shakespeare, the article declares that his plays cannot be called "tragedies," [56] for they do not conform to the accepted rules for tragedy. There is no unity of effect, the spectators being alternately moved and calmed by pathetic and light scenes. All is confusion, and no attention is paid to rules of time and space. Yet Shakespeare sometimes hits off inimitable strokes.[57] Among contemporary English playwrights the article mentions Addison, Rowe, and Philips and commends particularly Addison's *Cato.*[58] In surveying other fields of English literature it mentions Dryden for his extraordinary talent for satire,[59] but observes that an odious malignity and a disgusting obscenity spoil his productions. The licentiousness of the court of Charles II, says the article, is portrayed in Dryden's *Absalom and Achitophel.*

The Abbé Du Bos, in his *Réflexions critiques sur la poësie et la peinture,* accepts the current theory that the stage is a means of teaching morality through precepts and examples.[60] Just as the Lacedemonians

---

[51] *Ibid.,* p. 161.   [52] *Ibid.,* p. 162.   [53] *Ibid.,* p. 177.

[54] *Ibid.,* pp. 198–99, Doralice, in Dryden's *Marriage a-la-mode,* Act III, scene 3 (Nonesuch ed., III, 46), says that French poetry "is the very Leaf-gold of Wit, the very Wafers and whip'd Cream of sense, for which a man opens his mouth and gapes, to swallow nothing."

[55] *Ibid.,* p. 199.   [56] *Ibid.,* p. 202.   [57] *Ibid.,* p. 203.

[58] *Ibid.,* p. 215.   [59] *Ibid.,* pp. 171–72.

[60] References are to an English translation: Du Bos, *Critical Reflections on Poetry, Painting and Music, tr. into English by Thomas Nugent.*

Brunetière, in *L'Evolution des genres,* p. 144, says that Voltaire owed much to Du Bos.

in ancient times exhibited drunken slaves to their sons to teach them temperance, so *Le Cid* teaches us not to converse of things we have much at heart when the discussion may terminate in a quarrel, and *Phèdre,* although the heroine is a criminal against her will, that we should control our passions so that we shall not be dominated by them.[61] To purge the passions means to remove those passions which are prejudicial to society.

Du Bos reveals an unprecedented intimacy with English drama and quotes the opinion of a celebrated English poet, apparently Dryden, that the Romans and Greeks of Racine's tragedies are all French courtiers.[62] He agrees that gallantry and an exaggerated purity of taste have injured the French theater,[63] and he protests that it was not amorous intrigue that shook down the Roman empire.[64]

In conformity with the theory of the parallel of poetry with painting, Du Bos emphasizes, as does Voltaire, the necessity of appealing to the eye and ear in the theater.[65] Poetry must delight, else the moral will go neglected, and to delight there must be an appeal to the senses. The English carry this to an extreme.[66] In Dryden's time it was customary to show Julius Caesar stamping his foot in rage, and tragic declamation called for a sullen wild carriage and frantic gestures. But the French stage does not have enough appeal to the senses. He agrees with Addison that for Camille to be slain behind the scenes after Horace crosses the stage is to give the impression of a murder in cold blood.[67]

The English and the French carry things to opposite extremes in

---

Voltaire himself once spoke of the *Réflexions* (*Œuvres*, XIV, 66), as "le livre le plus utile qu'on ait jamais écrit sur ces matières."

Texte in *Jean-Jacques Rousseau et les origines du cosmopolitisme littéraire*, p. 40, notes that Du Bos was in London in 1698 and 1702 and that he translated several scenes from Addison's *Cato* for the *Nouvelles littéraires de la Haye*, VIII (October, 1716), 285.

Jusserand, in *Shakespeare en France sous l'ancien régime*, p. 256, comments that the *Réflexions* had a wide sale throughout the century and that between 1719 and 1746 there were five editions. Faguet, in "Comment Voltaire a conçu l'épopée," *Revue des cours et conférences*, IX, 1st ser. (January, 1901), 484–85, considers the possibility that Voltaire talked with Du Bos about the requirements of an epic poem before he composed the *Henriade*. Voltaire speaks of Du Bos as follows in *Le Siècle de Louis XIV* (*Œuvres*, XIV, 553): "L'abbé Du Bos, homme d'un très-grand sens qui écrivait son traité sur la poésie et sur la peinture vers l'an 1714, trouva que dans toute l'histoire de France il n'y avait de vrai sujet de poëme épique que la destruction de la Ligue par Henri le Grand."

[61] Du Bos, *Critical Reflections on Poetry, Painting and Music*, I, 355–57.

[62] *Ibid.*, pp. 111 ff.   [63] *Ibid.*, pp. 109–10, 254 ff.

[64] *Ibid.*, pp. 101–2.   [65] *Ibid.*, pp. 230 ff.

[66] *Ibid.*, pp. 344 ff.   [67] *Ibid.*, p. 347.

style also.[68] English style is too pompous, and English dramatists use metaphor and comparison to such an extent that their plays are strained and unnatural. But the French are not daring enough, Du Bos says, and he quotes a certain Marquis to the effect that reading French poetry after reading Latin is like drinking water. Du Bos thinks that in *Athalie* Racine was able to employ with good effect a figurative and majestic style suitable to an oriental subject.[69]

Father Brumoy's *Le Théâtre des Grecs,* a translation of a number of Greek tragedies with a discourse on the origin of tragedy, appeared in 1730. Brumoy's critical ideas are those of his age. "Il est aisé de voir en effet que la tragédie n'est que le poème épique en raccourci," he states.[70] Tragedy was derived from the epic poem, and its purpose is the same as that of the epic, to teach "une vérité morale, revêtue d'une fable." [71] In ancient tragedy the chorus served to point out the moral of the action,[72] and Racine is to be commended for reviving the chorus in *Athalie.*[73] Epic and tragedy are governed by the same rules, but the style of tragedy, while it should be "rempli d'expressions fortes, de couleurs vives, de traits hardis, de figures énergiques," [74] should not be as majestic as that of the epic. Aeschylus borrowed to an excessive degree the pomp of the epic.[75] Brumoy regrets, with Dacier, that the French must use the same Alexandrian verse for both epic and tragedy.[76]

Texte, in his study of the relations of Rousseau and English literature,[77] accepts Muralt, Prévost, and Voltaire as the most important figures in introducing the taste for English literature into France. Muralt's letters were finally printed in 1725. Prévost's *Mémoires et aventures d'un homme de qualité* also preceded Voltaire's *Lettres philosophiques,* the first volume appearing in 1728 and the seventh and last in 1731. Prévost started publishing the *Pour et contre,* a literary review in the manner of Addison's *Spectator,* in 1733, the year preceding the publication of Voltaire's *Lettres philosophiques,* promising to give in each issue "quelque particularité intéressante touchant le génie des Anglois." [78] The *Pour et contre* continued until 1740. George R. Havens,

---

[68] *Ibid.,* pp. 234 ff., 256 ff., 283 ff.   [69] *Ibid.,* II, 409.

[70] Brumoy, "Discours sur l'origine de la tragédie," in *Le Théâtre des Grecs,* I, 80.

[71] *Ibid.,* p. 65.   [72] *Ibid.,* p. 106.   [73] *Ibid.,* p. 108.

[74] *Ibid.,* p. 129.   [75] *Ibid.,* p. 128.   [76] *Ibid.,* p. 124.

[77] Texte, *Jean-Jacques Rousseau et les origines du cosmopolitisme littéraire,* pp. 43 ff.

[78] *Pour et contre,* I, 11, cited by Havens, *The Abbé Prevost and English Literature,* p. 25.

in his study of Prévost's relations with English literature, although he emphasizes the essential narrowness of Prévost's taste, says that Prévost embraced the doctrine that France had something to learn from England as well as from Greece and Rome and that his liberalizing spirit was instrumental in preparing the age to substitute imitation of England for imitation of the ancients.[79]

In the second volume of the *Mémoires et aventures d'un homme de qualité* Prévost notes the flourishing condition of the English theater and says that he has seen several English plays "qui m'ont paru ne le céder ni aux grecques, ni aux françaises. J'ose même dire qu'elles les surpasseraient, si leurs poètes y mettaient plus de régularité." [80] He cites *Hamlet,* Dryden's *Don Sebastian,* and Otway's *Venice Preserved* among English tragedies and names Congreve and Farquhar among writers of comedies, the same authors whom Voltaire mentions in the *Lettres philosophiques.*[81] In an early number of the *Pour et contre* he discusses Milton's *Paradise Lost,* but says that Dryden is better known than Milton.[82] The only play that Prévost translated in the *Pour et contre* was Dryden's *All for Love,* in 1735.[83] Later he translated Dryden's *Alexander's Feast*[84] to illustrate the sublime style of English poetry, an example that Voltaire also uses. But he is not in favor of too epic a style in the theater, and he admonishes Voltaire that his dramatic style is too brilliant.[85] In 1738 he devoted entire numbers of his periodical to Shakespeare, going farther in his praise than Voltaire ever went.

If the instruction in liberal arts which Voltaire received at the college of Louis-le-Grand may be judged by a discourse in Latin made in 1733 by Father Charles Porée, under whom Voltaire studied and with whom he corresponded in later years,[86] the epic theory of tragedy was part of Voltaire's academic background. The dramatist is superior to the philosopher, according to Father Porée, for the philosopher makes a profession of teaching and relies upon dry precepts, whereas the dramatist wins the soul to virtue in a hidden artful way.[87] The dramatist is also

---

[79] Havens, *op. cit.,* p. 125.
[80] See Texte, *Jean-Jacques Rousseau et les origines du cosmopolitisme littéraire,* p. 57.
[81] *Ibid.*   [82] *Ibid.,* p. 66.   [83] *Pour et contre,* VII (1735), 123–24, 146–68, 170–240.
[84] Texte, *Jean-Jacques Rousseau et les origines du cosmopolitisme littéraire,* p. 67.
[85] *Pour et contre,* I, No. 5 (1733), 113n.
[86] Voltaire wrote to Porée in 1730 that when he composed *Œdipe* he was "plein de la lecture des anciens et de vos leçons" (*Œuvres,* XXXIII, 198).
[87] Porée, *An Oration in Which an Enquiry Is Made Whether the Stage Is, or Can Be*

superior to the historian, for the stage proposes nothing but what may be of advantage, whereas the historian must often exhibit vice unpunished and virtue unrewarded.[88] Voltaire argues the same points in similar language. Porée asserts that this was the view of drama held by Aristotle, who wrote the laws of the drama.[89] Socrates went to see Euripides's tragedies that he might hear his own precepts repeated by the actors. Richelieu employed the pen which ruled the fate of Europe in writing tragic verses that he might establish a school in which to form the minds of the king and his subjects. Louis XIV commanded Racine to return to the stage that the young ladies of Saint-Cyr might be provided with precepts and examples of piety. There would be no controversy over the morality of the stage if dramatists took *Athalie* as their model.[90]

That the English language and the style of English poetry are particularly well suited to epic poetry was also the opinion of the Abbé Le Blanc, whose *Lettres d'un François* were published in 1745.[91] He writes that the English language is more copious, more hardy, better adapted to poetry than the French and that the mechanism of English verse is less rigid.[92] He thinks that the extreme boldness of English poets in using figurative expressions gives an epic tone to English tragedy, and he mentions Addison's *Cato* as an example. If La Motte objects to the epic style of the "récit de Théramène" in *Phèdre,* what would he think of the epic style so common on the English stage? [93] The English possess a superior genius for poetry, and *Paradise Lost* would have been a masterpiece if Milton had written with prudence and taste.[94]

Le Blanc displays a close knowledge of Dryden's critical essays,[95] and one of his letters is a mock art of dramatic poetry directed largely against Dryden.[96] The way to write a successful play for the London stage

---

Made a School for Forming the Mind to Virtue: and Proving the Superiority of Theatric Instruction over Those of History and Moral Philosophy, p. 22.

[88] *Ibid.,* pp. 26 ff. [89] *Ibid.,* p. 40. [90] *Ibid.,* p. 42.

[91] See Monod-Cassidy, *Un Voyageur-philosophe au XVIIIᵉ siècle,* p. 56. F. C. Green in *Minuet,* p. 92, says that Le Blanc's views on English drama represent a "well and long deserved French *riposte* to Dryden's jingoistic attack on the seventeenth-century French theatre" and that Le Blanc wrote "the shrewdest, the best informed, and the most devastating criticism of our dramatic manner ever penned by a Frenchman."

[92] Le Blanc, *Letters on the English and French Nations,* I, 92, 232.

[93] *Ibid.,* p. 238. [94] *Ibid.,* p. 242.

[95] See Jusserand, *Shakespeare en France,* p. 275.

[96] Le Blanc, *Letters on the English and French Nations,* II, 235 ff.

is to take a subject from Racine or Corneille, change the title, blow up
the speeches, invent numerous extra characters, and write clownish
scenes between the serious scenes. Dances, ballets, and songs should
be added. There should be battle scenes, prodigies in the heavens, and
ghosts. To paint the passions, imitate Dryden, who had Cleopatra and
Octavia quarrel like market women; this is what is meant by following
nature in the manner of Shakespeare. The pathetic of the French language should be kept, but the characters should be made to talk against
kings. There should be satirical remarks about priests, tirades against
the laws, attacks upon the ministers, and a eulogy of English liberty.
To get rid of some of the numerous characters, have them kill each
other, poetic justice being served by having the wicked die first.

Interest in Dryden seems to outweigh interest in Shakespeare in some
of the minor critical writings of the period. Boyer, in his *Grammaire*
(1700), had named Shakespeare, Ben Jonson, Dryden, and Milton, and
he preferred Dryden.[97] Destouches, who was sent by the regent to England in 1717, where he stayed until the death of the regent, in 1723, wrote
some comedies in the English manner, and in his prefaces he praised
the English theater, but named only Ben Jonson, Dryden, and Congreve.[98] Du Resnal, in his "Essai sur la critique," printed in *La Bibliothèque françoise,* in 1744, unreservedly puts Dryden above Shakespeare.

Dryden est plus connu & plus estimé que Shakespear; il est regardé comme
le plus grand Poëte d'Angleterre, du moins par le prodigieux nombre de
vers qui sont sortis de sa plume. On l'accuse d'avoir quelque fois abusé de
sa facilité. Il est plein d'inégalités. Mais dans ceux des ses ouvrages où il
s'est le plus negligé, on le plaint quelquefois, dit un homme d'esprit de son
pays, mais on l'admire toujours. Nous avons de lui quelques tragédies &
un grand nombre de comédies.[99]

In 1752 Louis Racine's *Traité sur la poësie dramatique et moderne* [100]
sets forth the case for epic tragedy in concise terms and serves to sum up
the period. It tends to confirm that Dryden's critical essays were a
primary source of information on the English theater and that, to a

[97] Texte, *Jean-Jacques Rousseau et les origines du cosmopolitisme littéraire,* p. 39n.
[98] Villemain, *Cours de littérature française; tableau de la littérature au XVIIIᵉ siecle,*
I, 283–84.
[99] *Bibliothèque françoise; ou, Histoire de la littérature françoise,* VIII (1744), 274–75.
[100] Racine, *Remarques sur les tragédies de Jean Racine suivies d'un traité sur la
poësie dramatique ancienne & moderne.* It seems probable that this work inspired Voltaire's *Commentaire sur Corneille* in which the critical method is similar.

considerable degree, Dryden represented the English theater in the minds of French critics. One of his chief concerns is to prove that his father's *Athalie* represents absolute perfection in spite of the fact that it is more epical than tragical, judged by the rules of Aristotle.[101] According to Aristotle, Louis Racine says, tragedy should properly excite pity and fear.[102] The peril of Joas does arouse these emotions, but the catastrophe resolves them into admiration and tranquillity, which is the function of the epic.[103]

Epic-tragedy, contends Louis Racine, is actually the logical culmination of the development of tragedy.[104] In ancient times the poets had to cater to thousands of ignorant spectators. Pity and terror were found to have the strongest emotional effect, and Aristotle accepted them as proper to tragedy. In modern Europe a more refined society deserves a more intellectual appeal. "Notre Tragédie sans doute," he says, "est plus propre que celle des Grecs à faire les délices de l'Esprit." [105] He would prefer to have tragedies composed only for a reading public and is opposed to the playing of his father's tragedies, with the possible exception of *Athalie*.[106]

Louis Racine thought that Corneille was more to blame than Racine for the gallantry of the stage.[107] Hardly a tragedy of Corneille but has a love intrigue, while the word *Maîtresse* occurs only twice in all the plays of Racine. All tragedies are dangerous in their effect, a fact which his father recognized when he retired from the theater.[108] *Athalie*, however, arouses admiration as well as pity and terror and thus realizes the moral utility of the epic poem, as well as the emotional force of tragedy.[109]

Maintaining that the style of his father's plays is always perfectly adapted to their subjects, ranging from its most pompous form in the legendary material in *Phèdre* to the simple sublimity of *Athalie*, Louis Racine is distinctly not in favor of raising dramatic style.[110] He denies absolutely that Du Bos was correct in saying that the style of *Athalie* is pompous and oriental.[111]

With regard to the English theater Louis Racine observes that one

101 *Ibid.*, III, 7.
102 *Ibid.*, pp. 83–84, 96 ff., 104.
103 *Ibid.*, pp. 93 ff., 328, 333–34.
104 *Ibid.*, pp. 7, 83 ff., 104, 388 ff.
105 *Ibid.*, pp. 325–26.
106 *Ibid.*, I, 1 ff., III, 389.
107 *Ibid.*, III, 251 ff.
108 *Ibid.*, p. 128.
109 *Ibid.*, p. 389.
110 *Ibid.*, pp. 294 ff.
111 *Ibid.*, p. 295.

can say of England what Horace said of Rome, *Spirat tragicum*.[112] But the English theater is an example of a primitive theater that appeals to the cruder emotions. He mentions only three English plays by title, Dryden's *Antony and Cleopatra*, Dryden and Lee's *The Duke of Guise*, and Addison's *Cato*. He shows some respect for Dryden, but says that he could not have known much about the theater, judging by his plays and by his remarks upon the French drama.[113] In *Antony and Cleopatra* Dryden reveals his complete misconception of the moral purpose of the stage, for the proper aim of this tragedy should have been to inspire a horror of guilty love, not to show its triumph.[114] Antony, dying, asks Cleopatra for a kiss, and Cleopatra, expiring, asks that her body be laid close to that of Antony. "Est-ce là respecter les Mœurs, la Raison & la Tragédie?" And yet, Louis Racine adds, it is in the preface of this play that Dryden accuses the French of lack of genius for tragedy. *The Duke of Guise* is a piece proper to cause revolution and civil war and was written to turn ridicule on religion.[115] That the English have not progressed farther in the theater is not because genius is lacking, however, but rather because of the example offered by that early English dramatist Shakespeare, who founded the English theater and whose genius and ignorance led the English astray.[116] That the English still lack taste is shown by Dryden's opinion that the refusal of Hippolytus to accuse Phèdre in Racine's play is against common sense.[117]

Our survey of dramatic criticism in France during the first half of the eighteenth century has brought out facts which are important for their bearing upon Voltaire's plays and dramatic criticism. The proposition of the most respected critics of the previous quarter century that epic and dramatic poetry are one in purpose, subject, and style is the foundation upon which the dramatic criticism of the period rests, and it will everywhere be implied in the critical ideas and plays of Voltaire. The corollary, to the effect that drama is a branch of moral philosophy and that its purpose is to teach by precept and example, is often all that appears in critical writings, but sometimes a critic will return to the original proposition and will avow again the identity of tragedy with the epic poem. Du Bos's conception of tragedy is fundamentally that of

[112] *Ibid.*, p. 201.
[114] *Ibid.*, p. 226.
[116] *Ibid.*, pp. 190, 197, 224.
[113] *Ibid.*, p. 199.
[115] *Ibid.*, p. 227.
[117] *Ibid.*, p. 227.

Dacier, but he draws no analogy to epic poetry. Ramsay, Brumoy, and Louis Racine, however, are conscious of the epic source of the didacticism which underlies their conception of tragedy, and they say so explicitly.

A sense of the failure of the French theater to attain the high seriousness and majesty considered essential to tragedy permeates much of the critical comment of the period. It was the general conviction that even Racine, *Athalie* excepted, had failed to measure up to the elevated conception of the theater established by the ancients. It was generally agreed that it would be well to turn back to the example of the Greeks, yet it was clearly perceived that the Greeks were to be imitated only in a general way, because their theater was a primitive theater, and their religion, which was the foundation of their theater, was a crude and barbarous religion. The English came to be substituted for the example of the ancients. This trend, initiated by Rapin, is increasingly evident in the comments of succeeding critics. The English were viewed as a forceful and serious-minded race whose liberty of thought and expression permitted them to deal with subjects suitable for heroic poetry, even to portray their own history upon the stage. The poetic style of the English was considered admirable in its vigor, its use of metaphor, its extensive vocabulary, and its freedom from rigid rules. A decade before Voltaire returned from England the opinion prevailed that a combination of English genius and French taste would bring perfection to the **theater.**

CHAPTER IV   ENGLISH THEORY AND PRACTICE, 1660-1725

THE ENGLISH poets who returned from exile with Charles II in 1660 [1] had been in France during the very years when the epic fever had been at its height and Chapelain, Desmarets, Le Moyne, and Scudéry were bringing out their heroic poems and expounding the theory of the didactic epic. There can be no doubt that English neoclassicism was based to a great extent upon English Renaissance materials. There had been plenty of sentiment before the Commonwealth, for example, in the direction of the dramatic unities and the moral epic.[2] But the critical writings of Davenant, Hobbes, Dryden, Rymer, Rowe, Addison, Blackmore, Steele, Gildon, Dennis, and Pope give abundant evidence that the French critics were their chief authorities.[3]

[1] Harvey-Jellie, in his *Les Sources du théâtre anglais à l'époque de la Restauration,* pp. 29–30, lists the following as among English men of letters who were refugees at the French court: Waller, Denham, Cowley, Davenant, Hobbes, Killigrew, Shirley, Fanshawe, Cleveland, and Crashaw. Later, Roscommon, Rochester, Buckingham, Wycherley, and Vanbrugh resided in France. Harvey-Jellie mentions that some of them preferred to settle at Rouen rather than at Paris.

[2] See Spingarn, *A History of Literary Criticism in the Renaissance,* pp. 253 ff., 286. See also Tillyard, *The Miltonic Setting,* pp. 141 ff.

[3] With regard to the Restoration theater, emphasis is placed on the continuance of English stage tradition in the following studies: Dowlin, *Sir William Davenant's Gondibert;* Harbage, *Cavalier Drama;* McManaway, "Philip Massinger and the Restoration Drama," *E L H; a Journal of English Literary History,* I (Dec., 1934), 276–304; Ward, "Massinger and Dryden," *E L H; a Journal of English Literary History,* II (Nov., 1935), 263–66; Wilson, *The Influence of Beaumont and Fletcher on Restoration Drama.* The following tend to stress the influence of France and the Continent on the Restoration theater: Beljame, *Le Public et les hommes de lettres en Angleterre au dix-huitième siècle, 1660–1744,* pp. 40 ff.; Charlanne, *L'Influence française en Angleterre au dix-septième siècle;* Chase, *The English Heroic Play;* Clark, William Smith, "Definition of the 'Heroic Play' in the Restoration Period," *Review of English Studies,* VIII, pp. 437–44, 1932; William Smith Clark, "Historical Preface," in Roger Boyle, *The Dramatic Works,* 2 vols., Cambridge, Mass., 1937; William Smith Clark, The Sources of the Restoration Heroic Play, *Review of English Studies,* IV (Jan., 1928), 49–63; Hill, *La Calprenède's Romances and the Restoration Drama;* Parsons, "The English Heroic Play," *The Modern Language Review,* XXXIII, No. 1 (Jan., 1938), 1–14; Pendlebury, *Dryden's Heroic Plays.*

Nicoll, in his *A History of Restoration Drama 1660–1700,* p. 20, says that from 1660 to 1680 English writers came as near to the French literary spirit as any body of men in England before or after. The heroic play, he writes (pp. 82 ff.) is explained by a threefold formula: Elizabethan substratum, the spirit of the age, and foreign influence. The chief foreign influence he says (pp. 86–87), were the French heroic romance and the example of Corneille. Deane, in his *Dramatic Theory and the Rhymed Heroic Play,* stresses

In England the conception of the epic poet as a political force had a significance which did not exist in France. The assumption by French critics and writers of an important role in the realm of polity was little more than a scholarly pose, for the social order was regimented under Louis XIV with a thoroughness which effectively discouraged the expression of any individual views stirring in literary minds.[4] In contrast to the situation among French authors, English writers were participants in a desperate battle of ideas and parties.[5] The fierce Catholic-Protestant controversy which raged during the Restoration was followed by the Whig-Tory quarrels of the Augustan Age, and a renewal of civil war was a constant threat. Questions of divine right, the subordination of the church to the state, and the obligation of the citizen to give unquestioning obedience were issues which excited passionate expression of opinion. Newton's conception of the universe as a vast machine, operating by mathematical law, startled English minds and gave rise to speculations about mind and matter which had an intimate connection with questions of politics and religion.[6] Religious skepticism, firmly repressed in France, was openly debated in England, and Democritus, Epicurus, and Lucretius, as well as modern skeptics, such as Charron and Montaigne, were quoted extensively.[7] The rationalism of the age is manifest in its literature, and the Enlightenment, which is nowhere reflected in Racine, is everywhere present in Dryden, his almost exact contemporary. Dryden ranks among the great ratiocinative poets in English literature, and his surpassing ability to argue in heroic verse made him a powerful figure in an age of reason.

the complexity of the pattern represented by the heroic play, but recognizes the importance of French critical theory in its development. Montague Summers, in his introduction to the Nonesuch edition of Dryden's plays (I, xlv), remarks that "it appears well nigh impossible to overestimate the importance of the heroic romance in its relations to our dramatists, and in particular to Dryden."

[4] Gustave Lanson, in his *Esquisse d'une histoire de la tragédie française*, p. 82, comments that in the epoch of Racine "La société polie se désintéresse de la politique et des matières d'Etat. La vie est remplie par l'intrigue et l'amour: l'amour seul (sauf pour le vieux Corneille) fournit la matière tragique."

[5] See Nicoll, "Political Plays of the Restoration," *Modern Language Review*, XVI (July–Oct., 1921), 224; also Teeter, "Political Themes in Restoration Comedy," unpublished Johns Hopkins thesis, 1936; Hughes, "Dryden as a Statist," *Philological Quarterly*, VI, No. 4 (Oct., 1927), 335–50; Hartsock, "Dryden's Plays; a Study in Ideas," in *Seventeenth Century Studies*.

[6] See Van Doren, *The Poetry of John Dryden*, p. 19.

[7] Bredvold, *The Intellectual Milieu of John Dryden*, pp. 27 ff. See also Stephen, *Hobbes*, p. 67.

The theory of heroic tragedy, inherent in neoclassic doctrine and dogmatized by Rapin, Le Bossu, and Dacier permeated the Restoration theater quickly. English stage tradition had been broken by the closure during the Commonwealth, and the appeal of the reopened theaters was to a considerable extent artificial.[8] Charles II favored drama in the French manner, sketched out plots, made suggestions with regard to stage scenery, and lent costumes to the actors.[9] The two theaters, established by royal decree, were patronized almost exclusively by court followers who went to the theater partly to ape the manners of the French and to distinguish themselves from the Puritans. The heroic play, defined and established by Dryden, flattered the courtiers by choosing to pretend with them that there was an innate quality in kings and heroes which raised them above common men.

With the coming of William and Mary the era of brilliant court life, which had provided the setting and justification for Dryden's heroic tragedies, was gone, but the moral viewpoint of the new age found literary justification in neoclassic doctrine. Attacks on the immorality of the Restoration stage were based, at least in part, on the ethical theories of the neoclassic school of criticism,[10] and the formal tragedies of the late seventeenth and early eighteenth centuries are epic in their elevated style and their embodiment of Le Bossu's conception of heroic poetry as moral instruction. An unprecedented willingness to submit to the dramatic unities as interpreted in France also marks the new period and was a step farther toward a completely artificial theater. Addison's *Cato* is probably the outstanding example of the reign of correctness and moral propriety in formal tragedy which followed Dryden.

Epic didacticism governed the approach of men of letters to their profession. Civilization against fanaticism and royalism against mob rule had been epic doctrines since Virgil.[11] Dryden supported the rule of the Stuarts in the conviction that he was fulfilling the epic poet's role, to praise and support the sovereign and relieve the country from the threat of civil strife. He looked upon the Whigs as imprudent flatterers

---

[8] Stephen, *English Literature and Society in the Eighteenth Century*, p. 58.

[9] Nicoll, *A History of Restoration Drama, 1660–1700*, pp. 8–9.

[10] Kathleen Ressler, in "Jeremy Collier's Essays," *Seventeenth Century Studies*, 2d ser., p. 254, says that Collier based his attacks against the English stage "upon a thorough knowledge of seventeenth-century classical criticism—that of Corneille, Rapin, Boileau, Molière."

[11] Tillyard, *The Miltonic Setting*, p. 167.

of human nature and upon democracy as a dangerous delusion.[12] He was anti-priest because he viewed bigotry as the chief cause of civil war. The following couplet in *Tyrannic Love* well expresses his attitude toward the dangerous religious quarrels of his time.[13]

> T'infected zeal you must no mercy show:
> For, from Religion, all Rebellions grow.

It is this conception of the epic poet and of his function that Thomas Hobbes and William Davenant propose in their letters preceding *Gondibert*. Davenant's work is a heroic poem in dramatic form, implying the identity of epic poem and drama, and the prefatory letters are the first exposition of French neoclassic theory in England.[14] In composing his medley of epic and romance Davenant was doing just what Chapelain, Le Moyne, and other French poets were doing at that time in Paris, and the prefixed letters form a discussion of epic poetry in the manner prevalent among French critics for more than a generation.[15] The letters are typical of English neoclassicism in their mixture of French doctrines and English empiricism, for they reveal not only the influence of such neoclassic critical writings as Chapelain's preface to the *Adonis*, and Scudéry's preface to *Ibrahim*, but also an English tendency toward pragmatic and independent thought.[16] The letters were first published in Paris in 1650, where both Hobbes and Davenant were members of the court in exile; they were republished in London in 1651, along with the first three books of Davenant's poem.[17]

The pragmatic element in the letters was probably due to Hobbes, who was such a powerful figure in the literature of the Restoration that his relation to the period has been compared to that of Descartes to French literature of the seventeenth century.[18] Hobbes asserted that he applied principles of scientific inquiry to human nature and thereby provided a scientific basis for government.[19] He declared that man was

---

[12] Bredvold, *The Intellectual Milieu of John Dryden*, pp. 144 ff.

[13] Act II, scene 1, Nonesuch ed., II, 347.

[14] Saintsbury, *A History of English Criticism*, p. 107. See Van Doren, *The Poetry of John Dryden*, p. 30.

[15] *Ibid.*, p. 108.

[16] Stephen, *Hobbes*, p. 12. See Spingarn, *Critical Essays of the Seventeenth Century*, I, xxxiii–xxxvi; II, 331.

[17] Spingarn, *Critical Essays of the Seventeenth Century*, II, 331.

[18] Taine, *Histoire de la littérature anglaise*, III, 27 ff.

[19] Stephen, *Hobbes*, pp. 136–37, 181.

a desiring animal in a mechanical and morally neutral universe. Man's natural state, he said, was one of constant warfare for the good things of life, a state from which he had managed to escape by contracting with his fellow men for an absolute ruler who would devise the necessary laws to maintain society.

Hobbes believed that war was the greatest of all evils and that the chief cause of war was religious strife.[20] His writings, although pretending to be wholly abstract, were actually attempts to justify an absolute government in which the church would be subordinate to the state. He had been in France in 1610, when Ravaillac assassinated Henry IV, and he used the murder as an apt illustration of the effects of religious fanaticism.[21] The Protestant rebellion in England had forced him to flee to France and served to fortify his conviction. In France he attacked the Roman Catholic Church, was promptly accused of atheism,[22] and fled back across the Channel. Under Charles II, whom he had tutored in mathematics during the exile, he was again accused of atheism and was forbidden to express his doctrines, but he lived fairly peacefully, due to the indulgent favor of the King and the large number of Hobbists at court.[23]

"Religion," said Hobbes, "has been generally taken for the same thing with divinity (that is, with metaphysical theology), to the great advantage of the clergy." [24] The church, he said, had profited by "phantasms" and dreams to claim supernatural powers and had succeeded in obscuring and confusing men's thinking.[25] For Hobbes religion, as far as it concerned the state, was a system of beliefs and observances imposed by the sovereign. He favored complete tolerance, but in view of the crisis of the times he said that the only way to end rivalry in temporal affairs was to make the church subordinate.[26] He attacked the claims of the papacy, but he detested the Presbyterians even more because of their doctrine of superiority to the state.[27] He insisted that his own beliefs were within the bounds of the Church of England and took sacrament regularly according to the Anglican rite.[28]

In his letter to Davenant, published with *Gondibert,* Hobbes agrees with Davenant that poetry is a branch of moral philosophy.[29] Among

[20] *Ibid.,* pp. 29–30. [21] *Ibid.,* p. 8. [22] *Ibid.,* pp. 44–45.
[23] *Ibid.,* p. 58. [24] *Ibid.,* p. 31. [25] *Ibid.,* p. 232.
[26] *Ibid.,* pp. 233–35. [27] *Ibid.,* pp. 30–31. [28] *Ibid.,* p. 46.
[29] Spingarn, *Critical Essays of the Seventeenth Century,* II, 54–55.

the Greeks, he recalls, the prophets and priests were poets, and they used heroic verse.[30] Unskillful divines, says Hobbes, are often less effective teachers of morality than poets, "for when they call unseasonably for *Zeal,* there appears a Spirit of *Cruelty;* and by the like error, instead of *Truth* they raise *Discord;* instead of *Wisdom, fraud;* instead of *Reformation, Tumult;* and *Controversie* instead of *Religion."* [31]

Hobbes justifies Davenant's merger of epic and dramatic by dividing poetry into three kinds—heroic, comic, and pastoral, corresponding to the three fields of human life, court, city, and country.[32] Each type, says Hobbes, has a narrative and dramatic form, epic poem and tragedy being the two forms of heroic poetry. Hobbes's statement identifying tragedy with epic is as follows: [33]

For the Heroique Poem narrative, such as is yours, is called an *Epique Poem.* The Heroique Poem Dramatique is *Tragedy.* . . . The Figure therefore of an Epique Poem and of a Tragedy ought to be the same, for they differ no more but in that they are pronounced by one or many Persons. Which I insert to justifie the figure of yours, consisting of five books divided into Songs, or Cantoes, as five Acts divided into Scenes has ever been the approved figure of Tragedy.

Davenant, in his prefatory letter, asserts that the world is ill-governed in modern times because the "four chief aids of Government, *Religion, Armes, Policy* and *Law,"* not only have been defectively applied but also have failed to take advantage of the collateral help of heroic poetry.[34] They have tried to prevail upon the bodies of men rather than upon their minds. Poetry, says Davenant, works through persuasion, and its operations are as "resistlesse, secret, easy and subtle as is the influence of Planets." [35] The examples of virtue offered in heroic poetry are often more effective in inculcating morality than is religion itself, which is universally rather inherited than taught.[36] Davenant accepts the theory that heroic poetry is allegory, reminds his readers of the use of fable in the Scriptures, and recalls that Demosthenes once saved Athens by recounting the fable of the dogs and the wolves.[37]

Davenant draws upon the political philosophy of Hobbes for his explanation of the nature of man and the origin of the state. Society is an armed camp which has been organized for protection against those

[30] *Ibid.,* pp. 56–57.   [31] *Ibid.,* pp. 58–59.   [32] *Ibid.,* p. 55.
[33] *Ibid.*   [34] *Ibid.,* p. 44.   [35] *Ibid.,* p. 45.
[36] *Ibid.,* p. 12.   [37] *Ibid.,* p. 49.

passions which control man in a state of nature and are still to be feared when men gather in multitudes.[38] Courts and camps maintain civilization by offering patterns of conduct which it is the business of the heroic poet to hold up for admiration and imitation.[39] The princes and the gentry, reformed and made noble by heroic poetry, serve in turn as examples for the multitude, which cannot but choose to imitate them "as Glowworms take in and keep the Suns beams till they shine and make day to themselves." [40] Thus, heroic poetry is meant primarily for the grandees of the state rather than for the wolfish mob, which surrounds the courts and camps and stares like animals at a hunter's torch.[41]

While Davenant admits the pre-eminence of the epic poem, he divides his allegiance between it and tragedy, which is natural, in view of his early activities as a producer of plays and as collaborator with Inigo Jones under Charles I.[42] He is convinced not only that the heroic poem is the most acceptable literary work to God and man [43] but also that no nation "hath in representment of great actions, either by *Heroicks* or *Dramaticks*, digested Story into so pleasant and instructive a method as the English by their *Drama.*" [44] In *Gondibert* he proposes to combine the advantages of drama and epic poem by proportioning his poem according to dramatic structure, writing five books to correspond to the acts of a play, with cantos to correspond to scenes and secondary actions to correspond to the under-plots of English tragedy.[45]

Dryden continued the work of Davenant and Hobbes in introducing the tenets of French neoclassicism into England.[46] He aided in translating Boileau's *Art poétique*, emending it by the substitution of English names for French.[47] He turned to Rapin and Le Bossu especially, and on one occasion said that were all other critics lost, Rapin alone would suffice "to teach anew the rules of writing." [48] In *An Essay of Dramatick*

---

[38] *Ibid.,* pp. 13, 44.
[39] *Ibid.,* p. 14.
[40] *Ibid.,* p. 45.
[41] *Ibid.,* pp. 12, 14.
[42] Nethercot, *Sir William D'Avenant,* p. 118.
[43] Spingarn, *Critical Essays of the Seventeenth Century,* II, 4.
[44] *Ibid.,* pp. 16–17.
[45] *Ibid.,* p. 17.
[46] Saintsbury, *A History of English Criticism,* pp. 111 ff., cf. Spingarn, *Critical Essays of the Seventeenth Century,* I, xxvi, lxiii.
[47] The translation was made in 1680 by William Soame, who asked Dryden to revise it. Dryden's opinion was that it would be better to apply the poem to English writers. The change was made by Dryden, and the work was published in 1683. See Dryden, *Works,* XV, 223.
[48] Dryden, "The Author's Apology for Heroique Poetry, and Poetique Licence," prefixed to *The State of Innocence and Fall of Man,* Nonesuch ed., III, 418.

Poesie (1668) he introduced French precepts for tragedy.[49] His view was that the French excelled as critics and the English as poets. His greatest ambition was to write an epic poem, which he recognized as "undoubtedly the greatest work which the soul of man is capable to perform." [50] It was only because he could not obtain the patronage which would allow him to devote his energies to composing an epic poem that he resorted to the stage for a living [51] and turned out twenty-eight plays. The epic tone, the grand manner, is in nearly everything he wrote, and when at the royal summons he turned to political satire, it was still in accordance with his epical conception of the poet's function. He considered the writing of pamphlets undignified, and he developed the mock heroic into an effective political weapon.[52]

Dryden's conception of the purpose, subject, and style proper to epic poetry was the stock conception of neoclassicism. He agreed with Rapin, Le Bossu, and Dacier that Virgil wrote the *Aeneid* with the political purpose of providing an example of mild rule to Augustus and of infusing "an awful respect into the people towards such a prince; by that respect to conform their obedience to him, and by that obedience to make them happy." [53]

The duty of the epic poet, according to Dryden, is "to form the mind to heroic virtue by example." [54] Although Le Bossu's treatise on the epic poem was not translated before 1695, Dryden was familiar with it as early as 1679, when he called Le Bossu "the best of modern Critics," [55] and on several occasions he submits to Le Bossu's theory that the poet should pick a moral maxim before thinking of the action of his poem. Dryden says in this respect in one instance:

For the moral (as Bossu observes) is the first business of the poet, as being the groundwork of his instruction. This being formed, he contrives such a design, or fable, as may be most suitable to the moral; after this he begins to think of the persons whom he is to employ in carrying on his design; and

---

[49] Spingarn, *Critical Essays of the Seventeenth Century*, I, lxiii.

[50] "Dedication to the *Aeneis*," *Works*, XIV, 129.

[51] Dryden appealed on several occasions for the necessary patronage. See Dryden's dedication addressed to the Earl of Mulgrave, prefixed to *Aureng-Zebe*, Nonesuch ed., IV, 84.

[52] See Brower, "Dryden's Epic Manner and Virgil," *PMLA*, LV, No. 1 (March, 1940), 131.

[53] "Dedication to the Aeneïs," *Works*, XIV, 152–53.

[54] *Ibid.*, p. 129.

[55] In "The Grounds of Criticism in Tragedy," prefixed to *Troilus and Cressida*, Nonesuch ed., V, 16.

gives them the manners which are most proper to their several characters. The thoughts and words are the last parts, which give beauty and colouring to the piece.[56]

He regrets on another occasion that Spenser had been without the aid of Le Bossu's treatise, for, he says, "Spenser wanted only to have read the rules of Bossu; for no man was ever born with a greater genius, or had more knowledge to support it." [57]

If Dryden had written his epic poem, he would no doubt have embodied in it the conservative principles of philosophy and polity central to epic tradition and to his own temperament.[58] Dryden took a keen interest in the new scientific ideas of the era, was a member of the Royal Society and a follower of Hobbes, yet it is clear that he put his faith in the classics as a sufficient and final source of wisdom, eloquence, and beauty and that he accepted the new knowledge as useful chiefly in clearing away factors in modern thinking, which tended to obscure the truths which had been established by the ancients. He belonged to the Enlightenment, but he went to Greece and Rome not only for his literary principles but for his philosophical conceptions as well.[59] In this his position is essentially that of Voltaire two generations later. In a passage on religion, for example, which has a close parallel in Voltaire's writings, Dryden says:

I have ever thought, that the wise men in all ages have not much differed in their opinions of religion; I mean, as it is grounded on human reason: for reason, as far as it is right, must be the same in all men; and truth being but one, they must consequently think in the same train. Thus it is not to be doubted but the religion of Socrates, Plato, and Plutarch was not different in the main; who doubtless believed the identity of one Supreme Intellectual Being, which we call God.[60]

Frustrated in his desire to devote himself to composing an epic poem, Dryden found a partial outlet for his ambition in the heroic play, which

---

[56] Preface to his translation of Du Fresnoy, "Art of Painting," *Works*, XVII, 303.

[57] "Dedication of the Aeneïs," *Works*, XIV, 210.

[58] See Van Doren, *The Poetry of John Dryden*, pp. 181 ff.

[59] Saintsbury remarks concerning Dryden's "Life of Lucian" that Dryden "had a soul congenial to Lucian's," *Works*, XVIII, 57. Dryden himself says (*Works*, XVIII, 70), that he read Lucian more than once and that in his opinion all knowing ages are "naturally sceptic, and not at all bigotted; which, if I am not much deceived, is the proper character of our own."

[60] "Life of Plutarch," *Works*, XVII, 33.

he defined as "an imitation, in little of an Heroick Poem." [61] He accepts the neoclassic view of the identity of epic poem and tragedy and writes on one occasion as follows:

> The Genus of them is the same . . . so is the end, namely for the delight and benefit of Mankind. The Characters and Persons are still the same, *viz.* the greatest of both sorts, onely the manner of acquainting us with those Actions, Passions and Fortunes is different. Tragedy performs it *viva voce,* or by action, in Dialogue, where in it excels the Epique Poem which does it chiefly by narration, and therefore is not so lively an Image of Humane Nature.[62]

Dryden's comments on the nature of epic poem and tragedy in the dedication to his translation of the *Aeneid* also indicate how near he was to the theories of the French critics. At times he goes the whole way with Bossu and Dacier and accepts tragedy as allegory. In the "Grounds of Criticism in Tragedy," prefixed to his adaptation of *Troilus and Cressida*,[63] he declares in precise terms that "the first Rule which *Bossu,* prescribes to the Writer of an Heroic Poem, and which holds too by the same reason in all Dramatic Poetry, is to make the moral of the work; that is, to lay down your self what that precept of morality shall be, which you would insinuate into the people." If the purpose of the heroic poem, argues Dryden on another occasion,[64] is to present heroes as models of conduct, a play written on the same design should be even more effective, since the heroes are present before the eyes of the spectators. He modeled his heroic plays by the rules of the heroic poem, he says, because the heroic poem is the most instructive way of writing and presents the highest pattern of human life.[65] In inscribing *The Conquest of Granada* to the Duke of York, later James II, Dryden is again close to the doctrine of Rapin.

> The feign'd Heroe inflames the true: and the dead vertue animates the living. Since, therefore, the World is govern'd by precept and Example; and both these can onely have influence from those persons who are above us, that kind of Poesy which excites to vertue the greatest men, is of greatest use to humane kind.[66]

---

[61] "Of Heroique Playes, an Essay," prefixed to *The Conquest of Granada,* Nonesuch ed., III, 20.

[62] "An Essay of Dramatick Poesie," Nonesuch ed., I, 53.

[63] Nonesuch ed., V, 18.   [64] "Of Heroique Playes; an Essay," Nonesuch, III, 22–23.

[65] *Ibid.*, p. 22.   [66] Nonesuch ed., III, 15.

The moral of his play, Dryden states, is the same as that of the *Iliad:* to show that union preserves a commonwealth and discord destroys it.[67]

Dryden, like most Englishmen of the period, preferred Corneille to any other French dramatist [68] and considered that the course of the French drama had been downward since Corneille had ceased to write. Dryden knew the critical writings of Corneille very well. He refers to Corneille's opinions frequently and evidently had Corneille's *Discours des trois unités* before him when composing *An Essay of Dramatick Poesie*.[69] As Corneille had done before him, Dryden admitted only a limited belief in the necessity of fixed rules and he defended himself by recourse to Corneille's arguments.[70]

Dryden's derogatory remarks upon the effeminacy of Racinian tragedy aroused the ire of generations of French men of letters. Voltaire observed that critical comment in England was often taken from the observations of the French themselves, and Dryden, at any rate, is probably referring to Rapin's *Réflexions* in his dedication to the *Aeneid* when he says that "The want of genius, of which I have accused the French, is laid to their charge by one of their own great authors, though I have forgotten his name, and where I read it." [71] In the same passage Dryden declares that since Ronsard's time the French have found their tongue too weak to support their epic poetry and that in general the genius of French poets, like their tongue, is light and trifling in comparison with that of the English and more proper for sonnets, madrigals, and elegies than for heroic poetry.[72] He is saying no more than had often been said by French critics when in his "Grounds of Criticism in Tragedy" he charges that Bajazet is a French courtier.[73]

The present *French* poets are generally accus'd that wheresoever they lay the Scene, or in whatsoever Age, the manner of their Heroes are wholly *French:* Racin's Bajazet is bred at *Constantinople;* but his civilities are convey'd to him by some secret passage, from *Versailles* into the *Seraglio.* But our Shake-

---

[67] "Grounds of Criticism in Tragedy," prefixed to *Troilus and Cressida*, Nonesuch ed., V, 18.

[68] Ker, in *Form and Style in Poetry*, p. 109, calls Dryden, Corneille's disciple. See also Spingarn, *Critical Essays of the Seventeenth Century*, I, lxiii–iv. See also Legouis, "Corneille and Dryden as Dramatic Critics," in *Seventeenth Century Studies*, pp. 269–91.

[69] See Montague Summers's explanatory note, Nonesuch ed., I, 376.

[70] Ker, "Introduction," in Dryden, *The Essays*, p. xx.

[71] *Works*, XIV, 209–10.   [72] *Ibid.*, pp. 208–9.

[73] Prefixed to *Troilus and Cressida*, Nonesuch ed., V, 20–21.

spear, having ascrib'd to *Henry the Fourth* the character of King, and of a Father, gives him the perfect manners of each Relation, when either he transacts with his Son, or with his Subjects.

His most celebrated attack on Racine comes in his preface to *All for Love,* written after he had thrown off much of his subservience to the French school. In this preface Dryden says that French critics have censured his scene between Octavia and Cleopatra on the ground that their verbal exchange offends against the greatness of their characters and the modesty of their sex. In reply he quotes Montaigne to the effect that the French dwell too much on ceremony and not enough on the substance of things, and he is comforted to think, after reading Montaigne, that "by this opinion my Enemies are but sucking Critiques, who wou'd fain be nibbling ere their teeth are come." [74] Dryden then proceeds to his celebrated attack on *Phèdre.* He accuses French dramatists of being civil, but dull, and remarks concerning Racine's hero:

In the mean time we may take notice, that where the Poet ought to have preserv'd the character as it was deliver'd to us by Antiquity, when he should have given us the picture of a rough young man, of the *Amazonian* strain, a jolly Huntsman, and both by his profession and his early rising a Mortal Enemy to love, he has chosen to give him the turn of Gallantry, sent him to travel from *Athens* to *Paris,* taught him to make love, and transform'd the *Hippolitus* of *Euripides* into Monsieur *Hippolite.* [75]

Dryden's expressed aim in his heroic play is to raise tragedy to a more epic plane. He would impose upon it the epic function of presenting an ideal hero to inspire admiration and imitation. He would avoid gallant subjects and would draw his heroes after those of Homer and Tasso. [76] In style he would take advantage of the strength and elevation of the English language, load his verse with metaphors and comparisons and strive for the sublimity of the epic poem.

In practice, however, Dryden was eminently practical, and he insured his success by employing all the elements which would please and flatter his audience. [77] No critic has ever been impressed with the moral teaching of his plays. As Walter Scott remarked, [78] the extraordinary prin-

---

[74] "Preface" to *All for Love,* Nonesuch ed., IV, 182.

[75] *Ibid.,* p. 183.

[76] "Of Heroique Playes," prefixed to *The Conquest of Granada,* Nonesuch ed., III, 23–24.

[77] See Deane, *Dramatic Theory and the Rhymed Heroic Play,* pp. 58 ff.

[78] Dryden, *The Works,* ed. by Walter Scott, IV, 4.

ciples and motives of his characters are those of the heroic romances which were the rage of the day. In contrasting the extravagant bombast of Dryden's heroes with the ranting of Shakespeare's characters Scott comments [79] that the outburst of Hotspur concerning the pursuit of honor paints his enthusiastic character and is quite different from the exuberant confidence in his own prowess and contempt of every one else exhibited by Dryden's Almanzor in *The Conquest of Granada.* When his heroes were accused of performing gross impossibilities, Dryden justified them as being drawn according to the heroes of the *Iliad,*[80] and he reminds his critics that the aim of the epic poet is to arouse admiration, a more manly passion than pity and terror.[81]

Dryden made little attempt at historical accuracy, and his plays are in this respect closer to the opera of his day than to the historical tragedies of Shakespeare. He went to history for some of the events in *The Conquest of Granada,* but the drama has the general atmosphere of extravagant gallantry that is typical of the romances. The evolution of the heroic play in England is actually closely linked with that of opera.[82] Davenant had been Inigo Jones's collaborator in contriving masques at the court of Charles I, and his *Siege of Rhodes,* which Dryden called the first heroic play,[83] was staged as an opera during the Commonwealth. Dryden's *The Indian Emperour* was, perhaps, derived ultimately from a series of opera-like scenes entitled *The Cruelty of the Spaniards in Peru,* which Davenant had devised to escape the ban on theatrical performances under Cromwell.[84] Dryden had to compete with the growing popularity of opera, and he took full advantage of the opportunity for exotic mountings and decoration which the romances provided, making frequent use of songs, dances, and supernatural manifestations, all of which were features of operatic performances.[85]

Dryden's greatest achievement in the theater was his heroic style. He won his way through sheer metrical genius, says a modern critic,[86] who

[79] *Ibid.*

[80] "Of Heroique Playes," prefixed to *The Conquest of Granada,* Nonesuch ed., III, 23–24.

[81] "Dedication of the Third Miscellany," *Works,* XII, 66.

[82] Chase, *The English Heroic Play,* "Appendix 'A,' " "Relation between the Heroic Play and the Opera," pp. 195 ff.

[83] "Of Heroique Playes," Nonesuch ed., III, 19–20.

[84] Nethercot, *Sir William D'Avenant,* pp. 325 ff.   [85] Chase, *op. cit.,* pp. 201 ff.

[86] Van Doren, *The Poetry of John Dryden,* p. 110.

adds that *The Indian Emperour* must have sounded suddenly like a gong on English ears. In a sense, this critic remarks, Dryden created Pope, who learned versification from Dryden's works.[87] It is in the "full resounding" style of Dryden that the eighteenth century will show most interest, and it was Dryden's heroic style that Voltaire especially appreciated. Dryden emphasized particularly the value of metaphor for heightening poetic style [88] and said that the French had failed in epic poetry because they hesitated to use figurative expressions. In the dedication to the *Aeneid* he comments:

I said before, and I repeat it, that the affected purity of the French has unsinewed their heroic verse. The language of an epic poem is almost wholly figurative: yet they are so fearful of a metaphor, that no example of Virgil can encourage them to be bold with safety.[89]

In seeking to give to his tragedies the majesty of the heroic poem Dryden borrowed heavily from the epic style of the poet whose works he knew best, his "master," Virgil.[90] In the early plays he is most obviously indebted to Virgil when he describes a martial exploit or an act of divine intervention.[91] Then Virgilian comparisons are frequent, and at times he translated directly from the *Aeneid*. In later plays he tended to limit his most epic passages to exposition, probably feeling that in an opening scene he might adopt a more expansive and leisurely manner than in the heart of the action. The opening scene of *The Conquest of Granada,* in which the audience learns of Almanzor's feats in a bull fight, is a long epic narrative mechanically split up into speeches, in obvious imitation of the games in the *Aeneid*.[92] There are Latinisms, such as the "darted cane," and even "Virgilian" hemistichs.[93] In later years, after he had quit the theater, Dryden regretted somewhat the bombast of his earlier style. He recognized that a hero in the heat of action should not speak like a poet, and he repents having had Montezuma die with a simile upon his lips. It is a fine one, says Dryden, but "ambitious, and out of season." [94]

---

[87] *Ibid.,* p. 325.

[88] "The Author's Apology for Heroique Poetry, and Poetique Licence," prefixed to *The State of Innocence and Fall of Man,* Nonesuch ed., III, 424.

[89] "Dedication to the Aeneïs," *Works,* XIV, 221.

[90] "Account of Ensuing Poem," prefixed to "Annus mirabilis," *Works,* IX, 99.

[91] Brower, "Dryden's Epic Manner and Virgil," *P M L A,* IV, No. 1 (March, 1940), 119–38. My remarks and examples are taken from this article.

[92] *Ibid.,* p. 124.   [93] *Ibid.*   [94] "Preface to Art of Painting," in *Works,* XVII, 317.

Since Voltaire was especially interested in passages in Dryden's plays and poems which have a skeptical cast, it is useful to turn, before leaving Dryden, to this aspect of his theater. Neoclassic critics held that the epic poet must look about upon his nation and choose a useful moral lesson before assembling plot and characters. The fierce religious disputes of the time were the chief peril of Restoration England, and Dryden, like Davenant and Hobbes, seems to have found literary justification for dealing with religious and political questions in the neoclassic theory that the epic poet should act as advisor to the prince and philosopher for the state. A recent critic has wondered that Dryden chose such an awkward method of discussing the Catholic-Protestant controversy as that in *The Hind and the Panther,* in which the rival churches are represented as forest animals. May not *The Hind and the Panther* be considered a natural consequence of Dryden's respect for the fable theory of epic poetry?

The skeptical passages in Dryden's plays, which usually stand out as set pieces which can be shortened or even removed without injury to the play, doubtless reflect Dryden's skeptical turn of mind. He remarked in the preface to *Religio Laici* that he was skeptical by nature.[95] Scott's opinion was that Dryden was skeptical concerning revealed religion and that his conviction hovered between natural religion and the faith of Rome.[96] Dryden's entrance into the Roman Catholic Church was finally on a fideistic basis [97] in accordance with his skeptical views; before and after his conversion to Catholicism he was anti-clerical. His position in the religious controversy of the period ranged from the rabid Protestantism of *The Spanish Fryar* to the orthodoxy of *Tyrannic Love,* a range of opinion which was unified by his uniform dislike for priests; it was, perhaps, not much wider in its variation than were the views of Charles II, who wavered between the rival churches. In 1681, for example, *The Spanish Fryar,* which had attracted special attention, obtained the protection of the king.[98]

Many passages relating to religion in Dryden's plays are marked by a rationalistic bent. In *Tyrannic Love* Saint Catherine, when disputing among the pagans, converts Apollonius by showing the rational and

---

[95] *Works,* X, 11.   [96] *Works,* I, 258–62.
[97] Bredvold, *The Intellectual Milieu of John Dryden,* p. 121.
[98] Nicoll, "Political Plays of the Restoration," *Modern Language Review,* XVI (July–October, 1921), 233.

ethical superiority of Christianity, hardly going beyond the principles of natural religion.[99] There are frequent references in his plays to the dilemma of free will and necessity, the great ethical problem raised in a new form by Hobbes deterministic doctrines.[100] Almanzor, for example, in *The Conquest of Granada,* exclaims,

> O Heaven, how dark a Riddle's thy Decree,
> Which bounds our Wills, yet seems to leave 'em free!
> Since thy fore-knowledge cannot be in vain,
> Our choice must be what thou did'st first ordain:
> Thus, like a Captive in an Isle confin'd,
> Man walks at large, a Pris'ner of the Mind:
> Wills all his Crimes, while Heav'n th' Indictment draws;
> And, pleading guilty, justifies the laws.[101]

There are references to the same problem in *The Indian Queen* and in *Tyrannic Love.*[102] Almahide in *The Conquest of Granada* approaches the scaffold with a deistic sentiment which anticipates Voltaire's Zaïre.

> Thou Pow'r unknown, if I have err'd, forgive:
> My infancy was taught what I believe.[103]

In the dedication to *Aureng-Zebe* Dryden's words would seem to reveal a familiarity with the skeptical viewpoint of Montaigne when he remarks, "Our minds are perpetually wrought on by the temperament of our Bodies, which makes me suspect: they are nearer alli'd, than either our Philosophers or School-Divines will allow them to be." [104] He was accused of irreligion after the playing of *Tyrannic Love* [105] and charged with atheism on the basis of a passage in *The Duke of Guise.*[106] In *The Indian Emperour* the celebrated scene in which a fanatical Spanish priest tries to force Montezuma to renounce his pagan faith and at the same time reveal his store of hidden gold is typical of Dryden's charge that greed was at the bottom of religious fanaticism and that the church should limit its interest to the souls of men.[107] The arguments of Montezuma, spoken on the torture rack, are near to deism and were widely

---

[99] Bredvold, *The Intellectual Milieu of John Dryden,* p. 114.

[100] Bredvold, "Dryden, Hobbes, and the Royal Society," *Modern Philology,* XXV (May, 1928), 432.

[101] Act IV, Nonesuch ed., III, 141.

[102] Bredvold, "Dryden, Hobbes, and the Royal Society," *Modern Philology,* XXV (May, 1928), 433.

[103] Act V, Nonesuch ed., III, 149.   [104] Nonesuch ed., IV, 80.

[105] Bredvold, *The Intellectual Milieu of John Dryden,* p. 107.

[106] *Ibid.,* p. 108.   [107] *Ibid.,* p. 110.

quoted in Restoration circles.[108] Dryden frequently indicated contempt for the priesthood, as in his alteration of Shakespeare's *Troilus and Cressida,* where Calchas is described not as simply a "priest," but as a "rascally rogue Priest," good for nothing but keeping a mistress.[109]

Dryden's skepticism in religion and his conservatism in politics stemmed to some extent from Hobbes. According to Richard Leigh,[110] Hobbes gave Dryden the reasons and the political ornaments of *The Conquest of Granada,* and Aubrey, in the notes he collected toward a life of Hobbes,[111] says that Dryden was a great admirer of Hobbes and often "makes use of his doctrine in his plays—from Mr. Dryden himself." As they had seemed to Hobbes, the activities of the League and Ravaillac's assassination of Henry IV seemed to Dryden apt illustrations of the evil resulting from the interference of priests in politics. As early as 1660 he had sketched out a play about the Duke of Guise, leader of the League, which he designed to be a political parallel, but he put the play aside.[112] With Lee's aid he finished the play quickly in 1682 and presented it as a parallel of the Whigs' attempt to pass an Exclusion Bill against the Duke of York.[113] Dryden displayed an intimate knowledge of Davila's history of the League in his *Defense of the Duke of Guise,*[114] and in 1684, at the request of Charles II, he translated Maimbourg's *History of the League* in a further effort to build up a case against the Whigs.[115]

As did Voltaire, Dryden often expressed a mild view of royal prerogative that was close to approval of a limited monarchy.[116] In the dedication of *All for Love* he says that "no Christian Monarchy is so absolute, but 'tis circumscrib'd with Laws," [117] and in the *Vindication of the Duke*

[108] *Ibid.,* p. 112.

[109] Nicoll, "Political Plays of the Restoration," *Modern Language Review,* XVI (July–October, 1921), 233*n.*

[110] Bredvold, *The Intellectual Milieu of John Dryden,* p. 118*n.*

[111] Teeter, "The Dramatic Use of Hobbes's Political Ideas," *E L H; a Journal of English Literary History,* III, No. 2 (June, 1936), 149.

[112] See Dryden's comments in "The Vindication of the Duke of Guise," Nonesuch ed., V, 299 ff.

[113] See Montague Summers's explanatory note on the prologue, Nonesuch ed., V, 459.

[114] See Montague Summers's note, Nonesuch ed., V, 208.

[115] *Works,* XVII, 81–82.

[116] Hughes in his article "Dryden as a Statist," *Philological Quarterly,* VI, No. 4, (October, 1927), 349, comments: "The author of *Absalom and Achitophel* was no democrat, but his independence of extreme royalist ideas in that satire is striking."

[117] Nonesuch ed., IV, 178.

of Guise, in referring to current Whig propaganda to the effect that those who had property should have the political power, Dryden says with regard to the authority of Charles that "preservation of his right destroys not our propriety, but maintains us in it." [118] Further substantiation of the view that Dryden was in favor of a limited monarchy is provided in his correspondence,[119] where he speaks with approval of his grandfather's opposition to an unjust tax levied by Charles I and takes pride in his having gone to prison for it. But if Dryden was unconvinced of the divine right of kings to rule with absolute authority, he was no less so of the ability of the people to rule themselves. He had a Hobbesian distrust of human nature and spoke of his "loathing to the specious Name of a Republic." [120]

Since Voltaire showed an especially keen interest in the anti-priest sentiments and deistic arguments of The Indian Emperour, excerpts from the play are given for reference in an appendix.[121] Voltaire went chiefly to Act I, scene 2, in which Cortez and Vasquez announce to Montezuma the nature of their claims to his gold and territory, and to the celebrated episode in Act V, scene 2, in which a Christian priest attempts to torture the Indian emperor into accepting the Christian religion and revealing at the same time a store of hidden gold.

In 1674, six years after Dryden had introduced the arguments of French critics in An Essay of Dramatick Poesie, Thomas Rymer made his translation of Rapin's Réflexions.[122] Rymer devotes part of his preface to discussing Rapin's brief, but flattering, remarks on the superior genius of the English for serious poetry. Rapin had said that English genius was due to a melancholy and brutal temperament resulting from English isolation and to a rich and figurative language. Rymer will not admit that the English are crude, but seizes upon the superiority of the language as the real reason for their superiority.[123]

The French tongue, in comparison with the English, says Rymer, "wants sinews for great and heroick Subjects, and even in Love-matters, by their own confession, is a very Infant." [124] The French try in vain

---

[118] Bredvold, The Intellectual Milieu of John Dryden, p. 149.
[119] Ibid., p. 148.   [120] Preface to All for Love, Nonesuch ed., IV, 178.
[121] Infra., Appendix, pp. 153–57.
[122] Since Rymer's preface in the original edition is without pagination, references are to the preface as given in Spingarn, Critical Essays of the Seventeenth Century, II, 163–81.
[123] Ibid., pp. 165–66.   [124] Ibid.

to make up for the weakness of their language by using the long Alexandrian verse, but the fact is that their language is faint and languishing
and has not the copiousness and dignity which heroic verse requires.[125]
The English tongue, in contrast, has the weight, the fullness, the force,
and the gravity which make it fit above all other languages for heroic
poetry.[126]

Rymer agrees with the French neoclassic critics that the aim of the
epic poem is political morality,[127] that its subject should be the career
of a national hero in whose success heaven itself is interested, that it
should inspire admiration and a desire to imitate, and finally that in
style it should be majestic and dignified. He agrees that the French
have a superior knowledge of the rules,[128] but he argues that despite
English neglect or ignorance of the rules of Aristotle, his fellow countrymen are superior.

Many of the greatest Wits of France have attempted the *Epick*, [says
Rymer] [129] but their performance answer'd not expectation; our fragments
are more worthy than their finish'd pieces. And though, perhaps, want of
encouragement has hinder'd our labours in the *Epic*, yet for the *Drama* the
World has nothing to be compared with us.

Rymer praises Dryden above all modern poets. In proving English
superiority in epic poetry, for example, he takes the familiar course of
comparing passages on night.[130] He chooses descriptions of night from
the *Argonautica* of Apollonius, the *Aeneid* of Virgil, the *Gerusalemme
liberata* of Tasso, the *Adonis* of Marini, *La Pucelle* of Chapelain, the
Saint Louis of Le Moyne, and finally from Dryden's heroic play *The
Indian Emperour*. His conclusion is that Dryden has greater variety
of matter, better choice of thoughts, and "something more *fortunate*
than the boldest fancy has reached, and something more *just* than the
severest reason has observed." [131]

In the advertisement of his own heroic tragedy *Edgar the English
Monarch*,[132] licensed in 1677, Rymer makes the essential features of
heroic tragedy praise of the monarch, a prosperous ending, and use of
the heroic couplet.[133]

Before writing his *Short View of Tragedy*, published in 1693, Rymer

---

[125] *Ibid.*, p. 167.   [126] *Ibid.*   [127] *Ibid.*, p. 168.
[128] *Ibid.*, p. 167.   [129] *Ibid.*, pp. 173–74.   [130] *Ibid.*, pp. 174 ff.
[131] *Ibid.*, p. 180.   [132] Rymer, *Edgar or the English Monarch.*
[133] *Ibid.*, "Advertisement" (no pagination).

evidently read Huet, Dacier, and other French and Italian critics,[134] and he couples Dacier with Le Bossu as the reformers of modern criticism.[135] He defends the moral utility of tragedy in the same terms as had Dacier, saying that it is basically an allegory and was so understood by the Greeks.[136] In its use of parable it is comparable to the Scriptures themselves.[137] Rymer concludes (as did Dacier): "The Medicine is not less wholesom, for the Honey, or the gilded Pill. Nor can a Moral Lesson be less profitable, when dressed and set off with all the advantage and decoration of the Theatre." [138] He considers Dryden the chief dramatist of England, and he outlines an ideal plot for a tragedy to be composed preferably by Dryden.[139]

Rymer is willing to commend the French theater for its decency and conformity to the rules, but he regrets that "some Scenes of Love must every where be shuffled in, tho' never so unseasonable." [140] He thinks that French tragedy is handicapped by the rhymed Alexandrian verse and is under the impression that there must be a regular pause in the middle of each line.[141] Their language, he concludes, is too weak for great tragedy.

In fine their language it self wants strength and sinews, is too feeble for the Weight and Majesty of Tragedy. We see their Consonants spread on Paper, but they stick in the Hedge; they pass not their Teeth in their Pronunciation.[142]

His attack upon Shakespeare [143] as vulgar and indecent will provide the principle source for Voltaire's critical method in dealing with Shakespeare.[144] Rymer, as did Voltaire, censures *Othello* especially, calling it low and undignified and barren of any moral lesson. His burly colloquial style makes his words sound strikingly abusive:

What can remain with the Audience to carry home with them from this sort of Poetry, for their use and edification? how can it work unless (instead of settling the mind, and purging our passions) to delude our senses, disorder our thoughts, addle our brain, pervert our affections, hair our imagina-

---

[134] Spingarn, *Critical Essays of the Seventeenth Century*, 3 vols., Oxford, 1908–9, "Introduction," I, lxxi.

[135] *Ibid.*, I, lxxiii.

[136] Rymer, *A Short View of Tragedy*, pp. 44 ff.

[137] *Ibid.*, p. 47.   [138] *Ibid.*, p. 50.   [139] *Ibid.*, p. 17.

[140] *Ibid.*, p. 62.   [141] *Ibid.*, p. 63.   [142] *Ibid.*, p. 64.

[143] Rymer calls *Othello* a bloody farce (*ibid.*, p. 146).

[144] Spingarn, *Critical Essays of the Seventeenth Century*, "Introduction," p. lxxviii.

tions, corrupt our appetite, and fill our head with vanity, confusion, *Tinta-marre*, and Jingle-jangle? [145]

Most other English critics, whose works Voltaire later read and some of whom Voltaire knew personally, joined Dryden and Rymer in doubting the adequacy of the French genius and language. William Temple found that the polish and refinement of the French had detracted from the former vigor of their language.[146] William Wotton asserted that Richelieu had improved the French tongue, but that it was not suitable for tragedy.[147] Roscommon, in his *Essay of Translated Verse,* repeats the common charge in lines that Voltaire later learned by heart.

> But who did ever in French authors see
> The comprehensive English energy?
> The weighty bullion of one sterling line,
> Drawn to French wire, would thro' whole pages shine.[148]

Blount quoted Dryden's derogatory opinion of the French language with approval and deemed it too feeble for fine tragedy, although he made the possible exception of Corneille's tragedies.[149] Buckingham considered the French language in its very nature incapable of fine poetry, and in a letter to Pope said that he considered La Motte capable of being a good epic poet, "if the French tongue would bear it." [150] Charles Gildon said that the faults of French poetry lay in the nature of the language, not in any lack of talent or art, and he found the English language much more copious and harmonious.[151]

The court life and pretensions of the Stuarts were abandoned after James II, and a more prosaic age of morality and social decorum began with the coming of William and Mary. Heroic romances were not approved, and tragedians turned to Republican Rome for their heroes. In the field of literary theory the morality of the age found expression in a growing respect for Le Bossu and the theory of poetry as moral instruction which he represented. Sir Richard Blackmore, to whom the English translation of Le Bossu was dedicated in 1695, wrote his epic poem *Prince Arthur* in accordance with Le Bossu's precepts [152] and said in his

---

[145] Rymer, *A Short View of Tragedy,* p. 146.
[146] Wollstein, *English Opinions of French Poetry 1660–1750,* pp. 90–91.
[147] *Ibid.,* p. 91.
[148] *Ibid.,* p. 38. Voltaire quoted Roscommon's lines to Martin Sherlock, an English visitor at Ferney, in 1776 (*Œuvres,* I, 392).
[149] *Ibid.,* pp. 89–90. [150] *Ibid.,* p. 80. [151] *Ibid.,* pp. 74–75.
[152] Clark, *Boileau and the French Critics in England 1660–1830,* p. 244.

preface that he had designed his poem as a source of entertainment for
young men and women and that it would be more beneficial than the
stage, whose morality was questionable.[153] Jeremy Collier's *A Short
View of the Immorality and Profaneness of the English Stage* (1698),
in which he lashed at Dryden, also reflected the didactic theories of the
French neoclassic critics.[154] John Sheffield, Earl of Mulgrave, in his
Essay upon Poetry (1682), is typical of the regard for Le Bossu when
he says that it was he who had first revealed the "sacred Mysteries" of
heroic poetry.[155] In respect to the *Iliad*, Mulgrave says,

> Had *Bossu* never writ, the world had still
> Like *Indians* view'd this wondrous piece of Skill.[156]

The *Athenian Mercury* of January 26, 1695, in answer to a subscriber's
question: "What is the nature of a true Epic Poem?" resorts to Le
Bossu's treatise on the epic.[157] John Dennis, who, like Rymer, criticized
Shakespeare on ethical grounds, published his *Remarks on Prince Arthur*
in 1696. He begins with Le Bossu's definition of an epic poem and then
asserts that Blackmore's poem fails to comply because it is not a universal
and allegorical action.[158] In his examination of the poem he set the
example for eighteenth-century reviewers by following Le Bossu's me-
chancial scheme of criticism.

Addison's most famous critical work, his series of papers on *Paradise
Lost*, with which Voltaire will show familiarity, is based on Le Bossu.[159]
The greatest critics have ruled that the epic should be founded on some
moral, he says.[160] He cannot agree with Le Bossu that a poet should
first choose a moral and then build a poem on it, but he agrees that every
heroic poem must teach a moral, and he uses Le Bossu's mechanical
divisions for his discussion. He considers Milton first among modern epic

[153] Spingarn, *Critical Essays of the Seventeenth Century*, III, 228 ff.

[154] Ressler, "Jeremy Collier's Essays," *Seventeenth Century Studies*, ed. by Robert
Shafer, 2d ser., p. 254*n*.

[155] Sheffield, "An Essay upon Poetry," in Spingarn, *Critical Essays of the Seventeenth
Century*, II, 296.

[156] *Ibid.*, p. 295.

[157] *Athenian Mercury*, XVI, No. 12 (Jan. 26, 1695), Question 4.

[158] Dennis, *The Critical Works*, ed. by Edward Niles Hooker, I, 46–144. Dennis shows
that the action of *Prince Arthur* is contrary to the doctrines of the Church of England, is
therefore immoral and hence contrary to Le Bossu, who said that an epic poem must be
a moral fable.

[159] Clark, *Boileau and the French Critics in England, 1660–1830*, p. 246.

[160] *Ibid.*, pp. 253–54. See also *The Spectator*, No. 369, Saturday, May 3, 1712.

poets and says that in attaining a sublime style Milton excelled in his use of bold metaphors, his transposition of words, his turning of adjectives into substantives, and similar devices which give elevation.[161]

Pope makes extended use of Le Bossu in the preface of his translation of the *Iliad,* and he entitles his preface to his translation of the *Odyssey* "A General View of the Epic Poem, and of the *Iliad* and *Odyssey,* extracted from Bossu." [162] He agrees that Homer meant to teach through allegory and that the purpose of the *Iliad* is to show the danger of discord among a country's leaders, of the *Odyssey* that virtue ultimately triumphs.

Tragedy is uniformly considered by English critics of the period to be close to epic poetry in purpose, subject, and style.[163] In the *British Apollo* for January 17–19, 1711, in answer to a reader's query as to the nature of epic, it is remarked that the chief difference between epic and tragedy is that in tragedy the persons say all.[164] The article then gives Le Bossu's definition of the epic poem. Joseph Trapp, first professor of poetry at Oxford, in his lectures, first printed in 1711, compares epic and tragedy, dwelling chiefly upon the distinction that an epic hero, since he represents the religion of the nation, should be successful.[165] Blackmore, in his *Essay on Several Subjects* (1716), identifies tragedy and epic in all essentials.[166] In providing rules for an epic poem Gildon, in *Laws of Poetry* (1721), finds it unnecessary to give specific laws for epic poetry, since they are the same as for tragedy.[167] Tragedy is represented, Gildon says, while epic is narrated; tragedy has limits of action, time, and place which epic poetry does not have, and epic poetry usually contains examples of the marvelous and wonderful, which tragedy does not ordinarily have.[168]

Richard Steele, in his *Tatler* papers, shows familiarity with French neoclassic criticism. Voltaire will quote an unspecified *Tatler* to the effect that Steele thought that a poet should pick a moral maxim before planning his poem,[169] and there are many occasions in which Steele is

---

[161] *The Spectator,* No. 285, Saturday, January 26, 1712.

[162] Clark, *Boileau and the French Critics in England, 1660–1830,* p. 247.

[163] Swedenberg, *The Neo-classic Theory of the Epic in England,* unpublished thesis, University of North Carolina, 3 vols., 1937, II, 394 ff.   [164] *Ibid.,* p. 295.

[165] *Ibid.,* p. 421.   [166] *Ibid.,* p. 406.   [167] *Ibid.,* p. 410.   [168] *Ibid.*

[169] In the preface to *Socrate* (1759) Voltaire wrote: "Richard Steel dit expressément, dans le *Tatler,* 'qu'on doit choisir pour le sujet des pièces de théâtre le vice le plus dominant chez la nation pour laquelle on travaille' " (*Œuvres,* V, 362).

close to the theory of Le Bossu.[170] In No. 156, April 8, 1710, he asserts, as Boileau and numerous French critics had declared, that Fénelon's *Télémaque* is "formed altogether in the spirit of *Homer,* and will give an unlearned Reader a Notion of that great Poet's Manner of Writing, more than any Translation of him can possibly do." [171] Fénelon, says Steele, wrote his work for the instruction of a young prince, insisting, as an epic poet should insist, on the misery of bad kings and the happiness of good kings.

Addison's *Cato,* which was held up by French and English critics alike as evidence that English poets had new regard for French rules, illustrates the degree to which the theory of epic didacticism actually permeated formal tragedy of the period.[172] The moral of the play, which Addison announces in the final lines, is the same as that which Le Bossu had assigned to the *Iliad* and Dryden had claimed for *The Conquest of Granada:*

> From hence let fierce contending nations know,
> What dire effects from civil Discord flow,
> 'Tis this that shakes our country with alarms,
> Produces fraud, and cruelty and strife,
> And robs the guilty world of Cato's life.[173]

Pope, in his prologue, recommends a moral.

> What Plato thought and God-like Cato was,
> Britain attend; be worth like this approv'd.[174]

He approves the small role that love plays and says that the business of tragedy is the offering of proper examples for imitation and admiration.

> To make mankind in conscious virtue bold,
> For this the tragic muse first trod the stage.[175]

John Dennis criticizes *Cato* with arguments drawn from Le Bossu and Dacier. It is not a moral tragedy, he says, for the hero destroys him-

---

[170] See, for instance *The Tatler,* No. 122, January 19, 1709, headed with a quotation from Martial "Cur in Theatrum, Cato severe, venisti?"

[171] *The Lucubrations of Isaac Bickerstaff,* Esq., 4 vols., III, 265.

[172] Voltaire asserted that Addison's *Cato* proved that a faultless hero could be the subject of a tragedy and that Addison aimed to demonstrate to his countrymen the dangers of liberty. In France, where the chief evil was religious persecution, Socrates would be a fitter subject for a play, added Voltaire (*Œuvres,* V, 361–62). In *An Essay on Epic Poetry* (ed. of Florence D. White, Albany, 1915, p. 102) Voltaire says that Addison drew his portrait of Cato after that by Lucan in the *Pharsalia.*

[173] Addison, *Cato,* Act V, scene 4, *The Miscellaneous Works of Joseph Addison,* London, 1914, I, 418.   [174] *Ibid.,* pp. 349–50.   [175] *Ibid.*

self while there is still opportunity for him to serve his country. *Cato* is not properly a tragedy at all, he says, in a passage directly inspired by Dacier, for a tragedy, like an epic poem, should be an allegory, and if the play has no moral, how can it be an allegory? Dennis argues as follows:

> As the action of this tragedy cannot be allegorical because it is not moral; so it is neither general or poetical, but particular and historical. The creation of the fable is that which distinguishes the poet from the historian and philosopher. He may form his characters, rhetorick, grammar, sentiments and expressions after the manner of the historian and philosopher, but there can be no fable, when the action is neither allegorical nor universal.[176]

John Pemberton, in defending *Cato,* agrees that the hero of an epic poem or tragedy should be allegorical.

> Thus the action of Achilles is to show what violence and anger would make all men of that character say or do. To make a just Hero of a tragedy, he must always be as general and allegorical as Achilles.[177]

Like Louis Racine, Pemberton is troubled by the opinion of Aristotle that there should be pity and terror in a tragedy.[178] He says that admiration may be admitted to tragedy, but to be truly tragic a tragedy must excite some pity and terror, for "admiration is too cold a passion for tragical effects." [179] He says that he had always considered Cato too perfect a figure to excite any other emotion than admiration, but on examining Addison's play, he finds that Cato's excess of pride and obstinacy bring his downfall, and this imperfection in character excites pity and terror.

A close relationship between Le Bossu and Augustan stage theory and practice is perceived by Breval in his *Epistle to Addison* in 1717.[180] He says that he is so absorbed by the moral theme of *Cato* that he forgets the love element.

> My wandering Eyes (such energy is there)
> Are fixt on Booth, and quite neglect the Fair,
> Of rising passions I let loose the rein,
> And weep the Wrongs of Rome in Drury-Lane.[181]

And the play pleases him better than any other because

> Here Bossu's Rules are mixt with Shakespeare's Fire,
> And critics rage, because they must admire.[182]

[176] Dennis, *Remarks upon Cato*, London, 1713, pp. 10–11.
[177] Pemberton, *Cato Examined*, p. 8.
[178] *Ibid.*   [179] *Ibid.*
[180] Breval, *An Epistle to the Right Honourable Joseph Addison Esquire.*
[181] *Ibid.*, p. 7.   [182] *Ibid.*, p. 6.

Addison's play was translated in 1714 by Boyer and produced on the Parisian stage. There it inspired Deschamps to write a *Cato,* which was published in Paris, with a parallel between it and Addison's *Cato.* Deschamps's play, along with the parallel, was in turn translated into English.[183] Deschamps, in his preface, says that the career of Cato is an ideal subject for tragic action, because the strictness of Cato's morals is a beautiful example to be presented to public view.[184]

The French author of the parallel prefers the French version.[185] He says that his ideal is Corneille and that his intention in making the parallel is to "excite between Mr. Addison and Mons. Deschamps, an emulation in the latter to tread in the steps of Corneille, and in the former to give a Corneille to England." [186] If the English, he says, would but restrain their fiery imagination beneath the yoke of French rules, not give way to metaphor, and beware of falling into the meannesses which even the Greek poets did not altogether avoid, the English stage would equal the French.[187]

England and France thus formed a single neoclassic community after 1650, and the theory of the didactic epic and its essential identity with tragedy, a basic neoclassic doctrine which had received much emphasis in France, was generally accepted by English critics. Hobbes's statement that epic poetry and tragedy were the narrative and dramatic forms of heroic poetry expressed the view of the age, and Rapin, Le Bossu, and Dacier came to have almost as much authority in England as in France. Dryden quoted frequently from Rapin and Le Bossu and even declared on several occasions that a tragedian should begin with a moral, as Le Bossu had recommended. His heroic play, designed to fulfill the neoclassic ideal, dominated the English stage until late in the century. In England men of letters participated in a bitter conflict of ideas and parties, which was marked by the new skeptical and scientific arguments of the Enlightenment. They found justification for their activity in the neoclassic theory that the poet is a more effective teacher of morality than the cleric. Dryden's ability to argue effectively in heroic verse brought

[183] The translation by John Ozell was published in London in 1716 under the following title: *Cato; a Tragedy as It Is Acted in the Theatre in Lincolns-Inn-Fields, Written in French by Monsieur Des Champs, Done into English by Mr. Ozell. To which Is Added a Parallel between This Play and That Written by Mr. Addison.*

[184] *Ibid.,* p. i.　　　　　　　　　　[185] *Ibid.,* pp. 3 ff.

[186] *Ibid.,* p. 28.　　　　　　　　　[187] *Ibid.,* p. 3.

him into the center of the conflict, and he frequently introduced discussions of natural religion, of the necessity for tolerance, and of the divine right of kings into his heroic plays.

After the departure of James II heroic tragedy faded, but the influence of Le Bossu enjoyed a mushroom growth. The critical writings of the first quarter of the eighteenth century mention Le Bossu oftener than any other French critic. Blackmore, Collier, Dennis, Addison, Steele, and Pope all go to him. English formal tragedy of 1700–1725 is epic by its elevation of style and by its exemplification of Le Bossu's ideal of poetry as a moral lesson offering precepts and examples for the instruction of the spectators. Addison's *Cato* perhaps best realized the epic ideal and was praised by one critic for its conformity to Le Bossu's rules.

Upon arriving in England in 1726 Voltaire was confronted with the unanimous judgment of English critics that the French stage had declined since Corneille and that the French language no longer possessed the strength and vigor necessary for heroic poetry. It was a conviction shared by French critics of that time, and the English attitude was apparently a reflection in part of the opinions of the French themselves. English critics, including Dryden, acknowledged the excellence of French critics and tended to think that a combination of English genius and French taste would bring new perfection to poetry, a point of view that Voltaire often adopted in his critical writings.

CHAPTER V   VOLTAIRE AND DRYDEN

WHEN VOLTAIRE's tragedies are under consideration there will be many occasions to speak of Voltaire's interest in the plays and dramatic criticism of Dryden, the leading exponent of heroic tragedy in neoclassic Europe. During the opening decades of the eighteenth century there was a tendency among French critics, as we have seen, to accept Dryden as the chief dramatist of England. There is at least good reason to believe that Voltaire, like Muralt and Prévost and other early critics of the century, had little contact with English literature antedating Dryden. By the middle of the century the spell cast by Rapin, Le Bossu, and Dacier had begun to lift, but even then the translations of Shakespeare by La Place in 1745 and by Le Tourneur in 1776 gave very faint and distorted reflections of Elizabethan tragedy.

Most modern commentators have emphasized that Voltaire, when he went to England at the age of thirty-one for a stay of some two and one-half years, found in England what he was prepared to find and that contact with English thought and literature, while it was vitally important in Voltaire's development, did not mold him, but served to strengthen and make more precise ideas which he already held.[1] Voltaire's approach to literature, like that of Dryden, was first of all critical, and he gathered material in England much as a journalist would collect material for a series of articles. Within the neoclassic frame of his literary conceptions he recognized a kindred spirit in Dryden, and the fact is that Dryden was particularly useful to him. There is no question of influence in the extreme sense against which students of comparative literature have been warned, but there is plenty of evidence to show that Voltaire knew at least some of Dryden's works intimately, that Dryden's example was often in his mind, and that Dryden's heroic tragedy loomed large in Voltaire's conception of the English theater. The basic impression left by a review of the relations of Voltaire with Dryden is that Voltaire was attracted to Dryden as a playwright who had accomplished the poet-philosopher role to which Voltaire himself aspired and had given just

[1] See Baldensperger, "Voltaire anglophile avant son séjour d'Angleterre," *Revue de littérature comparée,* IX (1929), 60.

the skeptical and deistic twist to the traditional epic message of anti-fanaticism which Voltaire was seeking.

Voltaire must have become acquainted with Dryden's reputation and, perhaps, with some of his works before he went to England in 1726. Rouen was a center of interest in English literature,[2] and Voltaire had a number of friends in Rouen with whom he was in close contact during his early years. Cideville and Formont were from Rouen, and so was Thieriot, to whom Voltaire ostensibly addressed the *Lettres philoso-phiques,* which were first printed secretly in Rouen, as was the first edi-tion of the *Henriade.* In notes that Voltaire gave to Du Vernet for writ-ing a biography Voltaire said that Thieriot was allowed to visit him in the Bastille during his incarceration in 1726, just before his departure for England. "Il est très-vrai que, dans ma seconde retraite à la Bastille," wrote Voltaire, "il me pourvut de livres anglais, et qu'il lui fut permis de venir dîner souvent avec moi." [3] Any writings of English critics which Thieriot might have brought, would have given prominent mention to Dryden, and there is the possibility that Thieriot actually brought some volumes of Dryden's works. Voltaire probably read Muralt's *Lettres sur les Anglois* [4] during his days in the Bastille, and these letters, which had been published in 1725, refer to Dryden as the chief dramatist of England.

There cannot be any doubt that Bolingbroke and Voltaire discussed the writings of Dryden as early as 1722, the date of Voltaire's stay at Bolingbroke's country estate near Orleans. In 1731, in his *Discours sur la tragédie à Mylord Bolingbroke,* Voltaire refers to Bolingbroke's judg-ment of English tragedy in these words: "J'ai entendu de votre bouche que vous n'aviez pas une bonne tragédie." [5] Bolingbroke, however, con-sidered Dryden very highly. Pope said that Bolingbroke was Dryden's friend and protector.[6] Bolingbroke was once at Dryden's home when the publisher Tonson called,[7] and there is an anecdote that it was Boling-broke who first received from Dryden's "trembling" hand the manuscript of *Alexander's Feast,* the ode which Voltaire later praised so highly.[8] Also, Bolingbroke wrote verses to be prefixed to Dryden's translation of the *Aeneid* (1697), in which he speaks as follows of Dryden:

---

[2] See Yvon, *Traits d'union normands avec l'Angleterre.*   [3] *Œuvres,* XLVIII, 6.
[4] See Texte, "Béat Louis de Muralt et les origines du cosmopolitisme littéraire au XVIIIᵉ siècle," *Revue d'histoire littéraire de la France,* I (1894), 16.
[5] *Œuvres,* II, 314.   [6] Hassall, *Life of Viscount Bolingbroke,* p. 10.
[7] *Ibid.*   [8] *Ibid.*

But Nature, grown extravagantly kind,
With all her fairest gifts adorned your mind.
The different powers were then united found,
And you the universal monarch crown'd.[9]

That Bolingbroke expressed views upon Dryden to Voltaire was inevitable and is, in fact, indicated by Voltaire's remarks in a letter to his friend Formont, in 1735, recommending the scene between Antony and Ventidius in Dryden's *All for Love* and referring to Bolingbroke's approval of it.[10] Voltaire wrote:

Je n'ai point encore vu la traduction en prose de la première scène de la *Cléopâtre* de Dryden. Tout ce que je peux vous dire, c'est qu'une traduction en prose, d'une scène en vers, est une beauté qui me montrerait son cul au lieu de me montrer son visage; et puis, je vous dirai qu'il s'en faut beaucoup que le visage de Dryden soit une beauté. Sa *Cléopâtre* est un monstre, comme la plupart des pièces anglaises, ou, plutôt, comme toutes les pièces de ce pays-là; j'entends les pièces tragiques. Il y a seulement une scène de Ventidius et d'Antoine qui est digne de Corneille. C'est là le sentiment de milord Bolingbroke et de tous les bons auteurs; c'est ainsi que pensait Addison.[11]

The translation of *All for Love* to which Voltaire refers is that of Prévost in his journal *Pour et contre*. Prévost, on the occasion of this translation, makes a statement which may be of some importance in its bearing upon Voltaire's knowledge of Dryden, for he seems to say that Thieriot, Voltaire's intimate friend, upon whom Voltaire depended to perform various missions in France and England, was planning to translate Dryden's plays. Prévost writes, referring to Act V of *All for Love*: [12] "Je ne doute point que ces Scènes détachées ne fassent souhaiter impatiemment la Traduction entière des plue belles Tragédies du même Théâtre, que M. Thiriot nous promet depuis son retour de Londres." If Thieriot contemplated translating other plays by Dryden, it may have been on Voltaire's suggestion, in view of the relations which existed between them during this period. The expression "du même Théâtre," however, may possibly refer to the English theater in general.

During his stay in England from May, 1726, to about November,

---

[9] Macknight, *The Life of Henry St. John, Viscount Bolingbroke,* p. 17.

[10] Dryden wrote that he himself preferred this scene "to anything which I have written in this kind" (Preface, *All for Love,* Nonesuch ed., IV, 187).

[11] *Œuvres,* XXXIII, 553.

[12] *Pour et contre,* V (1734), 168.

1728,[13] Voltaire had numerous literary irons in the fire, and an examination of some of his writings of this period is helpful in exploring his early knowledge of Dryden. One of the reasons for his going to England was his desire to publish a satisfactory edition of his epic poem the *Henriade,* which hitherto had had only clandestine printings in France. To prepare the way for the English edition, Voltaire first composed in English and published in London *An Essay upon the Civil Wars of France, Extracted from Curious Manuscripts and Also upon the Epick Poetry of the European Nations, from Homer down to Milton.* This appeared late in 1727,[14] and a handsome edition of the *Henriade* came out in the spring of 1728, with a subscription list of three hundred and fifty, headed by the king and the queen. While he was in England, Voltaire sketched out and partly completed *Brutus* and *La Mort de César,* his two plays imitative of the Roman themes then in vogue on the London stage. He was also at work on his impressions of England, which he brought out in 1734 as the *Lettres philosophiques.* While carrying on these projects he was collecting material for other works, such as his history of the age of Louis XIV.

A notebook in which Voltaire wrote down items relating to England was found among his papers in the Voltaire Library at Leningrad and is of value in tracing his literary projects of that period. In addition to this *English Notebook* there is a collection of five early notebooks bound together among Voltaire's papers, and some of the items in these notebooks were apparently written down by Voltaire before he left England. Voltaire's secretary, Wagnière, titled the latter collection of notes the *Sottisier.* The *English Notebook,* the *Sottisier,* the *Essay on Epic Poetry,* and the letter "Sur la tragédie," which is No. 18 in the *Lettres philosophiques,* apparently have some relation to each other with respect to the Dryden material contained in them. Voltaire seems to have transferred some Dryden items from the *English Notebook* to the *Sottisier.* Later he chose Dryden passages from the *Sottisier* to include in his *Essay on Epic Poetry* and in his observations on English tragedy in the *Lettres philosophiques.*

The *English Notebook* is not included in any printed editions of

---

[13] For a discussion of these dates see Foulet, *Correspondance de Voltaire (1726–1729),* pp. 28n, 278 ff.

[14] See Florence D. White, in *Voltaire's Essay on Epic Poetry,* Preface, p. v.

Voltaire's works, but was published in 1929 in *Modern Philology*,[15] by Norman L. Torrey, from a manuscript in the Voltaire Library in Leningrad. It is composed of seventy-seven items, most of them observations on English literature or quotations from English authors, which Voltaire wrote down while he was in England. Five of the items are quotations from Dryden, and two additional items, an opinion on the English drama and a remark on the development of the romance languages after the break-up of the Roman Empire, sound as though they were based on opinions expressed by Dryden in his *An Essay of Dramatick Poesie*. There are more items from Dryden than from any other author except Pope, from whom Voltaire quotes seven times and to whom he wrongly ascribes a passage of verse, referring to him in two other instances. There are no selections from Shakespeare, and only one line from Milton. Swift, Rochester, Waller, Denham, Jonson and Gay are represented by one or more selections each.[16] The quotations from Dryden, Voltaire evidently found either in *The Art of English Poetry,* the well-known anthology of English verse by Edward Bysshe, or in Addison's *Spectator.*

Three of the Dryden quotations, those included in Items X and XLVI, Voltaire doubtless found on the same page of Bysshe, under the heading "Religion." [17] Item X consists of two groups of verse: eight lines from *The Medal* and five lines from *The Indian Emperour*. Voltaire wrote down the thirteen lines as follows, leaving only a slight break between the two passages:

DRYDEN ABOUT RELLIGION

the common cry is ever rellgion's test
the Turk's at Constantinople best
Idols in India, Popery at Rome
and our own worship only true at home
and true but for the time, tis hard to know
how long we please it shall continue so
this side today, and that tomorrow burns
so all are God a'mighty in their turns [18]

---

[15] Torrey, "Voltaire's English Notebook," *Modern Philology*, XXVI, No. 3 (Feb., 1929), 307–25.

[16] *Ibid.*, p. 307.

[17] Bysshe, *The Art of English Poety,* II, 154.

[18] Torrey, "Voltaire's English Notebook," *Modern Philology*, XXVI, No. 3 (Feb., 1929), 310. For Dryden's lines, see *Works*, IX, 447.

> to prove religion true
> if either wit, or sufferings could suffice
> all faiths afford the constant, and the wise.
> and yet ev'n they by education sway'd
> in age deffend what infancy obeyd [19]

Item XLVI, two lines from Dryden's *The Hind and the Panther*, which Voltaire must have seen in Bysshe on the same page with the two above passages, is as follows:

> the priest continues what the nurse began
> and thus the child imposes on the man.[20]

Item XVI in the notebook consists of two lines from Dryden's *Œdipus*, which Voltaire probably found also in Bysshe under the heading "Woman," [21] for he misquotes them in the same manner as did Bysshe. Voltaire wrote them down as follows:

DRYDEN

> Our thoughtless sex is caught by outward form
> and empty noyse, and loves itself in man.[22]

Item XXX is a quotation from Dryden's prologue to *All for Love*, which no doubt Voltaire found in the *Spectator* of Saturday, February 2, 1712, since an anecdote which follows immediately after the lines in the *Spectator* was picked up by Voltaire and written down after the Dryden lines in his notebook.[23] Voltaire put down the two lines from Dryden as follows:

> errors like straw upon the surface flow
> he who would search for pearls must dive bellow.[24]

Item IX, Voltaire's first attempt to express himself in English upon the English theater,[25] is one of two passages which Voltaire may have based upon Dryden's *An Essay of Dramatick Poesie*. It reads: "theatre

---

[19] *Ibid*. For Dryden's lines see "Appendix," p. 156.
[20] *Ibid.*, p. 320. For Dryden's lines see *Works*, X, 221.
[21] Bysshe, *The Art of English Poetry*, II, 280.
[22] Torrey, "Voltaire's English Notebook," *Modern Philology*, XXVI, No. 3 (Feb., 1929), 312. Dryden's lines (Act I, Scene 1, Nonesuch ed., IV, 357) are as follows:
> That thoughtless Sex is caught by outward form
> And empty noise, and loves it self in man.
[23] *Ibid.*, p. 315n.
[24] *Ibid.*, p. 315. For Dryden's lines see Nonesuch ed., IV, 188.
[25] *Ibid.*, p. 310n.

in England is (boundless and temerarious) without decency etc." [26]
Torrey presents evidence which indicates that Voltaire was reading
Dryden's essay at the time.[27] Item LVI is a brief paragraph to the
effect that the romance languages arose from the breakdown of Latin.
Torrey notes that this opinion likewise may well have been based on a
similar passage in Dryden's essay.[28] Voltaire wrote:

> from the rubishes of the roman empire, several
> great kingdoms are formed, and grounded upon
> its ruines. in the same manner, italian tongue,
> the french, the spanish arose from the ruines of
> the roman language.[29]

The notebooks which form the *Sottisier,* some 137 pages in all, were
partially copied out by a Russian correspondent for Beuchot, the
scholarly editor of the 1828 edition of Voltaire's works. There are no
citations from Dryden in the fragmentary *Sottisier* as Beuchot and
subsequent editors have printed it, but in the photostatic copy of the
complete manuscript in the Library of Congress [30] there are eleven
quotations from Dryden, a total greater than that for Pope or for any
other English writer. There are none from Shakespeare. The Dryden
quotations, in the order in which they appear in the manuscript, with
the headings that Voltaire gave them, are as follows:

OF DRYDEN

> when I consider life, t'is all a cheat
> yet fool'd by hope, men favour the deceit
> trust on, and think to morrow will repay.
> to morrow comes, but worse than former day,
> gives less, and when she sais, we shall be blesst
> with some new joys, cut of what we possess.[31]
> strange cosenage. none would live past years again
> and all hope new pleasures from what yet still remain
> and from the dregs of life, think to receive
> what the first spritgly running could not give [32]

DRYDEN IN A TRAGEDY

> the common cry is ever relligion's test,
> the turk is at constantinople's best

---

[26] *Ibid.,* p. 310.   [27] *Ibid.,* p. 310n.   [28] *Ibid.,* p. 322n.   [29] *Ibid.,* p. 322.
[30] The Modern Language Association of America. *Collection of photographic facsimiles,
No. 183, 1931. A reproduction of Voltaire manuscript No. 240 in the Voltaire library of
the Public library, Leningrad, Russia.*
[31] *Ibid.,* Folio 17.   [32] (Lines 7–10), *ibid., verso.*

idols in india, Popery at Rome
and our own worship only true at home.
and true but for a time. t'is hard to know
how long we please it shall continue so
this side to day, and the other to morrow burns,
so all are god almighty in their turns [33]
if either wit or suffering could suffice
each faith afford the constant and the wise
and yet even they by education sway'd
in age deffend what infancy obey'd
the priest continues, what the nurse began
and thus the child imposes on the man [34]

OUT OF DRYDEN

the first phisicians by debauch were made
excess began, and sloth sustains the trade
by chace our long liv'd fathers earn'd their food
toil strung the nerves, and purified their blood
but we their sons a pamper'd race of men
are dwindled down to three score years and ten
better to hunt in fields for health unbought
than fee the doctor for the nauseous drought
the wise for cure on exercise depend
God never made his work for men to mend [35]

Down with him kill him, merit heaven thereby.
discourse of a priest in the conquest of mexico.[36]

in ancient times ee'r priestcraft did begin
before poligamy was taught a sin
when man on many multiplied his kind
eer one to one was cursedly confin'd
then israel's monarch after heaven's own heart
his vigorous warm did variously impart
to wives and slaves and wide as his command
scatter'd his maker's image through the land [37]

DRYDEN SUR MILTON

the force of nature coud not further go
to form the third, she join'd the former two [38]

DRYDEN, INDIAN EMPEROR

cessez de nous vanter vos faibles avantages,
nous avons comme vous nos martirs et nos sages.
il en est en tout temps, il en est en tous lieux

[33] Folio 17 verso.   [34] Ibid.   [35] Ibid., Folio 18.
[36] Ibid.   [37] Ibid., Folio 19.   [38] Ibid., Folio 57.

toute secte eut les siens, et tout peuple a ses dieux
nous naissons ignorants; lerreur de notre mere
sucee avec le lait nous en devient plus chere,
la nourrice commence, et le pretre finit
au joug des prejugez le temps nous endurcit
on se fait de l'erreur une triste science
l'age mur est encor la duppe de l'enfance
la superstition qui commence au berceau
tirannise la vie, et nous suit au tombeau [39]

FROM THE SPANISH FRYAR

jai peur que le mariage ne soit plustot
un des sept pechez mortels, qu'un des sept sacrements.[40]

DRYDEN

as if our world modestly witdrew
and here in secret had brought forth a new.[41]

There is no probability that the various parts of the *Sottisier* will ever be exactly dated, but it seems evident that certain of the sections given above represent notes that Voltaire took as early as 1727, for it is logical to suppose that the lines from Dryden which appear both in the *Sottisier* and the *Essay on Epic Poetry* were first copied down by Voltaire in his notebook and later transferred to the essay. A similar observation may be made about Dryden passages which appear in both the *Sottisier* and the *Lettres philosophiques.* As to the source of the Dryden quotations in the *Sottisier,* the ten lines from *Aureng-Zebe* which begin "when I consider life, t'is all a cheat" Voltaire could have found in Bysshe under the heading "Life." [42] The medley of fourteen lines which Voltaire grouped under the title "Dryden in a tragedy" were the lines from *The Medal, The Indian Emperour,* and *The Hind and the Panther,* which he had found in Bysshe and first copied out in the *English Notebook.* The lines which he noted simply as "out of Dryden" were from Dryden's epistle "To my honourd Kinsman, John Driden" and were available in Bysshe under the heading "Physick." [43] Neither the succeeding single line from *The Indian Emperour* [44] nor the eight lines regarding poligamy, from *Absalom and Achitophel,* [45] are in Bysshe. The lines on

[39] *Ibid.,* Folio 88, *verso.* [40] *Ibid.* [41] *Ibid.,* Folio 96.
[42] Bysshe, *The Art of English Poetry,* II, 9. For Dryden's lines see *Aureng-Zebe,* Act IV, Nonesuch ed., IV, 129.
[43] Bysshe, *The Art of English Poetry,* II, 117. For Dryden's lines see *Works,* XI, 75, 77.
[44] For Dryden's lines see "Appendix," p. 155. [45] For Dryden's lines see *Works,* IX, 219.

Milton were those which Dryden composed to be used as a caption beneath Milton's portrait in an edition by Tonson. They were frequently quoted and were in the 1715 edition of Bayle's dictionary.[46] The next twelve lines, headed "Dryden, indian emperor," are a paraphrase in French of the medley of lines which appeared above in English under the heading "Dryden in a tragedy." The two following lines, translated from *The Spanish Fryar*,[47] and the last two from *The Indian Emperour* [48] were not in Bysshe, and for them Voltaire may have gone to the plays themselves.

Some general observations may be hazarded on the basis of the Dryden citations in the *Sottisier*. Nearly all the passages have a bearing on religion. This was true of the quotations in the *English Notebook*, and it is no doubt an accurate indication of a central interest of Voltaire in Dryden. It may be inferred also, perhaps, that his interest in *The Indian Emperour* was first aroused by the passage in Bysshe which he copied in the *English Notebook* and that he then referred to the play itself for the additional quotations which appear in the *Sottisier*. At the time Voltaire was, perhaps, already sketching out *Alzire*, his adaptation of *The Indian Emperour*. In numerous places in his writings there is further evidence that his knowledge of this play was especially intimate. On the basis of the inaccuracies in the citations we may surmise also that Voltaire is often quoting Dryden by memory, a conclusion strengthened by the surprising ability he reveals late in life to recite verses from Dryden. Finally it may be concluded that certain passages in the *English Notebook* were made earlier than those which repeat them in the *Sottisier*, since in the latter there are more inaccuracies.

The fact that Voltaire makes no references to Shakespeare in the *English Notebook* or in the *Sottisier* must certainly be considered an indication of the nature of his interest in the English theater. The logical conclusion would seem to be that the references to Shakespeare in the *Lettres philosophiques* were due more to a desire to measure up to the expectations of the public than to satisfy any interest felt by Voltaire.

A question naturally arises with regard to Voltaire's interest in Dryden's thoughts upon religion. Why is there no evidence of interest in the *Sottisier* or elsewhere in Voltaire's writings, in Dryden's extensive

---

[46] Telleen, *Milton dans la littérature française*, p. 6.

[47] For Dryden's lines see *The Spanish Fryar*, Act V, Nonesuch ed., V, 197.

[48] For Dryden's lines see *The Indian Emperour*, Act I, scene 1, Nonesuch ed., I, 277.

expression of religious opinion in the *Religio Laici* and *The Hind and the Panther?* One answer must certainly be that Voltaire was interested in Dryden's skeptical turn of mind, not in his defense of Anglican doctrines in the *Religio Laici* and of Catholic doctrines in *The Hind and the Panther*. Moreover, these poems aroused little interest in Dryden's English readers,[49] and it is not likely that Voltaire would hear them quoted in English society. Another reason for Voltaire's lack of interest in these two poems is doubtless their style. All signs point to the fact that what Voltaire valued in Dryden was the combination of skeptical thought and heroic style which is especially evident in Dryden's plays. Elevation of style is markedly absent from both the *Religio Laici* and *The Hind and the Panther*.[50]

While preparing to write *An Essay on Epick Poetry*, which he published in London in 1727,[51] Voltaire read Dryden's celebrated *Dedication to the Aeneïs*. Early in his essay he asks indulgence for the author, "who has learned English but this year" and has "drawn most of his Observations from Books written in England." [52] Florence D. White, in her edition of the essay, observes that Voltaire spoke truly, for he drew many of his observations from Addison's *Spectator* and from Pope's preface to the *Iliad*.[53] It would have been natural for him to read Dryden's essay at the same time, and he says himself that he did so. He first quotes Dryden's lines on Milton which he had noted down in the *Sottisier* and then remarks with astonishment that Dryden, in his *Preface to the Aeneïs,* ranks Milton with Chapelain and Le Moyne, who, Voltaire says, were "the most impertinent Poets who ever scribbled." [54] Another indication that Voltaire knew Dryden's preface is, perhaps, offered by his references to Denham's poem *Cooper's Hill*.[55] Dryden had quoted lines from Denham's poem to show the sweetness of English verse.[56] Voltaire quotes the same lines with the two preced-

---

[49] See comments of Scott in *Works*, X, 6, 8.

[50] In the preface to "Religio Laici" Dryden remarks that he has imitated the epistolary style of Horace and has not attempted to give his poem "the numbers, and the turn of heroic poetry" (*Works*, X, 32), and in the preface to "The Hind and the Panther" he comments that he gave the first part the majestic turn of heroic poetry, made the second part "plain and perspicuous" and the third part still more free and familiar (*Works*, X, 117).

[51] White, in *Voltaire's Essay on Epic Poetry*, p. 8.

[52] *Ibid.*, p. 88.　　　　　　　　　　[53] *Ibid.*, p. 88n.

[54] *Ibid.*, p. 134.　　　　　　　　　　[55] *Ibid.*, p. 111.

[56] Dryden, "Dedication to the *Aeneïs*," *Works*, XIV, 207.

ing ones and compares them with similar lines in Camoëns's epic poem, as a proof that "Wit is of the Growth of every Country." [57]

That Voltaire was also reading Dryden's *An Essay of Dramatick Poesie* at this time is probably indicated by the similarity of a passage in his essay to a passage in Dryden's. Dryden, after weighing the tumult of activity on the English stage against the solemn narrations and long discourses of the French stage, concludes that if the English are to be blamed for showing too much action, the French are as much at fault for discovering too little and that a "mean betwixt them should be observed." [58] He suggests that the English should avoid showing such unrealistic occurrences as the death of a character, at which English audiences cannot forbear laughing, and the French should avoid having the actors "speak by the hour-glass," since it is unnatural to speak for a long time in a gust of passion. Voltaire comments similarly that the English and the French theaters might mutually profit by an exchange of ideas.

Would each Nation attend a little more than they do, to the Taste and the Manners of their respective Neighbours, perhaps a general good Taste might diffuse itself through all *Europe* from such an intercourse of Learning, and from that useful Exchange of Observations. The *English* Stage, for Example, might be clear'd of mangled Carcasses, and the Style of their tragick Authors, come down from their forced Metaphorical Bombast to a nearer Imitation of Nature. The *French* would learn from the *English* to animate their Tragedies with more Action, and would contract now and then their long Speeches into shorter and warmer Sentiments.[59]

Voltaire devotes the letter "Sur la tragédie," No. 18 of the *Lettres philosophiques,* to discussion of Shakespeare, Dryden, and Addison. In the section on Shakespeare he makes the usual statement with regard to the sublime genius of Shakespeare and qualifies it in the usual way by saying that Shakespeare completely lacked taste and knowledge of the theater.[60] The merit of Shakespeare, says Voltaire, has been fatal to the English theater, for "la plûpart des idées bizarres & gigantesques de cet auteur, ont acquis au bout de deux cens ans le droit de passer pour sublimes." [61] Voltaire mentions Otway's *Venice Preserved* to show that

[57] White, in *Voltaire's Essay on Epic Poetry*, p. 112.
[58] Nonesuch ed., I, 37.
[59] White, in *Voltaire's Essay on Epic Poetry*, p. 135.
[60] Voltaire, *Lettres philosophiques*, ed. by Gustave Lanson, II, 79.
[61] *Ibid.*

the buffoonery which marred the tragedies of Shakespeare was imitated even in the reign of Charles II, which, he says, was the "âge d'or des beaux arts" in England.[62] The only passage from Shakespeare that Voltaire quotes is the monologue of Hamlet, which, he says, is "sçu de tout le monde." [63] As he does for all his citations in the letter, Voltaire gives his own translation.

Voltaire turns to Dryden with the following introductory comment:

Voici encore un passage d'un fameux tragique anglais, Dryden poéte du tems de Charles Second, auteur plus fécond que judicieux qui auroit une réputation sans mélange, s'il n'avoit fait que la dixième partie de ses ouvrages, & dont le grand défaut est d'avoir voulu être universel.[64]

He then translates the passage from Dryden's *Aureng-Zebe*, which he had noted down in the *Sottisier*, and comments on the passage as follows, giving particular attention to Dryden's elevation of style:

C'est dans ces morceaux détachés que les tragiques Anglais ont jusqu'ici excellé: leurs pieces presque toutes barbares, dépourvues de bienséance, d'ordre, de vrai-semblance, ont des lueurs étonnantes au milieu de cette nuit. Le stile est trop ampoulé, trop hors de la nature, trop copié des écrivains hébreux si remplis de l'enflur asiatique; mais aussi il faut avouer que les échasses du stile figuré, sur lesquelles la langue anglaise est guindée, élévent aussi l'esprit bien haut, quoique par une marche irréguliére.[65]

In the 1742 edition of the *Lettres philosophiques* the section devoted to Dryden is considerably augmented by the addition of two passages from *The Indian Emperour*.[66] One is a reworking of the passage which Voltaire had already translated in the *Sottisier;* the other is the translation of a bit of dialogue between Pizarro and the Indian emperor from Act I, scene 2.[67] Voltaire's introductory comment to the first passage is as follows:

Voici un morceau de son Montézume, dans lequel cet infortuné Monarque réfute les argumens du Jacobin qui veut le rendre Chrétien pour le préparer doucement au supplice qu'on lui destine.

After giving the twelve lines, Voltaire continues:

Dans la même pièce Pizare dit à Montezume:

> L'envoyé du Très-Haut, le maître de ma loi,
> Le Pape a transporté ton Empire à mon Roi.

[62] *Ibid.*, p. 80.   [63] *Ibid.*, p. 81.   [64] *Ibid.*, p. 83.
[65] *Ibid.*, pp. 83–84.   [66] *Ibid.*, p. 83n.
[67] For Dryden's lines see "Appendix," pp. 153–54.

L'Empereur Mexiquain répond:

> Le Pape est l'ennemi du Dieu qu'il représente,
> S'il autorise ainsi ton audace insolente;
> Et c'est un insensé s'il donne mes Etats,
> Dont il n'est point le maître, & qu'il ne connoit pas.

In the edition of 1756 Voltaire adds still another Dryden passage,[68] this time the translation of a tirade against kings which Voltaire seems to have found himself in *Don Sebastian,* although part of the passage had appeared in Bysshe under the heading "Flattery." [69] By 1756 Voltaire believed that imitation of the English theater had gone too far, and the comment which he makes on the passage is the familiar charge that the English lack taste. Kings, says Voltaire, should never be addressed as Dryden makes his officer speak to Don Sebastian. The low tone of the passage illustrates how long it takes for a nation to achieve good taste. Even the Greeks showed such deplorable judgment in their tragedies that modern translators are at times embarrassed.

The original section devoted to Addison in the "Lettre sur la tragédie" is limited to a short paragraph in which Voltaire remarks that Addison's *Cato* was the first English play "raisonnable & écrite d'un bout à l'autre avec élégance" [70] and that the role of Cato is superior to that of Cornélie in Corneille's *Pompée.* The other personnages in *Cato,* Voltaire says, are inferior, and the play is injured by a cold intrigue of love "qui répand sur la piece une langueur qui la tue." In a later edition this paragraph is replaced by a new one of greater length in which Voltaire stresses particularly the scene in which Cato is shown in his *robe de chambre* reading to himself from *Plato.*[71] Voltaire doubts that a Parisian audience would enjoy Cato's fine monologue on the immortality of the soul. The play was addressed, says Voltaire, to an audience "un peu philosophique et tres Républicain." He then gives a translation of the monologue in some thirty lines.

The letter "Sur la tragédie" thus offers evidence that Voltaire's interest in Dryden outweighed his interest in either Shakespeare or Addison. He gives almost twice as much space to quotations from Dryden as to those from Shakespeare or Addison and reveals his continued interest

---

[68] *Lettres philosophiques,* ed. by Gustave Lanson, II, 84*n.*
[69] Bysshe, Edward, *The Art of English Poetry,* I, 185–86.
[70] *Lettres philosophiques,* ed. by Gustave Lanson, II, 84–85.
[71] *Ibid.,* pp. 85–86*n.*

in Dryden by new comment and new citations in 1742 and 1756, respectively. In speaking of Shakespeare he mistakes the date of his death by fifty years [72] and makes only the general critical remarks on his genius and lack of taste which had been made frequently by neoclassic critics of England and France. In his comments on Dryden he attacks with more precision, giving the particular attention to details of style which always marked his approach to works in which he was keenly interested.[73]

Voltaire was still putting the finishing touches upon the *Lettres philosophiques* when he composed *Zaïre* and *Alzire*, the former built around a theme contained in lines from Dryden which Voltaire had noted down in the *English Notebook* and in the *Sottisier*, the latter an adaptation of *The Indian Emperour*. In his letter to Falkener prefixed to *Zaïre* Voltaire speaks at length of Dryden and answers Dryden's attack on Racine by saying that Dryden showed by the indecency of his portrayal of love that he was unacquainted with the rules for tragedy.[74]

How closely Voltaire's conception of tragedy approached the heroic conception of Dryden is revealed by the similarity of Voltaire's *Dissertation sur la tragédie ancienne et moderne*, published with *Sémiramis*,[75] to Dryden's "Of Heroique Playes," the essay prefixed to *The Conquest of Granada*.[76] Dryden's essay represents his most advanced position, his farthest departure from the main tradition of English drama, and Voltaire's essay likewise represents, at least with regard to remarks on style, Voltaire's most extreme position. Dryden's play was followed by the *Rehearsal* which ridiculed heroic tragedy and did much to deflate Dryden's grandiose ideal.[77] Likewise, *Sémiramis* aroused critical disapproval and was followed by a forced retreat on Voltaire's part to a less elevated conception.

In his essay Dryden makes three main points in describing his conception of what heroic tragedy should be. He says that it should be marked by great elevation of character and of style,[78] that it should rise beyond the actualities of plain history and include "Gods and Spirits," as does the epic poem,[79] and finally that it should present examples of

[72] *Ibid.*, p. 79.   [73] See Naves, *Le Goût de Voltaire*, pp. 186 ff.
[74] *Œuvres*, II, 552–53.   [75] *Ibid.*, IV, 487 ff.
[76] Dryden, Nonesuch ed., III, 19 ff.
[77] Nicoll, *A History of Restoration Drama 1660–1700*, p. 235.
[78] Dryden, Nonesuch ed., III, 20–21, 23.   [79] *Ibid.*, pp. 21–22.

heroic virtue for admiration and imitation.[80] Voltaire's critical ideal, presented in his *Dissertation sur la tragédie ancienne et moderne,* is essentially that of Dryden, but there is no indication that he drew upon Dryden's essay. Like Dryden, he makes elevation of character and style, the use of the marvelous, and seriousness of moral purpose the requirements for tragedy. With regard to characters, he prefers the heroic figures of *Cinna* and *Athalie* to the gallant courtiers typical of the contemporary Parisian theater. He emphasizes the necessity for proper pomp and elevation of diction.[81] He advocates the use of ghosts, and his remarks reveal that he conceives a ghost to be a *deus ex machina* in the tradition of epic poetry. His final point is that tragedy should teach a moral, that "la véritable tragédie est l'école de la vertu." [82]

Dryden continued to be an example for Voltaire. In 1750 he used the episode of the Mexican prince and high priest on the torture rack which he had found in *The Indian Emperour* in his *Essai sur les mœurs.*[83] In the section on fine arts of the *Siècle de Louis XIV,* composed during the same period, he paid his highest tribute to Dryden as a poet, whose merit "aucun poëte de sa nation n'égale, et qu'aucun ancien n'a surpassé." [84] In the years when he was working on the *Commentaire sur Corneille* Voltaire lost some of his enthusiasm for grandiose rhetoric, and he aimed at Dryden the same kind of criticism which he directed against

---

[80] *Ibid.,* p. 23.   [81] *Œuvres,* IV, 498.

[82] *Ibid.,* 505.

[83] Voltaire, in *Alzire,* does not show the torture of the Indian prince, but mentions it in recital. But in the chapter on Cortez in the *Essai sur les mœurs (Œuvres,* XII, 396), he gives what is evidently the torture episode of *The Indian Emperour* and passes it off as authentic history, no doubt because he delighted in Dryden's satire. According to historical accounts, Cortez, after the capture of Mexico City, was forced by his fellow soldiers to consent to the torture of the young Mexican prince Guatemozin and of the Indian chief Tacuba. Only one historian, Lopez de Gomara (*Cronica,* cap. 145), gives any picturesque detail of the torture scene. Gomara portrays the prince as rebuking Tacuba for groaning when the Spaniards burn his feet. "Estoi yo en algun deleite, o bano?" he asks. Dryden, in *The Indian Emperour,* changes the circumstances and represents Montezuma as still alive and subjected to torture. On the rack with Montezuma Dryden places, not a fellow chieftain, but the Emperor's High Priest. Dryden changes the words of the tortured king, spoken when the High Priest longs for death, to:

> Think'st thou I lye on Beds of Roses, here,
> Or in a Wanton Bath stretch'd at my ease?
> Dye, Slave, and with thee dye such thoughts as these.

For Dryden's lines see Appendix. Voltaire in giving the scene in the *Essai sur les mœurs* is historically accurate in putting Guatemozin, not Montezuma, to torture, but cannot resist the temptation of placing the High Priest on the rack and having the Indian prince rebuke him with: "Et moi, suis-je sur un lit de roses?"

[84] *Œuvres,* XIV, 560.

Corneille. In the *Commentaire sur Medée,* for example, Voltaire condemns the inflated figures of speech used by Dryden and cites an example from *All for Love.*[85] But evidence of his special interest and high esteem for Dryden continued to issue from Voltaire's ever active pen. Like Dryden, he turned in his later years to Ariosto and Boccaccio with more and more pleasure, and in a letter to Damilaville in 1763 [86] he revealed that he was aware of Dryden's version of the *Wife of Bath's Tale* and that he had it in mind when he wrote his own version under the title *Ce qui plaît aux dames.*

There is good proof of his continued high esteem for Dryden's style in his words to James Boswell in 1764. When Boswell was in Geneva in December of that year he visited both Rousseau and Voltaire. Later, in reporting to Dr. Johnson on the hour he had spent in conversation with Voltaire at Ferney, Boswell said that Voltaire had distinguished Pope and Dryden thus: "Pope drives a handsome chariot, with a couple of neat trim nags; Dryden a coach, and six stately horses." Dr. Johnson's answer was: "Why, Sir, the truth is, they both drive coaches and six; but Dryden's horses are either galloping or stumbling: Pope's go at a steady even trot." [87]

Perhaps the most striking instance of Voltaire's late interest in Dryden is contained in a letter written in 1764 by the Chevalier de Boufflers, who seems to have spent several days at Ferney with Voltaire. While there he wrote to his wife an account of the visit of an Englishman to Ferney. Voltaire took delight, Boufflers wrote, in reciting "tous les poèmes de Dryden." The passage in Boufflers's letters is as follows:

Il est venu hier chez lui un Anglais qui ne peut se lasser de l'entendre parler anglais, et réciter tous les poëmes de Dryden comme Panpan récite la *Jeanne,* Cet homme là est trop grand pour être contenu dans les limites de son pays; c'est un présent que la nature a fait à toute la terre. Il a le don des langues et des *in-folio,* car on ne sait pas comment il a eu le temps d'apprendre les unes et de lire les autres.[88]

That at the age of seventy years Voltaire was able to recite a considerable number of verses from Dryden by memory is conclusive evidence of his special regard for Dryden.

[85] *Ibid.,* XXXI, 186.   [86] *Ibid.,* XLIII, p. 54.
[87] Boswell, *The Life of Samuel Johnson, LL.D.,* ed. by Percy Fitzgerald, I, 311.
[88] *Œuvres,* I, 354.

In 1768 Voltaire defended the use of rhyme in the theater in a letter to Horace Walpole by citing the example of Dryden.

Il faut que je vous dise encore un mot sur la rime que vous nous reprochez. Presque toutes les pièces de Dryden sont rimées; c'est une difficulté de plus. Les vers qu'on retient de lui, et que tout le monde cite, sont rimés: et je soutiens encore que *Cinna, Athalie, Phèdre, Iphigénie,* étant rimées quiconque voudrait secouer ce joug, en France, serait regardé comme un artiste faible qui n'aurait pas la force de le porter.[89]

In 1770, in writing the article "Blasphème" for the *Questions sur l'Encyclopédie,* in which he declares that the charge of blasphemy is the habitual weapon with which religious sects attack rival sects and that in accusing the Jansenists of blasphemy the Jesuits did just what the "joviens" did to the early Christians, the lines from Dryden's *The Medal* come back to Voltaire and he writes:

Dryden a dit:
> This side to day, and the other to morrow burns,
> And they are all God's almighty in their turns.

> Tel est chaque parti, dans sa rage obstiné,
> Aujourd'hui condamnant, et demain condamné.[90]

The errors in the English would indicate again that Voltaire relied on his memory, rather than on his *English Notebook,* the *Sottisier,* or any volume of Dryden which he had by him.[91]

Further evidence of Voltaire's intimate acquaintance with Dryden's *The Indian Emperour* is revealed in the article "Espace" in the *Questions sur l'encyclopédie* of 1771. In seeking to refute Leibnitz's assertion that "il n'y a point d'espace, point de vide," Voltaire recalls the words of Montezuma, and he writes:

Du moins Montézume raisonnait plus juste dans la tragédie anglaise de Dryden: "Que venez-vous me dire au nom de l'empereur Charles-Quint? il n'y a que deux empereurs dans le monde, celui du Pérou et moi." Monté-

[89] *Ibid.,* XLVI, 83.   [90] *Ibid.,* XVIII, 5.
[91] In "Voltaire's Books: a Selected List," *Modern Philology,* XXVII (August, 1929), 1–22, George R. Havens and Norman L. Torrey give a partial list of the books in Voltaire's library now in Leningrad. The only Dryden work included is the part of the first volume of *The Dramatick Works,* 6 vols., London, 1735, which contains the "Essay of Dramatick Poesy." The authors comment that the other volumes are no longer in Voltaire's library or perhaps never were (p. 10). They note that in Voltaire's eighteenth-century MS catalogue are listed: "Driden's *Fables,*" 1 vol., and Dryden's *Two Plays,* 1 vol.

zume parlait de deux choses qu'il connaissait; mais nous autres, nous parlons de deux choses dont nous n'avons aucune idée nette.[92]

It was in the same year, in the article "Enthousiasme," written for the *Questions sur l'Encyclopédie,*[93] that Voltaire retracted to a certain degree the charge of bombast which he had made against Dryden in the *Commentaire sur Médée.* He now praises Dryden's *Alexander's Feast* for falling "ni dans le faux ni dans l'ampoulé." In the following year Voltaire wrote to Chabanon that he valued Dryden's ode a hundred times more than all of Pindar.[94]

In the year 1776, only two years before Voltaire's death, another English traveler, Martin Sherlock, visited Ferney. To him Voltaire repeated his praise of Addison's *Cato* and his opinion that the English language is "énergique, précise et barbare." [95] He added that while he was not able to pronounce English perfectly, his ear was aware of the harmony of English poetry and that Pope and Dryden "avaient le plus d'harmonie dans la poésie, Addison dans la prose."

These are the only specific instances Voltaire's collected works yield to show his interest in Dryden. The only plays we can be sure that Voltaire read with some care are *The Indian Emperour,* which provided him with a model for *Alzire,* and *All for Love,* to which he refers with an authority which would seem too great to be gathered from the passages which were available in Bysshe. He also quotes from *The Spanish Fryar, Don Sebastian, Aureng-Zebe,* and *Oedipus,* but only once from each play, and, except for the single line from *The Spanish Fryar,* he mentions only passages which were wholly or in part in the anthology of Bysshe. As for the poems of Dryden, Voltaire praises *Alexander's Feast* so highly that it would seem that he knew it well. He also quotes one passage from *The Medal,* which he used later in *Zaïre,* two lines from *The Hind and the Panther,* and some lines on physicians from one of Dryden's epistles, but in each case, the lines are in Bysshe. There is also indicated in the *English Notebook* some familiarity with Dryden's *An Essay of Dramatick Poesie,* and, as might be expected, Voltaire's *Essay on Epic Poetry* indicates some familiarity with Dryden's preface to the *Aeneid,* Dryden's most extensive discussion of the epic.

These examples of Voltaire's direct knowledge of the works of Dryden

---

[92] *Œuvres,* XIX, 1–2. For Dryden's lines see "Appendix," p. 153.
[93] *Ibid.,* XVIII, 555–56.   [94] *Ibid.,* XLVIII, 42.   [95] *Ibid.,* I, 393.

reveal that two aspects of Dryden's poetry especially caught and held Voltaire's attention: Dryden's expression of skeptical thought and Dryden's magnificent style. Dryden represented to Voltaire an outstanding example of the hardiness of thought, freedom of expression and energetic style, which so impressed him in English literature. But when Voltaire, safe in Ferney, turned from *belles lettres* to propaganda, he did not depend on Dryden to supply him with philosophical ammunition, but went to the writings of the English deists.[96] Moreover, it is evident that Voltaire thought of Dryden principally as the author of tragedy. He applied the lessons he learned from Dryden chiefly in his own tragedies, and it is the similarity of their conceptions of tragedy which seems to be the key to their relationship. Dryden accepted the neoclassic theory that there is no fundamental distinction between epic poem and tragedy, and he explained and defended his theory in a number of essays. As the following chapters will show, Voltaire held the same idea, but did not theorize on the relationship of epic and tragedy, since their essential identity had long been accepted by critics in France.

In view of their similar conceptions of tragedy Voltaire's interest in Dryden's play *The Indian Emperour* can be easily understood. If Voltaire had been interested chiefly in a brutal and satirical attack on priests, he would have found much better material in *The Spanish Fryar*. But *The Spanish Fryar* is largely farce, and Voltaire was a tragedian. It is in blank verse and prose, and Voltaire's ambition was an elevated style in Alexandrines. *The Indian Emperour,* based on popular romance material, is full of arguments in heroic verse upon natural religion, and to Voltaire it was audacious in its introduction of such modern European figures as Cortez and Pizzaro, for this gave it an immediacy of application to contemporary society which no play had had in France for nearly century.

[96] See Torrey, *Voltaire and the English Deists.*

CHAPTER VI   VOLTAIRE'S MORAL CONCEPTION OF TRAGEDY

APPROACHING the drama critically rather than creatively, Voltaire tried to conform to the doctrine of Dacier that tragedy should teach delightfully by giving notable representations of virtue and vice. Whether he was treating the legends of Greek mythology, the stoical themes of Roman history, or the chivalric adventures of the heroic romances, the didactic purpose of his plays is always evident. Nearest to the theory of Dacier are his Greek tragedies; in composing them he seems actually to have started with a maxim. In their glorification of stoic patriotism and their declamatory style his Roman plays are epic in the sense that Addison's *Cato* was. With *Zaïre* he inaugurated a series of tragedies which may be called "heroic" in the manner of Dryden.

Whereas Dryden's attachment to the doctrine of epic didacticism had been more evident in his critical essays than in his dramatic practice, the contrary is true of Voltaire. What Voltaire says of the moral purpose of tragedy is always in accordance with the views of Dacier, but he nowhere takes the pains that Dryden did to justify and explain the theory underlying his conception. This is not surprising, since Dryden had been engaged in justifying an innovation in English criticism, while Voltaire was pursuing a doctrine that had been generally accepted by critics in France.

Voltaire's didactic conception of tragedy, however, is plainly enough stated in his essays and prefaces. The following, for example, in the preface to *Sémiramis* is typical and is in conformity with the precepts of Rapin and Dacier.

La véritable tragédie est l'école de la vertu; et la seule différence qui soit entre le théâtre épuré et les livres de morale, c'est que l'instruction se trouve dans la tragédie toute en action, c'est qu'elle y est intéressante, et qu'elle se montre relevée des charmes d'un art qui ne fut inventé autrefois que pour instruire la terre et pour bénir le ciel, et qui par cette raison, fut appelé le langage des dieux.[1]

Comments in his correspondence bear out this critical attitude and indicate that no doubt as to the didactic purpose of tragedy ever crossed

[1] *Œuvres*, IV, 505.

Voltaire's mind. Remarks such as the following in a letter to D'Argental in 1769 are continually recurring in his letters. "Les spectacles adoucissent les mœurs; et, quand la philosophie s'y joint, la superstition est bientôt écrasée." [2]

Voltaire's five plays on Greek themes are essentially parables illustrating that there is a "dieu vengeur" who punishes secret crimes. The necessity of encouraging a belief in a god of vengeance as a curb on unscrupulous actions is an idea central to the neoclassic conception of tragedy as a warning against wrongdoing. Voltaire consistently supported this belief, even though he doubted the existence of any such system of rewards and punishments.[3] Dryden discusses the question briefly in speaking of the philosophy of Lucretius.[4]

For the subject of his first play, written when he was barely twenty years old, Voltaire chose the "Oedipus" legend, which Rapin, Fénelon, and other critics, including Addison, had said, following Aristotle, is the best of all possible subjects for tragedy. Voltaire says that he consulted with Dacier about his play and that he went to Dacier's translation and comments.[5] He weighs Dacier's advice upon the use of a chorus to underline the moral lesson, but concludes that the modern demand for *vraisemblance* limits the utility of this device.[6] The play, which was a great success, is filled with lines which recall Racine and Corneille and served principally to announce the arrival in Paris of a new master in the theater.

Voltaire returned to Greek themes in *Eriphyle* (1732), *Mérope* (1743), *Sémiramis* (1748), and *Oreste* (1750). Lessing's remark that *Sémiramis* was built around the maxim that divine justice selects extraordinary means to punish extraordinary crimes applies equally well to *Eriphyle, Mérope,* and *Oreste*.[7] Of *Oreste* Voltaire himself says, in the *Dissertation sur les principales tragédies anciennes et modernes,* which accompanies the play, that it was "une maxime reçue chez tous les anciens que

---

[2] *Ibid.,* XLVI, 448.

[3] Voltaire wrote to the Duke of Richelieu in 1770 (*Œuvres,* XLVII, 240–41) regarding the deterministic doctrines of D'Holbach's *Système de la nature:* "Au reste, je pense qu'il est toujours très-bon de soutenir la doctrine de l'existence d'un Dieu rémunérateur et vengeur; la société a besoin de cette opinion. Je ne sais si vous connaissez ce vers: 'Si Dieu n'existait pas, il faudrait l'inventer.' "

[4] In the preface to *The Second Miscellany, Works,* XII, 292.

[5] *Œuvres,* II, 18–19, 25.

[6] *Ibid.,* p. 42. See also Voltaire's letter to Porée, *Œuvres,* XXXIII, 198.

[7] Lessing, *Hamburgische Dramaturgie,* in *Sämmtliche Schriften,* VII, 53–54.

les dieux punissaient la moindre désobéissance à leurs ordres comme les plus grands crimes."[8] In the same essay Voltaire quotes Rapin to the effect that tragedy "est une leçon publique, plus instructive, sans comparaison, que la philosophie."[9]

Voltaire declares in the *Dissertation sur la tragédie ancienne et moderne,* published with *Sémiramis,* that all men, because of an inborn sense of justice, like to believe that a Supreme Being punishes crimes which men are unable to bring to judgment and argues that a play portraying such divine intervention in the affairs of men is bound to bring pleasure to the spectators. From the first scene of *Sémiramis,* he says, one perceives that "tout doit se faire par le ministère céleste; tout roule d'acte en acte sur cette idée."[10] It is an avenging deity who inspires remorse in the queen "et c'est de là même que résulte l'instruction qu'on peut tirer de la pièce." Voltaire concludes:

> Je pourrais surtout appliquer à la tragédie de *Sémiramis* la morale par laquelle Euripide finit son *Alceste,* pièce dans laquelle le merveilleux règne bien davantage: "Que les dieux emploient des moyens étonnants pour exécuter leurs éternels décrets! Que les grands événements qu'il ménagent surpassent les idées des mortels!"[11]

Critics have often asserted that the ghost of the murdered king in *Sémiramis* was directly inspired by the ghost of Hamlet's father.[12] The ghost in *Hamlet* had made a strong impression upon Voltaire when he saw the play in London,[13] but his comments reveal that the ghost of Ninus represents fundamentally the introduction of the marvelous element of epic poetry and the opera and consequently resembles Dryden's use of the supernatural more than Shakespeare's. Shakespeare appealed to a folk belief in spirits in order to raise the spectators' hair, but Voltaire made of his ghost purely a *deus ex machina.*[14] When he withdrew

---

[8] *Œuvres,* V, 185.   [9] *Ibid.,* V, 169n.

[10] *Ibid.,* IV, 504.   [11] *Ibid.,* p. 504–5.

[12] See Lacroix, *Histoire de l'influence de Shakespeare sur le théâtre français,* p. 101; Lion, *Les Tragédies et les théories dramatiques de Voltaire,* pp. 67, 196–97; Jusserand, *Shakespeare en France,* pp. 206 ff.; Lounsbury, *Shakespeare and Voltaire,* p. 124; Sonet, *Voltaire et l'influence anglaise,* pp. 63 ff.

[13] See Voltaire's reference for example in the *Dissertation sur la tragédie ancienne et moderne, Œuvres,* IV, 502.

[14] See Gros, *Philippe Quinault,* p. 741n: "On pense à Shakespeare et à l'ombre d'*Hamlet,* qui a hanté Voltaire; on pense aux Grecs, dont il se réclamera bientôt; il faut penser aussi à l'opéra (l'ombre d'Ardan Canile dans *Amadis,* III, 3) et à sa machinerie." See also Lessing, *Hamburgische Dramaturgie,* in *Sämmtliche Schriften,* VII, 53.

Sémiramis for revision, he wrote significantly: "Je donne plus au tragique et moins à l'épique, et je substitue, autant que je peux, le vrai au merveilleux. Je conserve pourtant toujours mon ombre." [15] *Sémiramis* seems to have been the inspiration of a series of discussions in the *Nouvelles littéraires* and the *Correspondance littéraire* upon the proper use of the supernatural, the gist of which is that it should be limited to the epic poem and to the opera.[16] Grimm commented in 1754, for instance, that "Le merveilleux n'appartient de droit qu'au poëte épique qui peint sans couleur, non pas pour nos yeux, mais pour notre imagination." [17]

In England Voltaire sketched out and partly finished two plays on Roman themes, *Brutus* and *La Mort de César,* that he might give his fellow countrymen an idea of English tragedy.[18] It has been widely accepted that the plays were in imitation of Shakespeare, but the translation of Antony's speech from *Julius Caesar,* which forms the last scene of *La Mort de César,* is really an *hors d'œuvre,*[19] and there is little evidence in either play of any English influence save the didacticism so dominant in formal Augustan tragedy and notably in Addison's *Cato.*[20] The two

[15] In a letter to Formont in 1732, *Œuvres,* XXXIII, 274.

[16] See *Correspondance littéraire philosophique et critique,* I, 207; II, 343 ff.; III, 274 ff., 317 ff.

[17] *Ibid.,* II, 345.

[18] Of *Brutus* Voltaire remarked in the "Discours sur la tragédie à milord Bolingbroke" that he wished to "transporter sur notre scène certaines beautés de la vôtre" (*Œuvres,* II, 314). To the Abbé Asselin Voltaire wrote in 1735 concerning *La Mort de César:* "Cette pièce n'a d'autre mérite que celui de faire voir le génie des Romains, et celui du théâtre anglais" (*Œuvres,* XXXIII, 544).

[19] See Lion, *Les Tragédies . . . de Voltaire,* pp. 62–63.

[20] That *Brutus* and *La Mort de César* reflect the influence of Addison rather than of Shakespeare is the opinion of Villemain, Faguet, and Lanson. In "Voltaire et la littérature de la Reine Anne," *Revue des deux mondes,* 4th ser., X (April, 1837), 77, Villemain comments on Addison's *Cato:* "En tout, cette tragédie offrait, avec quelques beautés neuves, une imitation correcte, mais affaiblie, de la manière de Corneille. Conduite avec peu d'art, dans sa régularité, elle fut un effort remarquable, mais impuissant, pour changer la forme du théâtre anglais, une œuvre de critique, et non de fondateur. Elle ne fut pas inutile à Voltaire, pour le choix des ornemens qu'il a jetés dans ses pièces romaines, *Brutus, Catilina, La Mort de César, Rome sauvée.* Il en a même emprunté littéralement quelques beaux traits." In "Jugements particuliers de Voltaire sur plusieurs grands écrivains," *Revue des cours et conférences,* IX, 1st ser. (Nov. 29, 1900), 100, Faguet observes: "Voltaire a une affection particulière pour ce sage, discret et judicieux poète, pour cet excellent prosateur en vers. Addison, en somme, comprenait la poésie à sa manière, comme un enseignement clair, précis et grave, comme quelque chose de continuellement didactique. Sa tragédie de *Caton,* qui est surtout, à propos de la mort du héros d'Utique, une exposition de grands principes et de fortes idées, a servi de type aux tragédies de Voltaire. Il ne faut jamais oublier que celui-ci avait fait peu de pièces avant son départ pour l'Angleterre; c'est depuis seulement qu'il a donné au genre tragique

plays were little more than exercises; *Brutus* had little success, and *La Mort de César* did not achieve a performance before 1743. Their Republican ideas, hardly representative of Voltaire's own thinking, were far from any political actualities of the day in France. Lucius Junius Brutus, founder of the Republic, is presented in *Brutus* as an example of steadfast patriotism who condemns his own son to death for a conspiracy against the Republic. In *La Mort de César* the situation is reversed: Marcus Brutus, portrayed as the son of Julius Caesar, aids in the assassination of his father out of love of Republican principles, despite his father's affection for him and his father's proposal that he shall succeed to the throne.

Voltaire found it difficult to repeat the success he had enjoyed earlier with *Œdipe*. *Mariamne* was laughed out of the theater in 1724 because he introduced some action in the English style instead of using the traditional *récit*.[21] His two Roman plays aroused little interest, and *Eriphyle* lasted for only a few performances in 1732, even though Voltaire turned over the box office receipts to the actors in an attempt to spur them to do their best. Later in the same year he tried an entirely new approach in *Zaïre*(Abandoning the pompous themes of Greek mythology and the sententious moralizing of the Roman tragedies, he turned for subject matter to the heroic romances, whose situations still dominated the Parisian stage, despite the protests of the critics.[22] The overwhelming success of *Zaïre* insured his further working of the same vein.

---

ce tour dogmatique et cette allure d'apostolat renouvelés, non de Shakespeare, mais d'Addison. In *Histoire de la littérature française,* pp. 691–92, Lanson comments upon Voltaire's sojourn in England: "Les trois années qu'il y passa furent une contre-expérience qui précisa toutes les notions déjà élaborées en lui. L'Angleterre n'a pas créé Voltaire: elle l'a instruit. Il aimait trop les lettres pour ne pas s'apercevoir qu'il y avait là une grande littérature: il découvrit Shakespeare, et Milton, et les comiques de la Restauration, Wycherley, Congreve. L'époque de la reine Anne était faite pour lui plaire: c'est le temps ou l'ineffaçable originalité de l'esprit anglais se déguise le mieux sous le goût décent et la sévère ordonnance dont nos chefs-d'œuvre classiques donnaient le modèle. Ce que Dryden, Addison avaient de français, l'induisait à goûter dans une certaine mesure leurs qualités anglaises. Dryden lui donna l'idée d'un drame plus violent; Addison, par son *Caton,* l'instruisit à moraliser la tragédie, à y poser nettement la thèse philosophique."

[21] See Moland's note, in *Œuvres,* II, 161.

[22] There is evidence in the journals of the period that the vogue of the heroic romances had to some degree returned. In the *Pour et contre,* I, 260, Prévost remarks that the *Astrée* had been republished and that "si quelqu'un était capable de rapeller l'ancien goût de la nation pour les romans étendus," it would be this handsome new edition. The *Observations sur les écrits modernes,* VIII (1737), Lettre CVII, 25, speaking of the deplorable state of the republic of letters remarks: "On ne voit que des Romans vuides d'action & pleins de babil." The author of the article laments the effect of the romances and says (p. 28) that "il n'y a gueres que quinze ans qu'ils sont rentrés en grace." The article

Voltaire's new type of tragedy embodied the neoclassic faith in civilization as against fanaticism and in benevolent royalism as against mob-rule which was central to Voltaire's philosophy and to epic tradition. In France, Voltaire saw a modern Rome whose leadership in Europe was due to her civilizing mission and in bigotry he recognized a force which was compromising her effectiveness and undermining her hegemony.[23] The religious wars of the sixteenth century, when broiling Catholics and Huguenots brought France to the edge of ruin, were constantly in his mind, and the Duke of Guise and his Ligueurs were to him, as they had been to Hobbes and Dryden, symbols for ecclesiastical chicanery and hypocrisy. Contemporary instances of religious persecution shocked and exasperated him. In *Zaïre, Alzire,* and subsequent plays he sought to provide, as he had already done in the *Henriade,* an "école des mœurs" in which his countrymen might admire and imitate an ideal of civilized tolerance.

Voltaire's arguments for tolerance were, like Dryden's, based on natural religion, and he expressed the view on several occasions that all that could be said on the subject of religious belief could be found in Cicero. His words, written to a friend in 1776, recall those of Dryden: "La plupart des auteurs modernes ne sont que les fripiers des siècles passés. Tout l'athéisme est dans *Lucrèce,* et tout ce qu'on peut dire sur la Divinité est dans *Cicéron,* qui n'était que le disciple de Platon."[24] Where Dryden and Voltaire differ is in their conception of human nature. Dry-

---

credits Boileau with turning the public from the romances originally. Later in the same year the same journal, Lettre CXV, VIII, 234, remarks that "Les Romans qui depuis 15 ans regnent sur nos cheminées, veulent encore regner sur nos Théâtres; car enfin les Comédies dont il s'agit, sont-elles autre chose que des Romans Dialogués & en action?" The author of the article adds (p. 235): "Nous devons donc nous attendre à voir au premier jour *Zaïde* & la Princesse de Cleves sur le théâtre." The *Mercure de France,* Nov., 1730, p. 2459, notes a new edition of *Les Voyages de Cyrus;* in the issue of January, 1731, pp. 314–15, a new edition of *Les Avantures d'Aristée et de Telasie;* and in the issue of April, 1732, p. 743, a new edition of *Cassandre* by the same publisher who "vient de réimprimer de même les fameux Romans de *Clelie, Cyrus, Pharamond, Cléopatre, Astrée* &c."

[23] The following excerpt from a letter to the Marquis de Villevieille in 1768 is typical of hundreds of comments to be found in Voltaire's correspondence: "Je mourrai consolé en voyant la véritable religion, c'est-à-dire celle du cœur, établie sur la ruine des simagrées. Je n'ai jamais prêché que l'adoration d'un Dieu, la bienfaisance, et l'indulgence. Avec ces sentiments, je brave le diable, qui n'existe point, et les vrais diables fanatiques, qui n'existent que trop" (*Œuvres,* XLVI, 196–97).

[24] *Œuvres,* L, 76. See also Wade, *Voltaire and Madame du Châtelet,* p. 194: "In moral philosophy, on the other hand, Voltaire was the leader, Mme du Châtelet, the pupil, though the fundamental equipment of both was the same, a knowledge of Cicero."

den's attitude is based on a pessimistic Hobbesian conception of human nature as selfish and brutal, and government to him was a policing device contrived by the intellectual few to save man from himself. The basis of Voltaire's philosophy is an optimistic Lockian conviction of the natural goodness of man and of society as the expression of an inborn human instinct. But for Voltaire, as for Dryden, the mass of men who could not reason were not to be trusted with political power.[25]

In *Zaïre* and subsequent "heroic" plays the characters themselves symbolize Voltaire's ideas, and the action proves by its own evolution Voltaire's thesis that noble generosity of soul is an irresistible force. There is usually a character to represent European fanaticism, a Mohammedan, a Peruvian, or a native of some other exotic clime to represent natural man, noble at heart, but dominated by a primitive code of vengeance, and finally a character, often a tender and sincere heroine, to represent "grandeur d'âme." In several plays there is a venerable old man of ripened wisdom whose council of charity and tolerance is unheeded, but whose advice is proved sound by the dénouement of the play. This character often seems to represent Voltaire himself. The dénouement is brought about by the law of admiration and imitation, the Christian fanatic and the noble savage alike being converted by the high example of the hero or heroine.

In *Zaïre* Voltaire turned the exotic romance setting to his own purpose: to contrast two civilizations and show that religion is a matter of education and that nobility of soul is not an exclusively Christian quality. In so doing, Voltaire employed the medium in a manner which recalls Dryden, and there are indications that Dryden was, in part, the immediate inspiration of Voltaire's new dramatic formula. Central to the philosophical theme of *Zaïre* is a passage spoken by the heroine which paraphrases the lines from Dryden which Voltaire had copied into his *English Notebook*.[26] To indicate that Voltaire had Dryden in mind there is also the preface of the play, which is addressed to Voltaire's English friend Falkener. The chief point that Voltaire makes in this preface is that in England the poets enjoy higher esteem than in France and consequently fulfill their moral function with more seriousness and effectiveness.[27] Addison was made a minister of state, Prior was made an

[25] See Torrey, *Voltaire and the Enlightenment*, New York, 1931, p. 13.

[26] Torrey, "Voltaire's English Notebook," *Modern Philology*, XXVI, No. 3 (Feb., 1929), 310.   [27] *Œuvres*, II, 537 ff.

ambassador, Steele and "Wanbruck" [28] were not only authors of comedies but also members of Parliament. Voltaire then qualifies his approval of English tragedy and proceeds to reply to Dryden's celebrated attack on Racine in the preface to *All for Love*. He contrasts the good taste of French authors with the barbarity of the English, taking for illustrations the decency with which French dramatists portray love and the indecency of Dryden's play.[29] The crudity of the English, says Voltaire, is a result of the political and religious wars which raged in England while French manners were being polished and refined by the society of women and the cultured life of the court. Voltaire quotes two passages from *All for Love*, first Antony's words to Cleopatra, Act III, scene I, and then Cleopatra's answer, which he translates as follows:

Venez à moi, venez dans mes bras, mon cher soldat; j'ai été trop longtemps privée de vos caresses. Mais quand je vous embrasserai, quand vous serez tout à moi, je vous punirai de vos cruautés en laissant sur vos lèvres l'impression de mes ardents baisers.[30]

No doubt, says Voltaire, it was thus that Antony and Cleopatra spoke, but such indecency should never be portrayed on the stage. Some Englishmen call this following nature, but it is exactly this nature "qu'il faut voiler avec soin." [31] To portray such indecency is to show one's ignorance of the human heart, for the spectators are offended. This rule of art has long been known in France. Voltaire concludes, as had Rapin, Muralt, and other critics, that the French might well borrow English seriousness and philosophy and the English might well imitate French correctness and taste.

C'est, je crois, sur cet art que notre nation doit en être crue. Vous nous apprenez des choses plus grandes et plus utiles: il serait honteux à nous de ne le pas avouer. Les Français qui ont écrit contre les découvertes du chevalier Newton sur la lumière en rougissent; ceux qui combattent la gravité en rougiront bientôt.

Vous devez vous soumettre aux règles de notre théâtre, comme nous devons embrasser votre philosophie. Nous avons fait d'aussi bonnes expériences sur le cœur humain que vous sur la physique. L'art de plaire semble l'art des Français, et l'art de penser paraît le vôtre. Heureux, monsieur, qui, comme vous, les réunit! [32]

[28] John Vanbrugh, celebrated dramatist and architect.
[29] *Œuvres*, II, pp. 552–53.   [30] *Ibid.*
[31] *Ibid.*   [32] *Ibid.*, pp. 553–54.

If Voltaire had written "comme moi" instead of "comme vous," no doubt he would have been nearer to his real meaning.

In *Zaïre* the allegorical element does not obtrude as it does in later plays; the exotic background, the atmosphere of chivalric gallantry, the new and daring philosophical ideas are fused by Voltaire's sensibility and humanity and expressed in a brilliant and facile flow of verse. It was an immediate success and became one of the most popular plays of the century.

Zaïre, the captured daughter of a French nobleman, has been brought up from infancy in the court of the Sultan of Jersualem. Torn between her love for the Sultan, who has offered to make her his wife, and her loyalty to her father and brother, who insist that she be baptized and return to France, she meditates with pronounced deistic tendency upon the insignificance of religious differences and expresses her conviction that all men who worship God have a common bond. Her soliloquy when she is considering the choice which will make her either untrue to her blood or to her love, is a paraphrase of Dryden's lines noted down in Voltaire's *English Notebook* and in the *Sottisier*.

> La coutume, la loi plia mes premiers ans
> A la religion des heureux musulmans.
> Je le vois trop: les soins qu'on prend de notre enfance
> Forment nos sentiments, nos mœurs, notre croyance.
> J'eusse été près du Gange esclave des faux dieux,
> Chrétienne dans Paris, musulmane en ces lieux.
> L'instruction fait tout; et la main de nos pères
> Grave en nos faibles cœurs ces premiers caractères
> Que l'exemple et le temps nous viennent retracer,
> Et que peut-être en nous Dieu seul peut effacer.[33]

The belief that religion is a product of education had been frequently expressed by freethinkers in England and France. Voltaire's early friend and patron, the Abbé Chaulieu, had put it into verse.[34] But the lines from Dryden had an elevation and vigor which made Voltaire write them in his notebook and turn back to them later. If one were to make conjectures as to which lines of Dryden, Voltaire quoted to his English visitor in 1764,[35] the lines paraphrased in *Zaïre* and other similar pas-

---

[33] Act I, scene 1; *Œuvres*, II, 560.
[34] See Voltaire's citation, *Œuvres*, XIV, 54.
[35] *Œuvres*, I, 354.

sages which Voltaire had copied in his notebooks would seem logical surmises.

The dénouement of *Zaïre* represents a triumph for "grandeur d'âme." Orosmane, the Sultan, not understanding the reason for Zaïre's hesitation, stabs her in jealousy when he discovers that she has written to Nérestan and will meet him secretly. Finding that Nérestan is her brother and that Zaïre was actually true to her love, he is overcome with remorse. He sets his Christian captives free and stabs himself. His farewell words are to Nérestan.

> Porte aux tiens ce poignard, que mon bras égaré
> A plongé dans un sein qui dut m'être sacré;
> Dis-leur que j'ai donné la mort la plus affreuse
> A la plus digne femme, à la plus vertueuse,
> Dont le ciel ait formé les innocents appas;
> Dis-leur qu'à ses genoux j'avais mis mes Etats;
> Dis-leur que dans son sang cette main s'est plongée;
> Dis que je l'adorais, et que je l'ai vengée.
> > (*Il se tue*).
>
> (*Aux siens*)
> Respectez ce héros, et conduisez ses pas.[36]

Fanatical Nérestan is bewildered by the Sultan's noble sentiments, for to him there can be no virtue in an infidel. Standing over the expiring Mohammedan, he cries:

> Guide-moi, Dieu puissant! je ne me connais pas.
> Faut-il qu'à t'admirer ta fureur me contraigne,
> Et que dans mon malheur ce soit moi qui te plaigne! [37]

His enlarged vision represents a victory over bigotry and Zaïre and Orosmane seem to have died in a good cause.

The reaction to Voltaire's introduction of the issue of religious tolerance into the theater was generally unfavorable. The *Mercure de France,* for instance, remarked that there was some question as to whether Zaïre died as a Christian or a Mohammedan, but that there was no doubt that her dominating passion was love.[38] For J. B. Rousseau the play was harmful, for it showed that "tous les efforts de la grace n'ont aucun pouvoir sur les passions." [39] Nadal, in his parody of the play, said that it

[36] Act V, scene 10; *Œuvres*, II, 617.   [37] *Ibid.,* p. 618.
[38] *Mercure de France,* January, 1733, p. 144.
[39] Quoted in *Mercure de France,* April, 1733, p. 651.

concerned a "Tartar à l'eau-rose," who was "plus Celadon qu'un Heros de Roman," and a young princess

> Qui ne connoît de foi, de loi, que sa tendresse,
> Ou qui ne reconnoît d'autre religion,
> Que celle qu'on reçoit de l'éducation.[40]

Added weight is given to the evidence that Voltaire had Dryden in mind when composing *Zaïre* by the fact that his next important play, *Alzire*, is drawn after Dryden's *The Indian Emperour*. *Alzire*, like *Zaïre*, is Voltairian philosophy in action. The Spanish conquest of Mexico and Peru offered Voltaire in 1736, as it had offered Dryden, in 1665, an opportunity not only to use popular heroic romance material but also to illustrate again the deistic principle of the unimportance of different cults, and the thesis that all men who worship God have a basis for understanding. In *Alzire* the aged Spanish governor of Peru, Alvarez, with true Christian spirit, has succeeded in converting many Peruvians, including Montèze, Peruvian monarch, and his lovely daughter Alzire. Montèze sees the benefits which European civilization offers, and in order to have peace, he has consented that Alzire shall marry Alvarez's son Gusman, who is about to succeed him as governor. But Gusman is rapacious and cruel and is convinced that only by torture and oppression can the Peruvians be brought to accept Spanish rule. Alzire is resigned to the marriage with Gusman, though she is mourning the loss of Zamore, a young Peruvian leader, supposed to have been killed in battle, to whom she had long been betrothed. Alvarez, preparing to hand over the government to Gusman, recommends Christian mercy and pardon as the basis of peace and prosperity in the new Spanish possession.

> Ah! Dieu nous envoyait, quand de nous il fit choix,
> Pour annoncer son nom, pour faire aimer ses lois:
> Et nous, de ces climats destructeurs implacables,
> Nous, et d'or et de sang toujours insatiables,
> Déserteurs de ces lois qu'il fallait enseigner,
> Nous égorgeons ce peuple au lieu de le gagner.
>
> .   .   .
>
> Fléaux du nouveau monde, injustes, vains, avares,
> Nous seuls en ces climats nous sommes les barbares.
> L'Américain, farouche en sa simplicité,
> Nous égale en courage, et nous passe en bonté.[41]

[40] Nadal, "Arlequin au Parnasse," in *Les Parodies du nouveau théâtre italien*, I, 346.
[41] Act I, scene 1; *Œuvres*, III, 387–88.

To soften the heart of his son, Alvarez tells him how a brave Indian leader spared his life in battle. The Indian, it is revealed later, is Zamore, who had been taken prisoner by Gusman, tortured in an attempt to make him surrender hidden gold, and left for dead. Gusman is moved by his father's words and consents to spare those Indians who accept the Christian religion. But they must, he says, "tremblent sous un seul Dieu comme sous un seul roi." [42] Zamore is not dead, but is preparing to make a final and hopeless attack on the Spanish city. In addressing his men he reveals his primitive code of vengeance, as well as his nobility of soul.

> Après l'honneur de vaincre, il n'est rien sous les cieux
> De plus grand en effet qu'un trépas glorieux;
> Mais mourir dans l'opprobre et dans l'ignominie,
> Mais laisser en mourant des fers à sa patrie,
> Périr sans se venger, expirer par les mains
> De ces brigands d'Europe, et de ces assassins
> Qui, de sang enivrés, de nos trésors avides,
> De ce monde usurpé désolateurs perfides,
> Ont osé me livrer à des tourments honteux
> Pour m'arracher des biens plus méprisables qu'eux. [43]

The scene of the play, which the *Mercure de France* called "une des plus belles Scenes qui ayent paru au Théatre," [44] comes in the third act, when Alzire, after the wedding ceremony which has united her with Gusman, visits some Peruvian prisoners, who have been caught reconnoitering in the city. She finds Zamore among them. Alvarez has previously visited the scene and identified Zamore as the leader who spared his life in battle. Gusman comes upon the scene and finds that he has a rival—the Indian whom he had cruelly tortured. Zamore identifies himself to the astonished Gusman.

> Oui; lui-même, à qui ta barbarie
> Voulut ôter l'honneur, et crut ôter la vie;
> Lui, que tu fis languir dans des tourments honteux;
> Lui, dont l'aspect ici te fait baisser les yeux.
> Ravisseur de nos biens, tyran de notre empire,
> Tu viens de m'arracher le seul bien où j'aspire.
> Achève, et de ce fer, trésor de tes climats,
> Préviens mon bras vengeur, et préviens ton trépas. [45]

Alvarez is struck with horror at learning of the torture and exclaims to Gusman:

[42] Act I, scene 1; *ibid.*, III, 389.   [43] Act II, scene 1; *ibid.*, III, 397.
[44] *Mercure de France*, February, 1736, p. 354.   [45] Act III, scene 5; *Œuvres*, III, 413.

De ce discours, ô ciel! que je me sens confondre!
Vous sentez-vous coupable, et pouvez-vous répondre? [46]

It is then, in the words of the *Mercure de France,* that "Le Caractère
d'Alzire se dévelope tout entier à ses yeux; elle demande également la
mort à son Epoux et à son Amant, comme leur étant également infi-
delle." [47]

Gusman orders the death of Zamore, but when he calls his soldiers,
the Peruvians attack the city and he rushes off. In the confusion of the
attack Alzire frees Zamore by bribing a guard, but she is true to her
marriage vows and refuses to flee with him. She would take her own life,
but for the Christian law forbidding it. Zamore leaves with the bribed
guard, but instead of fleeing, he overpowers the guard, runs to the Spanish council chamber, and mortally wounds Gusman. Alzire and Zamore
are then held under guard to await the judgment of Gusman. An un-
expected dénouement is produced when Gusman is carried on the stage
in a litter, and, instead of pronouncing a decree of death, reveals that the
noble example of Alzire has converted him to Christian charity and
humility. He says:

> Le bonheur m'aveugla, la mort m'a détrompé.
> Je pardonne à la main par qui Dieu m'a frappé.
> J'étais maître en ces lieux, seul j'y commande encore:
> Seul je puis faire grâce, et la fais à Zamore.
> Vis, superbe ennemi, sois libre, et te souvien
> Quel fut, et le devoir, et la mort d'un Chrétien.
> Montèze, Américains, qui fûtes mes victimes.
> Songez que ma clémance a surpassé mes crimes.
> Instruisez l'Amérique; apprenez à ses rois
> Que les Chrétiens sont nés pour leur donner des lois.
> Des Dieux que nous servons connais la différence:
> Les tiens t'ont commandé le meurtre et la vengeance;
> Et le mien, quand ton bras vient de m'assassiner,
> M'ordonne de te plaindre et de te pardonner. [48]

Zamore, who had been unmoved under torture, is deeply stirred by
Gusman's words. He now recognizes the superiority of the Christian
God. The epic law of admiration and imitation works within his soul as
it had worked within that of Gusman, and he says:

[46] *Ibid.,* p. 414.
[47] *Mercure de France,* February, 1736, p. 354.
[48] Acte V, scene 7; *Œuvres,* III, 434.

Ah! la loi qui t'oblige à cet effort suprême,
Je commence à le croire, est la loi d'un Dieu même.
J'ai connu l'amitié, la constance, la foi;
Mais tant de grandeur d'âme est au-dessus de moi;
Tant de vertu m'accable, et son charme m'attire.
Honteux d'être vengé, je t'aime et je t'admire.[49]

In his preliminary essay Voltaire underlines the moral aim of his play.

On a tâché dans cette tragédie, toute d'invention et d'une espèce assez neuve, de faire voir combien le véritable esprit de religion l'emporte sur les vertus de la nature.

La religion d'un barbare consiste à offrir à ses dieux le sang de ses ennemis. Un chrétien mal instruit n'est souvent guère plus juste. Etre fidèle à quelques pratiques inutiles, et infidèle aux vrais devoirs de l'homme, faire certaines prières, et garder ses vices; jeûner, mais haïr; cabaler, persécuter, voilà sa religion. Celle du chrétien véritable est de regarder tous les hommes comme ses frères, de leur faire du bien et de leur pardonner le mal. Tel est Gusman au moment de sa mort; tel Alvarez dans le cours de sa vie; tel j'ai peint Henri IV, même au milieu de ses faiblesses.

On trouvera dans presque tous mes écrits cette humanité qui doit être le premier caractère d'un être pensant; on y verra (si j'ose m'exprimer ainsi) le désir du bonheur des hommes, l'horreur de l'injustice et de l'oppression.[50]

In a letter to D'Argental concerning the play Voltaire says he is persuaded that "la religion fait plus d'effet sur le peuple, au théâtre, quand elle est mise en beaux vers, qu'à l'église, où elle ne se montre qu'avec du latin de cuisine," [51] and that the more he considers the conversion of Gusman, the more he regards it as "un coup qui doit faire une très-grande impression." When Frederick II received the play, he saw clearly its philosophical purpose and wrote to Voltaire: "Vous faites voir, par le caractère de Gusman, qu'un christianisme mal entendu, et guidé par le faux zèle, rend plus barbare et plus cruel que le paganisme même." [52]

There is much evidence to indicate that *Alzire* was inspired by Dryden's *The Indian Emperour*. That Voltaire knew Dryden's play well is beyond doubt, since he quoted from it or referred to incidents in it in at least nine different instances between 1728 and 1771. That Dryden's torture scene made a lasting impression upon him is revealed by his use of it in the section on Cortez in the *Essai sur les mœurs*. Furthermore, his debt to Dryden seems to have been a fact accepted by Voltaire's con-

---

[49] *Ibid.*, p. 435.
[51] *Ibid.*, XXXIII, 471.
[50] *Ibid.*, 379.
[52] *Ibid.*, XXXIV, 104.

temporaries. In 1743 the Abbé Dubourg, in offering his translation of *The Indian Emperour* and *The Indian Queen,* changed the name of the Indian Queen to "Alsyre." [53] The Abbé Yart, in his *Idée de la poésie anglaise* (1753), recognizes the relationship between *Alzire* and *The Indian Emperour* when he says of Voltaire's knowledge of the English drama, "Ne sait-on point qu'il a appris, comme il l'avoue lui-même, à penser & à écrire vigoureusement dans l'étude de leurs livres, & à s'ouvrir, à leur exemple, un nouveau théâtre, en transportant comme Dryden la scène dans le nouveau monde?" [54]

The similar philosophical use to which similar heroic romance material is put in the two plays is the essential basis of their resemblance. In both plays the false zeal of the Christian conquerors, who hide their greed for gold behind a pretense of desire to win converts, is contrasted with the nobility of the native Americans. The torture of an Indian prince is the symbol in each play for the hypocritical cupidity of the Christians, and a spirit of understanding and charity is exemplified in *Alzire* by Alvarez and in *The Indian Emperour* by Cortez. In contrast to *Alzire,* in which the moral lesson is central, Dryden's play, although shot through with up-to-date discussions of natural religion and the relation of church and state, seems a hard and glittering operatic spectacle. The religious question is dropped when Cortez dismisses the High Priest, and only love and honor figure in the closing scenes.

In *Mahomet,* first performed in 1741, the didactic element tends to run away with the play, although Lord Chesterfield, when he was in Lille, [55] found that the spectators apparently did not realize that Mahomet represented religious chicanery and that Voltaire was making an attack on the church. Voltaire painted in an exotic background, always with an eye on Paris, and it has been said that he borrowed from Lillo's *The London Merchant* the central dramatic situation, the idea of having a youth murder his own benefactor. [56] When the play was attacked in Paris, Voltaire wrote the following in its defense.

C'est précisément contre les Ravaillac et les Jacques Clément, que la pièce est composée; ce qui a fait dire à un homme de beaucoup d'esprit que si *Mahomet* avait été écrit du temps de Henri III et de Henri IV, cet ouvrage

[53] *Mercure de France,* July, 1743, pp. 1583–84.
[54] Yart, *Idée de la poésie anglaise,* III, xxii.
[55] Desnoiresterres, *Voltaire et la société au XVIIIᵉ siècle,* II, 338.
[56] See note by editors of the Kehl edition in *Œuvres,* IV, 96.

leur aurait sauvé la vie. Est-il possible qu'on ait pu faire un tel reproche à l'auteur de *la Henriade*, lui qui a élevé sa voix si souvent dans ce poëme et ailleurs, je ne dis pas seulement contre de tels attentats, mais contre toutes les maximes qui peuvent y conduire?

J'avoue que plus j'ai lu les ouvrages de cet écrivain, plus je les ai trouvés caractérisés par l'amour du bien public. Il inspire partout l'horreur contre les emportements de la rebellion, de la persécution, et du fanatisme. Y a-t-il un bon citoyen qui n'adopte toutes les maximes de *la Henriade*? Ce poëme ne fait-il pas aimer la véritable vertu? *Mahomet* me paraît écrit entièrement dans le même esprit, et je suis persuadé que ses plus grands ennemis en conviendront.[57]

In *L'Orphelin de la Chine* (1755) the allegory is still more apparent, the historical coloring more false, the gallantry more artificial. Even the *Correspondance littéraire,* which seems to try to speak well of the play, called it "un recueil de beaux vers en cinq cahiers."[58] Voltaire's Tartar, says Grimm, "raisonne sur la religion et sur les arts, comme s'il avait passé sa vie à méditer et à réfléchir."[59] The play is again a triumph of "grandeur d'âme." Genghis-Khan is portrayed as so struck with admiration by the refinement of Chinese manners and by the nobility of Zamti, the mandarin, and of Idamé, his wife, that he abandons his program of subjugation and instead would preserve their country. Expressing his admiration for Chinese civilization, Genghis-Khan declares:

> Mon cœur est en secret jaloux de leurs vertus;
> Et, vainqueur, je voudrais égaler les vaincus.[60]

His change of heart comes when he finds that Zamti and Idamé prefer to die rather than be separated or reveal the whereabouts of the prince, whose safekeeping is in their hands. Genghis-Khan cries:

> En vain par mes exploits j'ai su me signaler;
> Vous m'avez avili: je veux vous égaler.[61]

His love for Idamé becomes a benevolent interest in her happiness, and he offers to share the government and protect the state. When Idamé, overcome with his generosity, asks what has inspired him to this action, he replies: "Vos vertus."[62]

In commenting upon the play, Voltaire declares that its purpose is the

---

[57] In the "Avis de l'Editeur," prefixed to *Mahomet*, which Voltaire himself wrote, *Œuvres*, IV, 99.

[58] *Correspondance littéraire philosophique et critique*, III, 84.

[59] *Ibid.*, p. 85.

[60] Act IV, scene 2; *Œuvres*, V, 336.

[61] Act V, scene 6; *ibid.*, V, 355.

[62] Act V, scene 6; *ibid.*, V, 356.

same as that of the *Henriade*. A tragedy is only a frivolous amusement, he says, if it does not inspire virtue. He concludes:

> J'ose dire que depuis *la Henriade* jusqu'à *Zaïre,* et jusqu'à cette pièce chinoise, bonne ou mauvaise, tel a été toujours le principe qui m'a inspiré; et que, dans l'histoire du siècle de Louis XIV, j'ai célébré mon roi et ma patrie, sans flatter ni l'un ni l'autre.[63]

After his first period of enthusiasm for the new play had passed, Voltaire remarked that "Gengis; c'est *Arlequin poli par l'amour.*" [64]

After Voltaire had retired within the comparative safety of the Swiss frontier to devote his energies to a furious campaign against intolerance, he did not abandon the drama, but his theater tends to fall apart into its various elements, each of which dominates in turn. Thus *Tancrède,* in 1760, is pure heroic romance on a theme of love and honor. *Olympie* is opera spectacle almost exclusively, and plays such as *Les Scythes, Les Guèbres,* and *Les Lois de Minos,* all three written during the last decade of his life, caricature his tendency toward allegory.

In *Tancrède,* as in *Zaïre,* Voltaire was successful in creating an atmosphere of valor and chivalry. There is no didactic element, unless the portrait of knightly generosity may be considered a pattern held up for imitation and admiration. The fundamental romance situation is very similar to that in Dryden's *The Conquest of Granada:* a hero fights for the honor of his lady, though he believes he has proof of her unfaithfulness. There is the same atmosphere of combat and changing fortunes and the same Christian-Mohammedan background of the Crusades. In each there is the prospect of the scaffold for the heroine; each hero in deciding to champion the cause of his lady in single combat, has a a similar thought. Tancrède says:

> J'ai dû sauver ses jours, et non lui pardonner.
> Qu'elle vive, il suffit, et que Tancrède expire.[65]

Almanzor says only:

> I'le leave her, when she's freed; and let it be
> Her punishment, she could be false to me.[66]

---

[63] In the dedication addressed to the Duc de Richelieu, *ibid.,* V, 299.
[64] In a letter to D'Argental in 1755, *ibid.,* XXXVIII, 356.
[65] Act IV, scene 2; *ibid.,* V, 543.
[66] *The Conquest of Granada,* Second Part, Act V, Nonesuch ed., III, 148.

It is a basic romance situation, common in heroic romance fiction,[67] but Voltaire may well have read Dryden's most celebrated heroic play and drawn some ideas from it. *Tancrède* was, perhaps, the outstanding dramatic success of the entire century. It was a favorite of Musset, Goethe translated it and, like *Zaïre*, it is still played.

Voltaire claimed a moral purpose for *Olympie,* declaring in a letter to D'Argental that the play was an emblem "plus mystérieux que vous ne pensez." [68] Its meaning, he said, was that "la confession, la communion, la profession de foi, etc., etc., sont visiblement prises des anciens." But he resorted to extended footnotes to point his moral, and he told D'Alembert that he chose the subject for the sake of the notes.[69] There is a high priest in the play who is unique among high priests of Voltaire and Dryden in that he has no political ambitions. Voltaire emphasizes the good example of this priest with the following note:

Cet exemple d'un prêtre qui se renferme dans les bornes de son ministère de paix nous a paru d'une très-grande utilité, et il serait à souhaiter qu'on ne les représentât jamais autrement sur un théâtre public qui doit être l'école des mœurs.[70]

Voltaire made no effort to conceal that *Les Scythes* (1767) was an attack on the intolerance of the Swiss Calvinists. Of one scene he wrote to D'Argental that he had made "un petit portrait de Genève pour m'amuser," [71] and in his preface he confesses that his play is "le tableau contrasté des anciens Scythes et des anciens Persans, qui peut-être est la peinture de quelques nations modernes." [72] Not satisfied that the fable was transparent enough, Voltaire wrote an allegorical dedication in which he pictured the author as a philosopher-farmer who cultivated his garden and who "avait le cœur bon, quoiqu'il se permit de rire quelquefois aux dépens des méchants et des orgueilleux." [73]

The allegorical element of *Les Guèbres* is no less evident and no less openly avowed. In correspondance with D'Argental concerning the possible production of the play Voltaire wrote that he trembled "pour les allusions, pour les belles allégories que font toujours messieurs du

[67] For a discussion of the source of Dryden's play see Hill, *La Calprenède's Romances and the Restoration Drama*, p. 72.

[68] *Œuvres*, XLII, 53–54.   [69] *Ibid.*, pp. 50–51.

[70] *Ibid.*, VI, 127n.   [71] *Ibid.*, 327n.

[72] *Ibid.*, p. 267.   [73] *Ibid.*, pp. 264–65.

parterre; qu'il se trouvera quelque plaisant qui prendra les prêtres païens pour des jésuites ou pour des inquisiteurs d'Espagne." [74] The setting of *Les Guèbres* is Syria at the time of the Roman conquest under the emperor Gallien, who arrives on the scene in time to save an innocent Syrian maid from being burned alive as a heretic by the priests. The emperor takes occasion to approve publicly the action of the philosopher-farmer who had come directly to him for relief from the fanaticism of the priests. Of the priests the emperor says:

> Les persécutions
> Ont mal servi ma gloire, et font trop de rebelles.
> Quand le prince est clément, les sujets sont fidèles.
> On m'a trompé long-temps; je ne veux désormais
> Dans les prêtres des dieux que des hommes de paix.[75]

The play has the air of a personal document in which Voltaire seems to symbolize his own role in France and the emperor's commendation of the good farmer sounds like wishful thinking:

> Et toi, qui fus leur père, et dont le noble cœur
> Dans une humble fortune avait tant de grandeur,
> J'ajoute à ta campagne un fertile héritage;
> Tu mérites des biens, tu sais en faire usage.
> Les Guèbres désormais pourront en liberté
> Suivre un culte secret longtemps persécuté:
> Si ce culte est le tien, sans doute il ne peut nuire
> Je dois le tolérer plutôt que le détruire.
> Qu'ils jouissent en paix de leurs droits, de leurs biens;
> Qu'ils adorent leur dieu, mais sans blesser les miens:
> Que chacun dans sa loi cherche en paix la lumière;
> Mais la loi de l'Etat est toujours la première.
> Je pense en citoyen, j'agis en empereur:
> Je hais le fanatique et le persécuteur.[76]

When the play was banned on the ground that its implications were dangerous, Voltaire wrote a preface in which he admits that he has composed an allegory, but argues that it is as a patriot concerned for his country that he advocates tolerance. He closes his preface as follows:

L'empereur, dans la tragédie des *Guèbres,* n'entend point et ne peut entendre, par le mot de *tolérance,* la licence des opinions contraires aux mœurs, les assemblées de débauche, les confréries fanatiques; il entend cette in-

---

[74] *Ibid.,* XLVI, 92.   [75] Act V, scene 6; *ibid.,* VI, 566.
[76] *Ibid.,* pp. 566–67.

dulgence qu'on doit à tous les citoyens qui suivent en paix ce que leur conscience leur dicte, et qui adorent la Divinité sans troubler la société. Il ne
veut pas qu'on punisse ceux qui se trompent comme on punirait des parri-
cides. . . . Plus on est absurde, plus on est intolérant et cruel; l'absurdité
a élevé plus d'échafauds qu'il n'y a eu de criminels. C'est l'absurdité qui
livra aux flammes la maréchale d'Ancre et le curé Urbain Grandier; c'est
l'absurdité, sans doute, qui fut l'origine de la Saint-Barthélemy. Quand la
raison est pervertie, l'homme devient un animal féroce; les bœufs et les
singes se changent en tigres. Voulez-vous changer enfin ces bêtes en hommes?
Commencez par souffrir qu'on leur prêche la raison.[77]

In his tragedies, as in the *Henriade,* Voltaire thus sought to fulfill the
neoclassic conception of the epic poet as a kind of official philosopher
and preceptor to the state. In his theater he began to use themes from
Greek drama and mythology to illustrate the maxim that a god of
vengeance intervenes in the affairs of men to punish secret crimes. On
visiting England, he found formal Augustan tragedy dominated by the
didactic ideal of the Le Bossu school, and he wrote two Roman
tragedies in the declamatory manner of Addison's *Cato.* Restoration
tragedy provided Voltaire with a more useful model, for he seems to
have had Dryden in mind when he initiated, with *Zaïre* and *Alzire,* a
new type of tragedy based, like Dryden's plays, on heroic romance
material. What impressed Voltaire most in the works of English poets
was their success in expressing philosophical ideas,[78] and he seems to
have gone to Dryden because he delighted in the skeptical arguments in
Dryden's plays and saw that Dryden's heroic formula was well adapted
to his own didactic purpose. In *The Indian Emperour,* which Voltaire
knew well, Dryden had used popular romance material to contrast two
civilizations and to illustrate that the false zeal of Christian bigots may
be more barbarous than a pagan creed of honor and vengeance. In *Zaïre,
Alzire,* and other plays Voltaire made similar use of similar material.
In the final period of his life, when, as the Patriarch of Ferney, he
deluged Europe with propaganda against intolerance, his plays become
more and more obviously parables against fanaticism and religious
bigotry.

[77] "Discours historique et critique," prefixed to the play, *ibid.,* VI, 502–3.
[78] In the *Siècle de Louis XIV* (*Œuvres,* XIV, 560), Voltaire writes:
"Nulle nation n'a traité la morale
en vers avec plus d'énergie et de
profondeur que la nation anglaise;
c'est là, il me semble, le plus
grand mérite de ses poëtes."

CHAPTER VII VOLTAIRE'S CHOICE OF SUBJECT MATTER

F<small>RENCH AND</small> English critics maintained that the tragedies of Racine, with the exception of *Athalie,* had robbed the French theater of its majesty by their emphasis on love, and Voltaire's early objective was tragedy without love. In accordance with the advice of Rapin and Dacier, he first sought to elevate the theater by going for his subjects to Greek mythology. Early in his career he also stated his preference for Corneille and favored events from Roman history as subject matter. He not only went to Corneille and the Greeks but he took Rapin's suggestion, which had been increasingly emphasized by critics of the first quarter of the eighteenth century, and looked to England for inspiration. He often spoke of Shakespeare's historical tragedies and said that he borrowed from the London theater the idea of using the names of his own countrymen in his plays. It is apparent, however, that a chasm separates Voltaire's conception of historical tragedy from that of Shakespeare—while the parallel between the tragedies of Dryden, Addison, and Voltaire is often close. Despite Voltaire's grandiose conception of historical tragedy there was gradually revealed an innate leaning toward the romanesque, and his best tragedies were more in the manner of Quinault than of Corneille, of Dryden than of Shakespeare. But Voltaire's "Quinauderie," a term which he himself used in referring to *Zaïre,*[1] was an original product. It was the tragedy of the successors of Racine, elevated and enlarged by philosophical and political implications.

The decadent state of French tragedy was a central theme of Voltaire's dramatic criticism and of his correspondance. In the *Discours sur la tragédie* preceding *Brutus* he wrote: "Nous avons en France des tragédies estimées, qui sont plutôt des conversations qu'elles ne sont la représentation d'un événement."[2] In 1741 he spoke of the "décadence

---

[1] Voltaire wrote to the Marquis de Villette in 1767: "On a joué *Zaïre* avec une grande perfection. Pour moi, je vous avoue que j'aime mieux une scène de César ou de Cicéron que toute cette intrigue d'amour que je filais il y a trente-cinq ans. Mais le parterre de Paris et les loges sont plus galants que moi: ils donnent la préférence à ma *Quinauderie"* (*Œuvres,* XLV, 397).

[2] *Œuvres,* II, 314.

du théâtre de Paris" and said that "Poésie, déclamation, tout y périt." [3]
In 1760 he asserted that "l'opéra-comique est devenu, ce me semble, le
spectacle de la nation," [4] and in 1767 he lamented, in a letter to
D'Argental, that "le spectacle de Paris, le seul spectacle qui lui fasse
honneur dans l'Europe, est tombé dans la plus honteuse décadence, et
je vous avoue que je ne crois pas qu'il se relève." [5]

The preface to *Mariamne,* in which Voltaire balances the practice of
Racine against that of Corneille, is largely an argument for banning love
as a subject of tragedy. Emile Faguet called the preface "le jugement
le plus profond de Voltaire sur la tragédie" and pointed out the epic
quality of Voltaire's conception of subject matter.

Il revenait, en somme, et avec beaucoup de raison à mon sens, aux théories
de Corneille. La tragédie doit être, avant tout, pensait-il, un poème historique,
ou même épique, mis sur la scène, et le danger qui la menace le plus est
qu'elle soit un roman, ou une espèce de drame bougeois, avec des noms
antiques. Racine est un grand homme, ce qui fait qu'on trouve très bien
tout ce qu'il a fait, et d'ailleurs on a parfaitement raison; mais l'esprit
général de son théâtre n'en reste pas moins fort dangereux pour l'imitation.
Il a jeté sur sa matière la merveilleuse pourpre de son génie poétique; mais
cette matière est plutôt celle du romancier, et Corneille apparemment a vu
plus juste, quand il a dit que la tragédie est une pièce de théâtre dans laquelle
interviennent les événements célèbres de l'histoire et les grand intérêts de
la société humaine.[6]

Voltaire wrote the preface to *Mariamne* in 1725, the year before his departure for England. He argues that Racine reduced tragedy to little
more than heightened comedy and that if the plot of *Mithridate,* for example, is laid bare by removing the pompous names of the characters, it
will be seen to be identical with that of *L'Avare.* Voltaire comments:

Les pièces tragiques sont fondées, ou sur les intérêts de toute une nation,
ou sur les intérêts particuliers de quelques princes. De ce premier genre sont
l'Iphigénie en Aulide, où la Grèce assemblée demande le sang de la fille
d'Agamemnon; *les Horaces,* où trois combattants ont entre les mains le
sort de Rome; *l'Œdipe,* où le salut des Thébains dépend de la découverte
du meurtrier de Laïus. Du second genre sont *Britannicus, Phèdre, Mithridate,* etc.

[3] In a letter to La Noue in 1741, *Œuvres,* XXXVI, 57.
[4] In a letter to Chabanon in 1766, *Œuvres,* XLIV, 406.
[5] *Œuvres,* XLV, 205–6.
[6] Faguet, "Voltaire—ses idées sur les genres épique et dramatique," *Revue des cours et
conférences,* 2d ser. (May 31, 1900), 486–87.

Dans ces trois dernières, tout l'intérêt est renfermé dans la famille du héros de la pièce; tout roule sur des passions que des bourgeois ressentent comme les princes; et l'intrigue de ces ouvrages est aussi propre à la comédie qu'à la tragédie.[7]

In general, Voltaire, as both his correspondence and formal critical writings prove, maintained his early preference for Corneille throughout most of his dramatic career. In 1735 he replied to Desfontaines, who had attacked *La Mort de César:*

La France n'est pas le seul pays où l'on fasse des tragédies, et notre goût, ou plutôt notre habitude de ne mettre sur le théâtre que de longues conversations d'amour ne plaît pas chez les autres nations. Notre théâtre est vide d'action et de grands intérêts, pour l'ordinaire. Ce qui fait qu'il manque d'action, c'est que le théâtre est offusqué par nos petits-maîtres; et ce qui fait que les grands intérêts en sont bannis, c'est que notre nation ne les connaît point. La politique plaisait du temps de Corneille, parce qu'on était tout rempli des guerres de la Fronde; mais aujourd'hui on ne va plus à ses pièces.[8]

In 1747 he sent *Sémiramis* to Frederick with the following comment:

Sire, eh bien! vous aurez *Sémiramis;* elle n'est pas à l'eau rose: c'est ce qui fait que je ne la donne pas à notre peuple de sybarites, mais à un roi qui pense comme on pensait en France, du temps du grand Corneille et du grand Condé, et qui veut qu'une tragédie soit tragique, et une comédie comique.[9]

In 1761 he observed to the Abbé d'Olivet:

Les étrangers se moquaient de nous; mais nous n'en savions rien. Nous pensions qu'une femme ne pouvait paraître sur la scène sans dire *j'aime* en cent façons, et en vers chargés d'épithètes et de chevilles. On n'entendait que *ma flamme,* et *mon âme; mes feux,* et *mes vœux; mon cœur,* et *mon vainqueur.* Je reviens à Corneille, qui s'est élevé au-dessus de ces petitesses dans ses belles scènes des *Horaces,* de *Cinna,* de *Pompée,* etc.[10]

That Voltaire turned to Greek and Roman subjects in order to avoid the love theme is confirmed by remarks with which he accompanied his productions. Of *Mérope* he wrote in 1738 that he had in mind a tragedy "qui ne soit point enjolivée d'une intrigue d'amour" and that he intended thereby to render "quelque service au théâtre français, qui, en vérité, est trop galant." [11] In regard to *Oreste* he wrote, in 1750,

[7] *Œuvres,* II, 167.　[8] *Ibid.,* XXXIII, 551–52.　[9] *Ibid.,* XXXVI, 483.
[10] *Ibid.,* XLI, 412.　[11] In a letter to Frederick, *ibid.,* XXXIV, 431.

Je demande après cela si la république des lettres n'a pas obligation à un auteur qui ressuscite l'antiquité dans toute sa noblesse, dans toute sa grandeur, et dans toute sa force, et qui y joint les plus grands efforts de la nature, sans aucun mélange des petites faiblesses et des misérables intrigues amoureuses qui déshonorent le théâtre parmi nous? [12]

In addition to the early plays based on Roman history, *Brutus* and *La Mort de César,* which had been in the didactic tradition of the English Augustan theater, Voltaire composed *Rome sauvée* (1752) and *Le Triumvirat* (1764). In the preface to *Rome sauvée* he said that his purpose was to remove the opprobrium which gallantry had brought upon the French stage.

On a voulu essayer encore une fois, par une tragédie sans déclaration d'amour, de détruire les reproches que toute l'Europe savante fait à la France, de ne souffrir guère au théâtre que les intrigues galantes; et on a eu surtout pour objet de faire connaître Cicéron aux jeunes personnes qui fréquentent les spectacles.[13]

Such a play would succeed in England, he says, mentioning Ben Jonson's *Catiline,* but he does not expect it to be acceptable in Paris, where "personne ne conspire aujourd'hui, et tout le monde aime." [14]

In these later Roman tragedies Voltaire attempted to paint in the historical background accurately, but the constraint he felt to make them at the same time moral lessons limited his success. Since tragedy must teach by precept and example, it could not be too close to reality, for reality was not, in Voltaire's eyes, moral. He frequently stated his belief that history demonstrated the triumph of the wicked and hence had to be altered by the artist. In portraying history too accurately, Voltaire believed, the English showed their ignorance of the very fundamentals of art. Shakespeare's kings talked like human beings, whereas in tragedy they should never depart from the elevation which should be characteristic of kings.[15] The purpose of the stage was not to portray reality, but to show what men ought to be. Voltaire's article "Fable" (1764) in the *Dictionnaire philosophique* is a clear statement of this point of view and is of great importance in understanding Voltaire's attitude toward the proper subject matter for tragedy. It is the epic conception as it had been handed down by neoclassic critics:

[12] In the *Dissertation sur les principales tragédies anciennes et modernes, Œuvres,* V, 189.
[13] *Ibid.,* p. 205.   [14] *Ibid.,* p. 209.
[15] See Voltaire's criticism of *Hamlet,* for instance, in the "Appel à toutes les nations de l'Europe, *ibid.,* XXIV, 203.

Les belles fables de l'antiquité ont encore ce grand avantage sur l'histoire, qu'elles présentent une morale sensible: ce sont des leçons de vertu, et presque toute l'histoire est le succès des crimes. Jupiter, dans la fable, descend sur la terre pour punir Tantale et Lycaon; mais, dans l'histoire, nos Tantales et nos Lycaons sont les dieux de la terre. Baucis et Philémon obtiennent que leur cabane soit changée en un temple; nos Baucis et nos Philémons voient vendre par le collecteur des tailles leurs marmites, que les dieux changent en vases d'or dans Ovide.

Je sais combien l'histoire peut nous instruire, je sais combien elle est nécessaire; mais en vérité il faut lui aider beaucoup pour en tirer des règles de conduite. Que ceux qui ne connaissent la politique que dans les livres se souviennent toujours de ces vers de Corneille:

> Ces exemples récents suffiraient pour m'instruire,
> Si par l'exemple seul on se devait conduire; . . .
> Quelquefois l'un se brise où l'autre s'est sauvé,
> Et par où l'un périt, un autre est conservé.
>
> (*Cinna*, acte II, scène 1.)

Henri VIII, tyran de ses parlements, de ses ministres, de ses femmes, des consciences et des bourses, vit et meurt paisible: le bon, le brave Charles Ier périt sur un échafaud. Notre admirable héroïne Marguerite d'Anjou donne en vain douze batailles en personne contre les Anglais, sujets de son mari: Guillaume III chasse Jacques II d'Angleterre sans donner bataille. Nous avons vu de nos jours la famille impériale de Perse égorgée, et des étrangers sur son trône. Pour qui ne regarde qu'aux événements, l'histoire semble accuser la Providence, et les belles fables morales la justifient. Il est clair qu'on trouve dans elles l'utile et l'agréable: ceux qui dans ce monde ne sont ni l'un ni l'autre crient contre elles. Laissons-les dire, et lisons Homère et Ovide, aussi bien que Tite-Live et Rapin-Thoiras. Le goût donne des préférences, le fanatisme donne les exclusions.

> Tous les arts sont amis, ainsi qu'ils sont divins:
> Qui veut les séparer est loin de les connaître.
> L'histoire nous apprend ce que sont les humains,
> La fable ce qu'ils doivent être.[16]

Voltaire's conception of tragedy was that it should portray to the spectators "ce qu'ils doivent être." In his prefatory comments to *Rome sauvée* he reveals his didactic point of view, saying that his purpose in composing the play is less to show the ferocious soul of Catiline than to present his audience with a portrait of the noble character of Cicero.[17] The play is thus a demonstration of "grandeur d'âme," and the emotion which Voltaire sought to inspire was principally admiration. In a

---

[16] *Ibid.*, XIX, 67–68. [17] *Ibid.*, V, 205 ff.

foreword to the play written for the Kehl edition of Voltaire's collected works Condorcet well interprets Voltaire's didactic point of view.

Cette pièce, ainsi que *la Mort de César,* est d'un genre particulier, le plus difficile de tous peut-être, mais aussi le plus utile. Dans ces pièces, ce n'est ni à un seul personnage, ni à une famille qu'on s'intéresse, c'est à un grand événement historique. Elles ne produisent point ces émotions vives que le spectacle des passions tendres peut seul exciter. . . Ce qui attache dans ces pièces, c'est le développement de grands caractères placés dans des situations fortes, le plaisir d'entendre de grandes idées exprimées dans de beaux vers, et avec un style auquel l'état des personnages à qui on les prête permet de donner de la pompe et de l'énergie sans s'écarter de la vraisemblance; c'est le plaisir d'être témoin, pour ainsi dire, d'une révolution qui fait époque dans l'histoire, d'en voir sous ses yeux mouvoir tous les ressorts. Elles ont surtout l'avantage précieux de donner à l'âme de l'élévation et de la force: en sortant de ces pièces on se trouve plus disposé à une action de courage, plus éloigné de ramper devant un homme accrédité, ou de plier devant le pouvoir injuste et absolu. Elles sont plus difficiles à faire: il ne suffit pas d'avoir un grand talent pour la poésie dramatique, il faut y joindre une connaissance approfondie de l'histoire, une tête faite pour combiner des idées de politique, de morale, et de philosophie.[18]

Voltaire confesses with regard to *Le Triumvirat* that he altered the characters to make them better moral examples. When Octavius pardons young Pompey, even though Pompey has attempted to assassinate him, Voltaire observes: "Mais assurément cette magnanimité n'était pas alors dans le caractère d'Octave: le poète lui fait ici un honneur qu'il ne méritait pas." [19] On another occasion he remarks of another character: "On lui donne des remords dans cette pièce; on lui attribue des sentiments magnanimes: je suis persuadé qu'il n'en eut point; mais je suis persuadé qu'il en faut au théâtre." [20] In the notes, which run to some 7,000 words, he contrasts the depraved conduct of the Roman consuls and emperors with the integrity of Cato and Cicero and with the high sense of honor which prevailed during the Age of Chivalry. In the preface to the play he fears that lack of love interest will doom any chance of success in Paris, where "une femme trahie intéresse plus que la chute d'un empire." [21]

Voltaire's great innovation in the field of historical tragedy was not in his Roman plays but in a series of tragedies in which he dared to intro-

[18] *Ibid.*, p. 202.
[20] *Ibid.*, p. 211*n.*
[19] *Ibid.*, VI, 241–42*n.*
[21] *Ibid.*, p. 178.

duce French heroes from the annals of chivalry. *Zaïre* (1732), *Adélaïde du Guesclin* (1734), and *Tancrède* (1760) were bold departures in this respect. In speaking of his use of French names Voltaire wrote in the dedication to *Tancrède:*

Je ne saurais trop recommander qu'on cherche à mettre sur notre scène quelques parties de notre histoire de France. On m'a dit que les noms des anciennes maisons qu'on retrouve dans *Zaïre,* dans *le Duc de Foix,* dans *Tancrède,* ont fait plaisir à la nation. C'est encore peut-être un nouvel aiguillon de gloire pour ceux qui descendent de ces races illustres. Il me semble qu'après avoir fait paraître tant de héros étrangers sure la scène, il nous manquait d'y montrer les nôtres. J'ai eu le bonheur de peindre le grand, l'aimable Henri IV, dans un poëme qui ne déplaît pas aux bons citoyens. Un temps viendra que quelque génie plus heureux l'introduira sur la scène avec plus de majesté.[22]

In a sketch of the origin of this new kind of tragedy the *Journal des savants* (August, 1781), recognizes the importance of Voltaire's contribution and asserts that Shakespeare's example inspired him.[23] Voltaire "fit entendre sur la scène française des noms français, comme Shakespeare avait mis sur la scène anglaise des personnages anglais." [24] The author of the article recognizes, however, that in historical accuracy Shakespeare far outdid Voltaire and comments that "on ne peut prendre aucune confiance pour l'histoire aux tragédies françaises; faits et caractères, tout est altéré, c'est-à-dire, orné," whereas one can trust oneself to Shakespeare "comme à un historien exact dans les sujets étrangers, comme à un historien partial et passioné dans les sujets nationaux." [25] Actually Voltaire's new type of tragedy was "heroic" tragedy in the same sense that the term is applied to Dryden's plays, for they were based, like Dryden's, not on history, but on the heroic romances. Voltaire himself had no pretensions as to the historical value of his plays and said of *Zaïre:* "Je n'ai pris dans l'histoire que l'époque de la guerre de saint Louis: tout le reste est entièrement d'invention." [26]

The use of French names was a courageous innovation. The only plays which were based on any modern or national sources during the classical period were Racine's *Bajazet* (1672) and the *Comte d'Essex*

[22] *Ibid.,* V, 497*n.*
[23] Cited in Brenner, *L'Histoire nationale dans la tragédie française du dix-huitième siècle,* p. 197.
[24] *Ibid.*   [25] *Ibid.,* p. 198.
[26] 1732, in a letter to La Roque, *ibid.,* XXXIII, 283.

(1678) of Thomas Corneille. Racine had been careful to excuse proximity in time by distance in space,[27] and the same claim could be made for the *Comte d'Essex*, as Voltaire himself pointed out.[28] Boursault discovered in 1678 that he had come too close to reality with his *La Princesse de Clèves*, and he transformed it by substituting Roman for French names and giving it the new title *Germanicus*.[29] Several other dramatists masked modern intrigues under classic disguise; Campistron, for example, converted the history of Don Carlos to *Andronic* in 1685.[30] From 1700 to 1732 there had not been a successful tragedy which drew upon modern or national history.[31] It is true that the tragi-comedies of the preclassic era of the French theater were not essentially dissimilar from Voltaire's formula, for they were based on the romances and depended for interest chiefly upon incident rather than character development, but they were not set in a classical frame, as were Voltaire's, and they were without any historical or moral pretensions. It has been generally conceded that Voltaire found his inspiration in the English theater, and he says so himself in the preface to *Zaïre*.

C'est au théâtre anglais que je dois la hardiesse que j'ai eue de mettre sur la scène les noms de nos rois et des anciennes familles du royaume. Il me paraît que cette nouveauté pourrait être la source d'un genre de tragédie qui nous est inconnu jusqu'ici, et dont nous avons besoin. Il se trouvera sans doute des génies heureux qui perfectionneront cette idée, dont *Zaïre* n'est qu'une faible ébauche.[32]

Yet to think of the Henry plays of Shakespeare or of *Richard II* or *Richard III* as in any way parallel to *Zaïre* is surely out of the question, and it is not surprising that Voltaire made no mention of Shakespeare in his preface to the play. Voltaire, significantly, did speak at length of Dryden in his preface, for Dryden had done in *The Indian Emperour, The Conquest of Granada, Don Sebastian,* and *Secret Love* what Voltaire did in *Zaïre, Adélaïde du Guesclin,* and *Tancrède:* he had utilized plots from the romances and had not hesitated to portray such modern European figures as Cortez, Pizzaro, the Duke of Arcos, Don Sebastian, and the kings of Aragon and Navarre. Moreover, he had anticipated Vol-

---

[27] Brenner, *L'Histoire nationale dans la tragédie française du dix-huitième siècle*, p. 209.
[28] In "Remarques sur le comte d'Essex," *Œuvres*, XXXII, 328, cited in Brenner, *L'Histoire nationale dans la tragédie française du dix-huitième siècle*, p. 210.
[29] Brenner, *L'Histoire nationale dans la tragédie française du dix-huitième siècle*, p. 211.
[30] *Ibid.*, p. 213.   [31] *Ibid.*, pp. 214, 218.   [32] *Œuvres*, II, 542.

taire in using the exotic material for political and anticlerical propaganda.

A feature of the evolution of Voltaire's theater that is especially obvious in his heroic-romance tragedies is his constantly increasing use of spectacle. He had very early lamented the lack of action in the French theater, and he remarked repeatedly upon the unfortunate tendency of French tragedy to become merely a long conversation divided into five acts. It is more and more obvious that what Voltaire meant by "action" was something very similar to operatic scenic effects. Thus, once more are revealed the abyss which separates Voltaire from Shakespeare and the parallel between Voltaire and Dryden.

That action and spectacle were nearly synonymous in Voltaire's mind is plainly indicated in his attitude toward the banning of spectators from the stage in 1759.[33] With regard to the custom of seating fops on the stage he wrote in 1735: "Notre théâtre est vide d'action et de grands intérêts, pour l'ordinaire. Ce qui fait qu'il manque d'action, c'est que le théâtre est offusqué par nos petits-maîtres." [34] He made similar remarks on the occasion of the presentation of *Sémiramis*.[35] When in 1759, with the stage cleared, Voltaire had his opportunity for more "action," he soon demonstrated that he meant little more than picturesque tableaux. In that year he wrote to Diderot concerning plans for *Tancrède:*

Mon Dieu! que je fus bien aise quand j'appris que le théâtre était purgé de blanc-poudrés, coiffés au rhinocéros et à *l'oiseau royal!* Je riais aux anges en tapissant la scène de boucliers et de gonfanons. Je ne sais quoi de naïf et de vrai dans cette *chevalerie* me plaisait beaucoup.[36]

Voltaire's static conception of "action" is revealed again in his letter to Damilaville concerning *Olympie.*

Je prie mon cher frère de dire au frère Platon [here Diderot] que ce qu'il appelle pantomime je l'ai toujours appelé action. Je n'aime point le terme de *pantomime* pour la tragédie. J'ai toujours songé, autant que je l'ai pu, à rendre les scènes tragiques pittoresques. Elles le sont dans *Mahomet,* dans *Mérope,* dans *l'Orphelin de la Chine,* surtout dans *Tancrède.* Mais ici toute la pièce est un tableau continuel. Aussi a-t-elle faite le plus prodigieux effet. . . . Je voudrais qu'on perfectionnât ce genre, qui est le seul tragique: car les

---

[33] In 1759 the Comte de Lauraguais gave the necessary sum of money to clear the stage of spectators. Voltaire dedicated *L'Ecossaise* to him.

[34] In a letter to the Abbé Desfontaines in 1735, *Œuvres,* XXXIII, 551–52.

[35] In the "Dissertation sur la tragédie ancienne et moderne," in *Œuvres,* IV, 499.

[36] *Œuvres,* XL, 125.

conversations sont à la glace, et les conversations amoureuses sont à l'eau rose.[37]

Voltaire's heroic-romance plays were generally preferred by the Parisian public to his more elevated tragedies on Greek and Roman subjects. *Zaïre, Alzire,* and *Tancrède* were, with *Mérope,* his most popular plays. This lack of appreciation of the tragedies from which he had been at pains to eliminate love was a matter for regret according to Voltaire's correspondence. In 1752 he wrote of *Rome sauvée:*

On se lassera bien vite d'une diable de tragédie sans amour, d'un consul en *on,* de conjurés en *us,* d'un sujet dans lequel le tendre Crébillon m'avait enlevé la fleur de la nouveauté. On peut applaudir, pendant quelques représentations, à quelques ressources de l'art, à la peine que j'ai eue de subjuguer un terrain ingrat; mais, à la fin, il ne restera que l'aridité du sol. Comptez qu'à Paris, point d'amour, point de premières loges, et fort peu de parterre.[38]

Twelve years later he remarked of *Le Triumvirat:*

La politique est une fort bonne chose, mais elle ne réussit guère dans les tragédies: c'est, je crois, une des raisons pour lesquelles on ne joue plus la plupart des pièces de ce grand Corneille. Il faut parler au cœur plus qu'à l'esprit. Tacite est for bon au coin du feu, mais ne serait guère à sa place sur la scène.[39]

Numerous comments in his correspondence indicate that Voltaire was regretfully departing from his elevated ideal of tragedy without love. He wrote to D'Argenson concerning *Zaïre* in 1739:

Il est vrai que, puisque ce spectacle est représenté et vu par des hommes et par des femmes, il faut absolument de l'amour. On peut s'en sauver tristement une ou deux fois, mais

"Naturam expellas furca, tamen ipsa redibit"
(Hor., lib. I, ep. x, v. 24)

Que diront de jeunes actrices? qu'entendront de jeunes femmes, s'il n'est

---

[37] 1762, *Œuvres,* XLII, 85. Voltaire was sensitive to the charge that he was loading the stage with useless spectacle. His defense in the "Dissertation sur la tragédie ancienne et moderne" was that when he spoke of action, he was speaking "d'un appareil, d'une cérémonie, d'une assemblée, d'un événement nécessaire à la pièce, et non pas de ces vains spectacles plus puérils que pompeux, de ces ressources du décorateur qui suppléent à la stérilité du poëte, et qui amusent les yeux quand on ne sait parler à l'oreille et à l'âme" (*Œuvres,* IV, 500). His claim was that he appealed to the eye, the ear, and the mind at the same time.

[38] In a letter to Cideville, *Œuvres,* XXXVII, 382–83.

[39] In a letter to the Marquis de Chauvelin, *Œuvres,* XLIII, 341.

pas question d'amour? On joue souvent *Zaïre*, parce qu'elle est tendre; on ne joue point *Brutus*, parce que cette pièce n'est que forte.[40]

Regarding *Zulime*, he wrote to Frederick in 1740 that he had not spoken of it because "je suis honteux de ma molesse." [41] He referred to *Tancrède* repeatedly as the "roman de Tancrède," [42] and when he revised *Adélaïde du Guesclin* as *Le Duc de Foix,* he commented apologetically to D'Argental: "Mon cher ange, puisqu'il faut toujours de l'amour, je leur en ai donné une bonne dose avec ma barbe grise. J'en suis honteux; mais j'avais ce reste de confitures, et je l'ai abandonné aux enfants de Paris." [43]

Even so, the comparative ease with which Voltaire turned out these romance tragedies probably indicates that they were not only more suited to the taste of his audience but to his own taste as well. To one correspondent he commented in 1732 in reference to *Zaïre* that "le sujet m'entraînait, et la pièce se faisait toute seule.[44] He remarked in another letter that 'le plan *d'Eriphyle* m'avait beaucoup coûté, celui de *Zaïre* fut fait en un seul jour; et l'imagination, échauffée par l'intérêt qui régnait dans ce plan, acheva la pièce en vingt-deux jours.' " [45]

Another passage in the same letter is particularly revealing. "Zaïre est la première pièce de théâtre dans laquelle j'aie osé m'abandonner à toute la sensibilité de mon cœur; c'est la seule tragédie tendre que j'aie faite." [46] He wrote in the same vein in the preface to *Rome sauvée* that "une seule scène entre César et Catilina était plus difficile à faire que la plupart des pièces où l'amour domine." [47]

It has frequently been pointed out that Voltaire grew less "Homeric" with the passing years. In his early literary criticism, when he was most under the influence of the Rapin school of thought, there was a tendency to prefer Homer to Virgil, Tasso to Ariosto, and Corneille to Racine. This preference was gradually reversed. Homer was more and more impugned for his crudity, Ariosto was gradually raised above Tasso, and Voltaire's preference for Corneille rather than Racine was less frequently expressed and in regard to style he flatly reversed his

[40] *Œuvres*, XXXV, 283.   [41] *Ibid.*, 442.
[42] See a letter to D'Argental in 1760, *Œuvres*, XLI, 98.
[43] *Œuvres*, XXXVII, 475.
[44] To Formont, *Œuvres*, XXXIII, 273.
[45] To La Roque in 1732, *Œuvres*, XXXIII, 283.
[46] *Ibid.*, p. 282.   [47] *Œuvres*, V, 209.

position and upheld Racine's style as equivalent to perfection.[48] Rigault says:

Dans sa jeunesse, il admirait Homère et l'appelait "un peintre sublime"; il plaignait les esprits philosophiques qui ne peuvent pardonner ses fautes en faveur de ses beautés. . . . Mais, en vieillissant, Voltaire devient moins homérique. Il trouve que si La Motte a mal traduit *l'Iliade,* il l'a très-bien attaquée. Les héros d'Homère lui paraissent fastidieux, et ses dieux ridicules. Les grandes images de *l'Iliade,* qui faisaient dire au sculpteur Bouchardon: "Lorsque j'ai lu Homère, j'ai cru avoir vingt pieds de haut," n'ont plus de prix à ses yeux. . . . Le seigneur *Pococurante* avouant à *Candide* qu'il a *l'Iliade* dans sa bibliothèque, par égard pour l'antiquité, comme on a de vieilles médailles, n'est pas loin d'exprimer la dernière opinion de Voltaire sur Homère. . . . Aujourd'hui nous admirons Homère d'avoir peint en traits immortels l'homme et la nature, parce que nous n'avons pas besoin que l'homme nous ressemble pour aimer les images qu'en trace la poésie. Nous tenons Hector, Achille, Ulysse, malgré leur barbarie, pour des exemplaires aussi vrais que nous-mêmes des passions éternelles de l'humanité. Pour le xviiie siècle, l'homme et la nature, c'étaient l'homme et la nature civilisés. Aux yeux de Voltaire, les héros d'Homère ne sont que des ébauches de l'homme véritable, qui est l'honnête homme du xviiie siècle, poli, sans préjugés, et collaborateur de *l'Encyclopédie.*[49]

André Morize, in his edition of *Candide,* traces Voltaire's increasing regard for Ariosto in the successive editions of the *Essai sur la poésie épique* (1726–56). Morize notes that in 1733 Voltaire wrote, "L'Europe ne mettra l'Arioste avec le Tasse que lorsqu'on placera l'Enéide avec le Roman comique," but that in 1756 the reference to Ariosto was altered to read, "L'Arioste a plus de fertilité, plus de variété, plus d'imagination que tous les autres ensemble; et si on lit Homère par une espèce de devoir, on lit et on relit l'Arioste pour son plaisir."[50] This change in attitude is also evident in Voltaire's correspondence. In 1769 he wrote to Mme du Deffand in praise of *Clélie* and the *Astrée,* for which he had had only scorn in earlier years,[51] and in the same letter he recommended that she read Ariosto.

Soyez très-sûre [advised Voltaire with regard to Ariosto] qu'il écrit beaucoup mieux que La Fontaine, et qu'il est cent fois plus peintre qu'Homère,

---

[48] See Voltaire's letter prefixed to *Irène* (1777), *Œuvres,* VII, 326.
[49] Rigault, "Histoire de la querelle des anciens et modernes," in *Œuvres complètes,* I, 504–5.
[50] André Morize, critical edition of *Candide,* p. 189n.
[51] See the "Essai sur la poésie épique," *Œuvres,* VIII, 362.

plus varié, plus gai, plus comique, plus intéressant, plus savant dans la connaissance du cœur humain que tous les romanciers ensemble, à commencer par l'histoire de Joseph et de la Putiphar, et à finir par *Paméla*.[52]

Doubtless one reason for Voltaire's gravitating toward romance material was the fact that it was more easily adapted to his didactic purpose. In treating the legends of Greek mythology he was bound by themes familiar to every spectator. In his tragedies based on Roman history he was likewise obligated not to depart too far from the accepted idea of the characters and events portrayed. But in tales of chivalry Voltaire not only found a tone suited to his taste but also a medium easily turned to his purpose. Although he introduced names from French chivalric annals, no one thought of looking for historical accuracy, and Voltaire had all the freedom of parable.

Voltaire's conception of the heroic romances as essentially epic fables in prose is indicated in precise terms in the twelfth conversation of the satirical *L'A, B, C* (1762). The title of this conversation is "Du code de la perfidie," [53] and B is maintaining that the Bible and history actually set up a code for the practice of perfidy. Did not Moses lie to the Egyptians in order to steal provisions to be used against the Egyptians? Did not the annointed King Clovis bargain basely with cutthroats for the assassination of a rival and then pay the bargain price in worthless money?

B declares:

Presque toutes nos histoires sont remplies de pareilles perfidies commises par des princes qui tous ont bâti des églises et fondé des monastères.[54]

A answers:

Il m'importe fort peu que Clovis et ses pareils aient été oints; mais je vous avoue que je souhaiterais, pour l'édification du genre humain, qu'on jetât dans le feu toute l'histoire civile et écclesiastique. Je n'y vois guère que les annales des crimes.[55]

C then observes that the romance is superior for teaching morality and says that he considers Homer's "romance," the *Iliad*, inferior in this respect to Fénelon's *Télémaque*.

[52] *Œuvres*, XLVI, 318.   [53] *Ibid.*, XXVII, 375 ff.
[54] *Ibid.*, p. 376.   [55] *Ibid.*

Oui, je conçois que le roman vaudrait mieux: on y est maître du moins de feindre des exemples de vertu; mais Homère n'a jamais imaginé une seule action vertueuse et honnête dans tout son roman monotone de *l'Iliade*. J'aimerais beaucoup mieux le roman de *Télémaque*, s'il n'était pas tout en digressions et déclamations.[56]

There is no indication that Voltaire here meant that the dramatic use of romance material would avoid the "digressions et declamations" of *Télémaque*, but the conversation indicates an attitude of mind which is important in understanding the use Voltaire made of romance material in his plays.

An inevitable consequence of Voltaire's underlying didacticism was that he had to rely on melodramatic situations to hold the interest of spectators. Gros, in his study of Quinault, declares that Racine was actually "à part" and traces the main line of descent to Voltaire from Thomas Corneille, through Quinault, Campistron, La Grange-Chancel and Crébillon.[57] The "vim tragicam" [58] for Voltaire was an added element by which an author sought to work on the emotions of the spectators in order that they might be pleased while they were instructed, an attitude identical with the sugared pill theory of Dacier. The characters became manikins maneuvered by the author and the dramatic effect a series of *coups de théâtre*. Voltaire was forced to rely on devices such as letters that fall into the wrong hands, mistaken identity, and a golden

[56] *Ibid.*, p. 377.

[57] Gros, *Philippe Quinault*, pp. 739–40. Gros writes: "On oublie un peu trop, quand on étudie l'influence de la tragédie lyrique sur la tragédie, que la plupart des défauts que l'on relève chez les auteurs de la fin du XVIIe siècle et chez ceux du XVIIIe viennent— autant et plus que de l'opéra—de la tragédie romanesque qui, elle-même, se rattache à la tragi-comédie. Nous l'avons dit ailleurs, la tragédie de Racine est, dans l'histoire du théâtre, une 'heureuse exception.' Elle ne rompt pas la continuité de l'évolution; elle se développe à part. La chaîne qui va de Quinault, auteur tragique, et de Th. Corneille à Campistron et à La Grange-Chancel, puis à Crebillon et à Voltaire, est ininterrompue. La tradition de la tragédie romanesque et de la tragi-comédie se continue, en dehors de Racine, grâce à Boyer, qui s'obstine à vivre, à Pradon, à l'abbé Abeille, à Ferrier, à l'abbé Genest et autres personnages, sans qu'il soit nécessaire de faire appel à l'opéra pour expliquer cette persistance. Il reste que l'opéra, qui n'est pas lui-même sans attaches avec la tragi-comédie et la tragédie romanesque, contribua par son succès à renforcer cette tradition, à la maintenir et à la faire triompher."

[58] In a letter to Saint-Lambert in 1773 (*Œuvres*, XLVIII, 447). Voltaire made this revealing comment upon his hastily composed *Les Lois de Minos*: "Vous vous doutez bien dans quel esprit j'ai fait cette rapsodie; il ne faut jamais perdre de vue le grand objet de rendre la superstition exécrable. J'aurais dû y mettre un peu plus de *vim tragicam;* mais un malade de quatre-vingts ans ne peut rien faire de ce qu'il voudrait en aucun genre."

cross given to Zaïre by her mother. His tragedy became a tragedy of situation rather than of character: a son is induced to murder his own father, as in *Mahomet,* a father condemns his own son, as in *Brutus,* a son condemns his own father, as in *La Mort de César.* The development does not depend upon character revelation, but rather upon simple intrigue. Will Zaïre marry the Sultan despite the opposition of her brother and father? Will Tancrède save Aménaïde, though he thinks her unfaithful. Voltaire doubtless mistook the essence of tragedy, but his mistake was the mistake of neoclassicism in general.

That his tragedies still have indubitable appeal is owing to the characteristic sensibility which animates them. His genuine humanitarian instinct always vibrated sympathetically with suffering mankind. There is an appeal to Zaïre's words:

> Mais, Fatime, à l'instant les traits de ce que j'aime,
> Ces traits chers et charmants, que toujours je revoi,
> Se montrent dans mon âme entre le ciel et moi.
> Eh bien! race des rois, dont le ciel me fit naître,
> Père, mère, chrétiens, vous mon Dieu, vous mon maître,
> Vous qui de mon amant me privez aujourd'hui,
> Terminez donc mes jours, qui ne sont plus pour lui! [59]

The accent of Alzire, when she bids Zamore escape, but says that she will remain true to her obligations as the wife of the detested Gusman, is touching and sincere: "Pars, emporte avec toi mon bonheur et ma vie." [60] Brunetière wrote concerning this quality of Voltairian drama:

Je pourrais m'étendre longuement sur ce thème. Un caractère essentiel de la tragédie de Corneille et de Racine, c'est, à mon sens, le peu de prix ou d'importance que leurs héros, le public du XVIIe siècle, et le poète lui-même y semblent attacher à la vie des autres. On y tue avec une facilité prodigieuse; la légende ou l'histoire y justifient les pires horreurs; et le bon vieux Corneille n'est pas plus ému de l'épouvantable catastrophe de sa *Rodogune* que le tendre, l'élégant, le délicat Racine de celle de son *Athalie.* Au contraire, l'âme cachée de la tragédie de Voltaire, le principe diffus de sa sensibilité, la source de son pathétique, c'est l'importance qu'il donne, c'est le prix qu'il met à l'existence humaine, si considérable à ses yeux que la passion en peut bien excuser quelquefois, mais que rien au monde, ni jamais, n'en saurait justifier la suppression violente: Voltaire a l'horreur du sang.[61]

[59] Act IV, scene 1; *Œuvres,* II, 595.   [60] Act IV, scene 4; *Œuvres,* III, 423.
[61] Brunetière, in a review of "Le Théâtre de Voltaire, par M. Emile Deschanel," *Revue des deux mondes,* CLXXXIX (September 1, 1886), 218.

Although Voltaire thought it was the amatory element of his plays which charmed the spectators, his sensibility was probably quite as effective: *Mérope,* where Voltaire departed from the formula of *Sémiramis* and *Oreste* to devote most of the tragedy to the touching recognition of the lost prince by the queen, was as popular as *Zaïre, Alzire,* or *Tancrède.*

Having agreed, in fine, that tragedy should be a public lecture more instructive than history or plain philosophy, Voltaire sought, as Rapin and Dacier had recommended, to choose for subject matter great events and admirable heroes. He turned first to Greek examples, which offered legendary accounts of historical episodes with strong moral implications. His use of Roman history was didactic after the manner of Addison, and his critical comments reveal that he believed the artist should rewrite history so as to justify the ways of Providence and offer a portrait of what men should be rather than of what they are. This conception Voltaire developed clearly and fully in the article "Fable" in the *Dictionnaire philosophique*. As he gravitated toward the use of the heroic tales of chivalry the newer material proved not only more adaptable to his conception of tragedy as a kind of parable or apologue but also more suited to his taste and to that of his age. That he conceived the heroic romances to be likewise epic fables in prose is revealed by a satirical conversation in *L'A, B, C,* in which he argues that *Télémaque* is superior to the *Iliad* because its moral is better. Voltaire's greatest triumphs were in this type of tragedy, which may be said to be "heroic" in the manner of the plays of Dryden. In introducing the names of actual chevaliers into his plays Voltaire did as Dryden had already done, and the affinity between the two is further emphasized by the similar political and philosophical implications.

CHAPTER VIII

VOLTAIRE'S EFFORT
TO RAISE DRAMATIC STYLE

Tʜᴇ ʜᴇʀᴏɪᴄ style of Voltaire's plays represents a conscious effort to
fulfill the neoclassic conception of tragedy and to disprove the critical
opinion prevalent in France and England that the French language
was too feeble for heroic verse. Early in his career Voltaire held up the
style of Corneille as an example of heroic sublimity, and he often spoke
with enthusiasm of the metaphorical style of the last act of *Rodogune*.
In defending his own attempts to elevate the style of tragedy he also
referred frequently to the vigor and energy of English drama. He expressed his admiration particularly for Dryden, and there is some evidence that he had Dryden's heightened style in mind in composing his
own dramatic verse.

Judging by critical writings in general, however, the movement in
favor of a more bold and figurative style, strong in the last quarter of
the seventeenth century, gradually lost momentum after 1700. Begin-
ning with La Motte's proposal for tragedy in prose early in the new
century, an idea which Voltaire attacked in the preface to *Œdipe* in
1730 and frequently thereafter, there was a constantly increasing volume
of sentiment in favor, not of raising, but of lowering the style of tragedy.
As the age advanced the campaign in favor of a more conversational
tone seems to have centered in the *Correspondance littéraire,* in whose
columns Grimm and Diderot maintained with growing conviction that
prose was the only medium for French tragedy. In 1770 Grimm declared
flatly that "toutes nos plus belles pièces sont de la poésie épique." [1]

This growing critical trend in favor of a more simple style was not
without its effect upon Voltaire. He removed many elevated passages
from his later plays, and in *Tancrède* he abandoned heroic verse for
alternating rhyme. He gradually shifted his allegiance from Corneille to
Racine, and in the preface to his last tragedy, *Irène,* he recognized
Racine's style as the perfect model for prose as well as for verse.[2] But his
dramatic style never lost a certain grandiose tone, and to the end he
gagged at the thought of tragedy in prose. Faced with the actuality of

[1] *Correspondance littéraire, philosophique et critique,* VIII, p. 460.
[2] *Œuvres,* VII, 326.

prose tragedy at the Comédie-Française, he hurled remarks such as "Voilà le coup de grâce donné aux beaux-arts." [3]

The age was extremely conscious of style, and every new tragedy was a signal for debate. The *Mercure de France,* in 1731, the year after Voltaire's *Brutus* was first played, is filled with comments upon questions of dramatic style. In the March issue a contributor writes that the opening scene of *Brutus* sounds like a passage from the *Henriade,* and the writer advises Voltaire not to attempt dramatic verse.[4] Voltaire has said that a tragedy in prose is not a tragedy. Verse is, perhaps, necessary to an epic poem, but the writer of the article does not think that it is necessary to tragedy. Attention is again drawn to the battle between prose and rhyme in the December issue of the *Mercure de France* for the same year,[5] the dispute being the subject of an allegorical poem of some length. Prose and rhyme are brought before the divinity of Mount Parnassus to argue the merits of prose tragedy. Rhyme is successful in its defense on the strength of examples cited from the tragedies of Corneille, Racine, and Voltaire.

In an article written for the Académie Royale des Inscriptions et Belles Lettres, in 1732, Louis Racine opposes too elevated a style. His position is approximately that of Voltaire twenty-five years later. Louis Racine writes that "le véritable stile de la Tragédie est peu connu. Il ne doit pas estre pompeux comme le stile du Poëme héroïque, il ne doit pas non plus estre simple comme le stile de la Comédie." He explains:

Nostre langue, dont la versification ne consiste pas dans la mesure des syllabes bréves ou longues, n'a point de vers propres à chaque espéce de Poëme, ce n'est que par un stile plus ou moins élevé, qu'on se conforme au goût du sujet qu'on traite; & la Tragédie estant un poëme en dialogues, ne doit point estre écrite en vers pompeux qui ne conviennent point à une conversation, ni en vers simples, parce que cette conversation est noble. C'est donc ce milieu entre la pompe du vers héroïque & la simplicité du vers comique, cette noblesse sans affectation, & ce naturel sans bassesse qu'il est difficile d'observer toûjours.[6]

In 1733, after the success of *Zaïre,* the Abbé Prévost, in his literary

---

[3] In a letter to D'Argental (1770), *Œuvres,* XLVII, 205.

[4] *Mercure de France,* March, 1731, pp. 429 ff.

[5] *Ibid.,* December, 1731, pp. 2964 ff.

[6] Racine, "Réflexions sur l'Andromaque d'Euripide et sur l'Andromaque de Racine," in *Mémoires de littérature, tirez des régistres de l'Académie Royale des inscriptions et belles lettres,* X, 320–21.

journal *Pour et contre,* observes that Voltaire "s'élève plus que Racine, mais il est moins tendre et gracieux. Il a plus de graces et de tendresse que Corneille, mais avec moins d'élévation. Il me semble donc qu'on peut marquer sa place entre ces deux grands hommes." [7] Prévost then adds in a footnote: "M. de Voltaire me permettra de remarquer encore, que ses pièces de théâtre sentent un peu trop le poème épique. Elles souffrent du talent principal de l'auteur." [8]

In 1735 the literary review *Observations sur les écrits modernes* finds it necessary to defend Voltaire against the charge of employing too epic a style.

C'est en vain que l'envie, & le triste sentiment de leur impuissance, leur font donner aux beaux vers d'un Poëte qu'on admire aujourd'hui sur la scene, le nom de vers *épiques.* Quelle erreur! Les vers de Sophocle & d'Euripide sont plus forts que ceux d'Homere & on trouve plus d'énergie dans quelques scenes de *l'Hippolyte* de Seneque, que dans tout *l'Eneïde.* Il n'y a donc que l'ignorance qui ait établi, quant à l'élegance & à l'harmonie, la distinction frivole des vers tragiques et des vers épiques.[9]

In the same year the *Mercure de France,* in speaking of *Sabinus,* by Richer, warns that the tone of tragedy has been raised in recent years "au delà des bornes qu'il faut lui prescrire, si l'on ne veut confondre la Tragédie avec l'Epopée." [10]

In the prologue to his tragedy *Teglis* (1734), Pierre de Morand mocks the pompous style of tragedy, and in 1738 the Comédie-Italienne presented a humorous allegorical skit by Morand in which Melpomene, the tragic muse, complains that Calliope, the muse of epic poetry, has invaded the theater and that "la tragédie enfin n'est qu'un monstre épique."

> On méprise aujourd'hui l'Art qui fit autrefois
> La gloire de la France, & le plaisir des Rois.
> Depuis que, sous mon nom, Calliope trop vaine
> A, d'un stile ampoulé, fait retentir la scène,
> Sans exiger encor la pitié, la terreur,
> Où je sçais, tour-à-tour, faire passer un cœur;
> Le Public, qu'a séduit son pompeux verbiage,
> Ne veut, de mots ronflans, qu'un bizarre assemblage,
> Que, d'Epithetes vains, de grands vers tout tissus,

---

[7] *Pour et contre,* I, No. 5 (1733), 111.   [8] *Ibid.,* p. 113*n.*
[9] *Observations sur les écrits modernes,* I, 311.
[10] *Mercure de France,* February, 1735, pp. 344–45.

Et des traits recherchés ensemble mal cousus;
Cette simplicité, tableau de la Nature,
Ces nobles sentimens ma plus chere parure,
Les Caracteres vrais jusqu'au bout soûtenus,
La Conduite, les Mœurs, sont-ils encor connus?
Racine est aujourd'hui traité de Prosaïque:
La Tragédie enfin n'est plus qu'un monstre épique.[11]

In the preface to *Teglis,* a marquis inquires of an actor as to the nature of the tragedy about to be presented. He asks whether there are any "vers ronflants, épithétiques, pompeux? de ces vers qui éblouissent, étourdissent, ravissent?"[12] The actor replies that there is only one passage which he considers "trop épique." Hopefully the marquis suggests: "C'est donc un sujet tiré de quelque Roman, puisqu'il y a de l'épique?" Disappointed again, he is off to inspect the audience with his lorgnette.

In 1748 Marmontel is praised by Raynal in the *Nouvelles littéraires*[13] as an apt pupil of Voltaire, and his first tragedy, *Denys le Tyran,* is recommended, even though there are found in·it a number of epic passages. This is recognized as a fault, but Raynal prefers good epic verse to flat verse. Why should one object to the artificiality of an epic style, he asks, when the monologues common in tragedy are not like actual conversation and no kind of verse, elevated or not, resembles reality. "Combien de pièces de Voltaire," he exclaims, "ne se soutiennent qu'à l'aide de plusieurs traits épiques, qui répandent sur elles un coloris plus fort, plus lumineux et plus éclatant!"[14]

The increasing boldness with which Grimm and Diderot in the *Correspondance littéraire* favored prose tragedy and dared to criticize even the style of Racine seems to reflect the course of critical opinion. In 1754 Voltaire's early play *Mariamne,* revived in that year, is praised for its simple style, which is contrasted with the epic style of current Parisian tragedy.[15] A letter of 1755 objects to an elevated style on the ground that a person does not stop to make a speech in an emotional crisis, but expresses himself in action, by broken words or exclamations.[16] Voltaire's *L'Orphelin de la Chine* languishes "quoique les acteurs disent les plus

---

[11] Morand, *Théâtre et Œuvres diverses,* II, 9.
[12] *Ibid.,* I, xxxii–xxxiii.
[13] In *Correspondance littéraire, philosophique et critique,* I, 134 ff.
[14] *Ibid.*   [15] *Ibid.,* II, 397.   [16] *Ibid.,* III, 83.

belles choses du monde." [17] In 1758 Grimm seizes upon Colardeau's *Astarbé*, based on an episode from *Télémaque*, as an example of verse too elevated for the theater.

Notre goût facile et corrompu passe aujourd'hui les plus grandes absurdités en faveur de ce qu'on appelle beaux vers. Pour moi, quand on me dit qu'il y a de beaux vers dans une pièce, peu s'en faut que je ne regarde ce propos comme une critique. En effet, que veulent dire les beaux vers dans un ouvrage dramatique? Ce sont des sentences, des maximes, des sentiments aussi pleins d'emphase que vides de naturel.[18]

If Horace banned these ornaments from epic poetry, Grimm concludes, what must one say of their use in tragedy?

An extended statement of the case against epic style comes in a letter of the *Correspondance littéraire* in 1764.[19] The occasion is an heroic poem by Dorat based on Lillo's *The London Merchant*. Grimm agrees with Diderot that the French version fails to convey the sublimity of the English prose. This is the fault of the language, not of the poet, says Grimm, for "le vers français sera toujours un langage trop apprêté, trop arrondi pour convenir à la poésie dramatique." Grimm continues:

C'est lui, n'en doutons point, qui a éloigné le théâtre français de cette simplicité, de ce naturel, de cette énergie concise et sublime, qui font le prix du théâtre ancien et le charme des gens de goût. Il a entraîné le poëte dans ces écarts épiques, dans ces tirades si contraires à la bienséance théâtrale.[20]

Grimm returns to the attack in an article entitled, "Réflexions sur la tragédie," in January, 1765.[21] Alexandrian verse, he reiterates, is too full and harmonious to be suitable for the stage. The first verse of a couplet is usually made for the second and even the finest passages of Racine, although they charm the ear, are not dramatic.

Diderot's comment upon De Belloy's highly successful tragedy *Le Siège de Calais,* in the same year, is that the characters, "au lieu de dire ce qu'ils doivent dire, disent presque toujours ce que leurs discours et leurs actions devraient me faire penser et sentir, et ce sont deux choses bien différents." [22] They should have been made to talk like the simple bourgeois they were.

---

[17] *Ibid.*
[19] *Ibid.*, V, 475 ff.
[21] *Ibid.*, VI, 170 ff.

[18] *Ibid.*, III, 483.
[20] *Ibid.*, V, 477.
[22] *Ibid.*, VI, 241.

In 1767 Grimm charges in the *Correspondance littéraire* that Voltaire's epic conception of the stage is old fashioned, that his point of view "est de l'évangile de l'autre siècle, et a passé de mode depuis que M. de Voltaire n'est plus en France." [23] The letter is commenting on the *Prosodie française* of the Abbé d'Olivet, academician. Voltaire had apparently agreed with D'Olivet's suggestion that subjects for the stage could be found in Ovid. Grimm protests.

J'ose soutenir encore que la poésie dramatique doit être essentiellement différente de la poésie épique. Tout poëte qui veut tirer ses sujets, pour le théâtre lyrique, des *Métamorphoses* d'Ovide, a déjà un projet absurde; et s'il veut imiter jusqu'au style d'Ovide dans les pièces faites pour être représentées, il peut se vanter de n'avoir pas les premières notions du goût véritable.[24]

The publication of Beaumarchais's prose drama *Eugénie* offered another opportunity for a discussion of epic tragedy in the same year. In reviewing the play, Grimm repeats that in his opinion there is no form of French verse suitable for the stage. He comments that

il est impossible qu'une langue qui n'observe point de prosodie dans ses vers, dont la prosodie est même toujours sourde, et qui se contente de compter les syllabes de ses vers sans s'embarrasser de leur mesure, qu'il est impossible, dis-je, qu'une telle langue ait jamais le vers dramatique[25]

In answer to those who would hold up ancient tragedy and Racine as examples of successful drama in verse, Grimm asserts that the ancients never used heroic verse in tragedy and that if a Greek dramatist had made the queen of Carthage speak on the stage as she spoke in the fourth act of the *Aeneid*, he would have been hissed.[26]

Even after this preparation it is still startling to have Grimm assert in the *Correspondance littéraire* in 1770 that France has yet to create real tragedy and that it will be impossible to achieve except in prose:

Je soutiens que toutes nos plus belles pièces sont de la poésie épique, et ne sont pas de la poésie dramatique; que ces deux poésies sont essentiellement différentes, et que, puisque les Français n'ont pas, comme les Grecs, les Romains, et les Italiens modernes, un vers dramatique, il faut qu'ils écrivent leurs tragédies en prose, ou qu'ils n'en aient jamais de vraies.[27]

The letter containing the above was inspired by the publication of La Harpe's *Mélanie*. The style of the play is so harmonious, Grimm says,

[23] *Ibid.*, VII, 212. [24] *Ibid.* [25] *Ibid.*, pp. 415–16.
[26] *Ibid.*, p. 416. [27] *Ibid.*, VIII, 460.

that it is worthy to be placed immediately after the tragedies of La Harpe's master Voltaire, "qui est notre maître à tous." But *Mélanie* only strengthens Grimm's conviction that prose is the only proper medium for French tragedy.

> Otez à son ouvrage la forme dramatique, donnez-lui celle d'une héroïde; conservez les discours, ils seront superbes, et je n'aurai plus d'objection à faire: car dans la poésie épique, c'est le droit du poëte de se montrer toujours à coté de ses héros, c'est lui qui parle lors même qu'il fait parler les autres; mais dans la poésie dramatique, le sublime de son art, c'est de ne se jamais rappeler à l'idée du spectateur.[28]

In 1772 it is observed that the divine harmony of Racine's verse recalls Virgil, but it is repeated that "cette poésie était toujours épique comme celle de Virgile, et jamais dramatique." [29]

From this review of opinions voiced in the *Mercure de France*, the *Pour et contre*, the *Observations sur les écrits modernes*, the *Nouvelles littéraires*, and the *Correspondance littéraire*, it is plain that the critical viewpoint of the period was moving in a direction opposite to that of Voltaire. Voltaire's aim was to raise the style of tragedy from the simple purity of Racine to a more bold and majestic, a more "epic" plane. Fellow critics considered that even the style of Racine was too elevated and that real tragedy would be achieved in France only in prose, since no form of French verse had the directness they judged to be necessary for the stage.

The history of Voltaire's style is marked by a series of shifts back and forth from a declamatory heroic manner reminiscent of Corneille to a more simple and conversational style which Voltaire and his age considered Racinian. The evidence indicates very clearly that he gradually modified his heroic ideal because of the increasing weight of critical opposition.

His concern with the alleged feebleness of the French language is expressed as early as 1727, in his essay on epic poetry, written and published in England to advance the sale of the English edition of the *Henriade*.[30] His opinions reflect the views of Racine, Dacier, Fénelon, Dryden, and other French and English critics. Voltaire says that he has heard the French tongue arraigned in England for insufficiency, as being neither

---

[28] *Ibid.*, p. 461.   [29] *Ibid.*, X, 113.
[30] Florence D. White, *Voltaire's Essay on Epic Poetry*, p. 7.

lofty nor strong enough to attain the sublimity of epic poetry.[31] He admits that the genius of the French language, its precision, its turn of phrase, which does not permit transposition, qualify it particularly well for conversation, whereas the English language, because its copiousness has been improved in variety and energy, because of its capacity for inversions, is naturally suited to elevated verse. Voltaire writes:

Our coy Language is not as copious as it should be. We have discarded a Multitude of old energetic Expressions, the Loss of which has weakened the Stock of the *French* Tongue, as the compelling our Protestants away hath thinned the Nation. The *English* have naturalized many of our antiquated Words, as they have done our Countrymen, and so they have increased their Language, as well as their People at our Expence.[32]

But the French tongue has strength and majesty enough in Corneille's tragedies, where it soars oftentimes beyond the true measure of the sublime.[33] The language does not lack force or grandeur, but freedom. Rigid rules for versification handicap the poet, and a narrow purity of taste robs the language of its natural abundance.[34] Lack of freedom of thought is also a serious disadvantage, for there is no sublimity of expression without sublimity of thought.[35] In England the force of the language is increased by the nature of the government, which allows the English to speak on questions of great concern to the nation. Religious tolerance has also strengthened the English language by endowing it with the metaphorical style of the Scriptures. If the French had the freedom of thought and expression which exists in England, the French language would not be lacking in the capacity for great and serious poetry.

In his "Epître à la Duchesse du Maine" in 1750, prefixed to *Oreste*, Voltaire declares that he was inspired to write his first tragedy when he heard a performance of *Iphigenia in Tauris* at the court of Sceaux.[36] A translation had been provided by the learned Malézieu, and the duchess herself played the leading role.[37] Voltaire writes that he was so impressed by the force and majesty of the French language in Malézieu's version that he was inspired to try his hand at composing an *Œdipe*.[38] He says of Malézieu:

[31] *Ibid.*, p. 144.   [32] *Ibid.*, pp. 149–50.   [33] *Ibid.*, p. 145.
[34] *Ibid.*, p. 149.   [35] *Ibid.*, pp. 144–45.   [36] *Œuvres*, V, 79–80.
[37] *Ibid.*, V, 81.   [38] *Ibid.*

Il prenait quelquefois . . . un Sophocle, un Euripide; il traduisait sur-le-champ en français une de leurs tragédies. L'admiration, l'enthousiasme dont il était saisi lui inspirait des expressions qui répondaient à la mâle et harmonieuse énergie des vers grecs, autant qu'il est possible d'en approcher dans la prose d'une langue à peine tirée de la barbarie, et qui, polie par tant de grands auteurs, manque encore pourtant de précision, de force, et d'abondance.[39]

Later in this prefatory letter Voltaire, with regard to his plans for his first play, says that he tried to "imiter cette pompe et cette magnificence vraiment tragique des vers de Sophocle, cette élégance, cette pureté, ce naturel, sans quoi un ouvrage (bien fait d'ailleurs) serait un mauvais ouvrage." [40] The tirades of Philoctète, which are the most pompous passages of *Œdipe,* are comparatively restrained in comparison with the bombastic tone which will characterize such later plays as *Mahomet* and *Sémiramis.* Philoctète, in spurning Œdipe's suspicions that he covets the throne, replies:

> Le trône est un objet qui n'a pu me tenter:
> Hercule à ce haut rang dédaignait de monter.
> Toujours libre avec lui, sans sujets et sans maître,
> J'ai fait des souverains, et n'ai point voulu l'être.[41]

It was probably of such passages that Fontenelle was thinking when he told Voltaire that *Œdipe* "était fort belle, mais que la versification en était trop forte et trop pleine de feu." [42]

Mariamne offers an early example of Voltaire's ability to vary his style. It is in a comparatively simple and fluid style which contrasts with that of *Œdipe.* Raynal in the *Nouvelles littéraires* remarked of *Mariamne:* "Ce ne sont pas de ces vers épiques qui, souvent déplacés, arrachent quelquefois des applaudissements passagers." [43] Voltaire, in a letter written in 1725 to Thieriot regarding the vigorous style of the *Henriade,* says significantly that it is "un peu autrement travaillé que *Mariamne*" and then continues: "L'épique est mon fait, ou je suis bien trompé, et il me semble qu'on marche bien plus à son aise dans une carrière où on a pour rival un Chapelain, Lamotte, et Saint-Didier, que dans celle où il faut tâcher d'égaler Racine et Corneille." [44]

[39] *Ibid.,* pp. 79–80.   [40] *Ibid.,* p. 87.   [41] Act II, scene 4, *Œuvres,* II, 78.
[42] As reported in the "Nouvelles littéraires," in *Correspondance littéraire, philosophique et critique,* I, 328.
[43] *Ibid.,* II, 397.   [44] *Œuvres,* XXXIII, 152.

In his *Dicours sur la tragédie à Mylord Bolingbroke,* prefixed to
Brutus, Voltaire again praises the energetic style of English tragedy and
of Corneille. He speaks of Corneille as "le grand Corneille" and seems
to be referring to Racine when he says, "Nous avons en France des
tragédies estimées, qui son plutôt des conversations qu'elles ne sont la
représentation d'un événement."[45] Voltaire opens his dedication to
Bolingbroke as follows:

Souffrez donc que je vous présente *Brutus,* quoique écrit dans une autre
langue, *docte sermonis utriusque linguae,* à vous qui me donneriez des
leçons de française aussi bien que d'anglais, à vous qui m'apprendriez du
moins à rendre à ma langue cette force et cette énergie qu'inspire la noble
liberté de penser: car les sentiments vigoureux de l'âme passent toujours dans
le langage, et qui pense fortement parle de même.[46]

In a letter in 1731 to the *Nouvelliste du Parnasse* with regard to his
dedication to *Brutus* Voltaire later qualifies somewhat his placing of
Corneille above Racine, and having said that both have their faults, he
concludes:

Le style fort et vigoreux, tel qu'il convient à la tragédie, est celui qui
ne dit ni trop ni trop peu, et qui fait toujours des tableaux à l'esprit, sans
s'écarter un moment de la passion.
Ainsi Cléopâtre, dans *Rodogune,* s'écrie (acte v, scène 1):

> Trône à t'abandonner je ne puis consentir;
> Par un coup de tonnerre il vaut mieux en sortir
>
> .   .   .
>
> Tombe sur moi le ciel, pourvu que je me venge!

Voilà du style très-fort, et peut-être trop.[47]

In the first scene of *Brutus* a resounding passage in which Brutus,
speaking before the Senate, scorns the demands of an emissary of the
deposed Tarquin is typically declamatory.

> L'ennemi du sénat connaîtra qui nous sommes,
> Et l'esclave d'un roi va voir enfin des hommes.
> Que dans Rome à loisir il porte ses regards:
> Il la verra dans vous: vous êtes ses remparts.
> Qu'il révère en ces lieux le dieu qui nous rassemble;
> Qu'il paraisse au sénat, qu'il écoute, et qu'il tremble.[48]

---

[45] *Œuvres,* II, 314.
[46] *Ibid.,* 311.   [47] *Ibid.,* XXXIII, 218.
[48] Act I, scene 1; *ibid.,* II, 328.

It was concerning this first scene that a commentator wrote in the *Mercure de France:*

Les grands Vers de la premiere Scene m'ont presque fait croire que je lisois un nouveau Chant de la Henriade. Est-ce là, me suis-je dit, le ton que prennent Corneille et Racine, et qu'ils doivent donner à tous ceux qui entrent dans une carriere qu'ils ont si dignement remplie? Je conviens que M. de V. quitte quelquefois le ton Epique, mais d'un excès il tombe dans un autre qui fait encore plus de tort, et l'on a de la peine à se figurer, qu'aprés s'être élevé si haut on puisse descendre si bas, d'où je conclus que sa vocation n'est pas pour le Théatre.[49]

The style of *La Mort de César* is raised to an equal pitch. In a letter to Asselin, in 1735, Voltaire says that the style of the play gives a true impression of the vigorous style of the English theater. It is, he comments, "l'ouvrage le plus fortement versifié que j'aie fait," [50] and in another letter, also addressed to Asselin, he remarks that the play is "de tous mes ouvrages celui dont j'ai le plus travaillé la versification." [51] He has imitated the style of Corneille particularly in the use of images.

Je m'y suis proposé pour modèle votre illustre compatriote, et j'ai fait ce que j'ai pu pour imiter de loin

> La main qui crayonna
> L'âme du grand Pompée et celle de Cinna.

Il est vrai que c'est un peu la grenouille qui s'enfle pour être aussi grosse que le bœuf; mais enfin je vous offre ce que j'ai.[52]

Eriphyle is in a similarly pompous style and, like *Brutus,* it was not well received. Voltaire furiously rewrote whole scenes between performances. When he remarked, in making revisions, "Je donne plus au tragique et moins à l'épique," [53] he was probably thinking of style as well as of subject matter, but commentators still found the style brilliant. *Le Nouvelliste du Parnasse* speaks of "des Vers magnifiques & pompeux . . . des Sentences admirables," [54] and the *Mercure de France* says of the play that "la diction en est mâle." [55]

After the cold reception given *Brutus* in 1730 and *Eriphyle* in 1732,

[49] *Mercure de France,* March, 1731, pp. 429–30.
[50] *Œuvres,* XXXIII, 548.   [51] *Ibid.,* p. 495.
[52] *Ibid.*
[53] In a letter to Formont (1732), *Œuvres,* XXXIII, 274.
[54] *Le Nouvelliste du Parnasse, ou Réflexions sur les ouvrages nouveaux,* II, 505.
[55] *Mercure de France,* March, 1732, p. 562.

Voltaire abruptly returned to a simpler style. Referring to *Zaïre*, his next play, he wrote to Cideville that he had loosened the strings of his lyre and that "pour le style, il ne faut pas s'attendre à celui de *la Henriade*. Une loure ne se joue point sur le ton de *la Descente de Mars*." [56] It was necessary, he explains, to "répandre de la mollesse de la facilité dans une pièce qui roule tout entière sur le sentiment. *Qu'il mourût* serait détestable dans *Zaïre; et Zaïre, vous pleurez*, serait impertinent dans *Horace*." [57] At about the same date the Abbé Nadal is quoted in a literary journal as having remarked that in *Zaïre* Voltaire "a passé du faste Epique, qui regne en presque toutes ses piéces, dans un *tissu de lignes prosaïques, sans cadence & mal rimées*." [58] The *Mercure de France* remarked that "on a sçû bon gré à M. de Voltaire d'avoir bien voulu descendre de l'Epique au Dramatique." [59]

Alzire, a few years later, is a mingling of Voltaire's elevated and simple styles. A passage in which Zamore encourages his followers to attack the Spaniards recalls the grandiloquent tirades of *Brutus*.

> Amis, de qui l'audace, aux mortels peu commune,
> Renaît dans les dangers et croît dans l'infortune;
> Illustres compagnons de mon funeste sort,
> N'obtiendrons-nous jamais la vengeance ou la mort?
>
> .   .   .
>
> J'ai porté mon courroux, ma honte, et mes regrets,
> Dans les sables mouvants, dans le fond des forêts.
> De la zone brûlante et du milieu du monde,
> L'astre du jour a vu ma course vagabonde
> Jusqu'aux lieux où, cessant d'éclairer nos climats,
> Il ramène l'année, et revient sur ses pas.[60]

The following words of Alzire, however, have a fluency and directness more typical perhaps of the general tone of the play.

> Cher amant, si mes pleurs, mon trouble, mes remords,
> Peuvent percer ta tombe, et passer chez les morts;
> Si le pouvoir d'un Dieu fait survivre à sa cendre
> Cet esprit d'un héros, ce cœur fidèle et tendre,
> Cette âme qui m'aima jusqu'au dernier soupir,
> Pardonne à cet hymen où j'ai pu consentir! [61]

[56] *Œuvres*, XXXIII, 310.   [57] *Ibid.*
[58] *Observations sur les écrits modernes*, XV, 350.
[59] *Mercure de France*, January, 1733, p. 143.
[60] Act II, scene 1, *Œuvres*, III, 396.   [61] Act III, scene 1, *Œuvres*, III, 407.

Mérope, although it was not performed until 1743, was finished, according to Voltaire, in 1736.[62] It was therefore composed during the period of *Zaïre* and *Alzire.* Its style is comparatively simple, a fact which is appreciated by the *Mercure de France* in its notice of the play. The *Mercure* reviewer comments that "on n'a trouvé dans cette Piéce ni de ces tirades, ni des ces morceaux détachés, qui sont en possession d'être applaudis. Le style ne nous a pas parû pompeux; tout y est simple, tout y est naturel." [63]

Yet there is reason to believe that Voltaire, even while composing *Mérope,* was planning to resume his elevated style. In a dedicatory letter to Maffei, the Italian dramatist, whose *Mérope* had preceded his own, Voltaire notes the use which Maffei had made of a simile taken from Virgil, and he remarks ruefully: "Si je prenais une telle liberté, on me renverrait au poëme épique: tant nous avons affaire à un maître dur, qui est le public." [64]

In 1739, before the publication of *Mérope,* Voltaire wrote a letter to a fellow dramatist, La Noue, praising the latter's tragedy *Mahomet II* and defending an elevated style for tragedy.[65] If the dramatist is portraying a French courtier, the simple and elegant style of Racine is appropriate, but if he is portraying a barbarian, he should make him talk with the vigor and force which primitive men of action employ. It is in vain that French critics protest that a strong, vigorous style is epic, for did not Sophocles and Euripides imitate the style of Homer in their tragedies? The letter contains Voltaire's clearest exposition of what he meant by "epic style," and the grounds upon which he justified its use in tragedy.

Il ne faut sans doute rien de trop hardi dans les vers d'une tragédie; mais aussi les Français n'ont-ils pas souvent été un peu trop timides? . . . J'aime un langage hardi, métaphorique, plein d'images, dans la bouche de Mahomet II. Ces idées superbes sont faites pour son caractère: c'est ainsi qu'il s'exprimait lui-même. . . . On a beau dire que ces beautés de diction sont des beautés épiques; ceux qui parlent ainsi ne savent pas que Sophocle et Euripide ont imité le style d'Homère. Ces morceaux épiques, entremêlés avec art parmi des beautés plus simples, sont comme des éclairs qu'on voit quelquefois enflammer l'horizon, et se mêler à la lumière douce et égale

---

[62] See Voltaire's prefatory letter to Maffei, *Œuvres,* IV, 189.

[63] *Mercure de France,* March, 1744, p. 561.

[64] *Œuvres,* IV, 188.   [65] *Ibid.* XXXV, 236.

d'une belle soirée. Toutes les autres nations aiment, ce me semble, ces figures frappantes. Grecs, Latins, Arabes, Italiens, Anglais, Espagnols, tous nous reprochent une poésie un peu trop prosaïque. Je ne demande pas qu'on outre la nature, je veux qu'on la fortifie, et qu'on l'embellisse. Qui aime mieux que moi les pièces de l'illustre Racine? Qui les sait plus par cœur? Mais serais-je fâché que Bajazet, par exemple, eût quelquefois un peu plus de sublime? [66]

That the letter to La Noue revealed Voltaire's thinking is substantiated by the elevated tone of *Mahomet,* in 1742, and of *Sémiramis,* in 1748. They represent the loftiest heights to which Voltaire's efforts carried him. The tone of *Mahomet* is softened in the scenes which concern the fate of Zopire's two children, where Voltaire used a more simple style suitable to their characters, but the bombastic tone of *Sémiramis* is unrelieved.

The most pompous passages of *Mahomet* are those in which a character, conscious of his own superiority, vaunts his worth like an epic hero. Mahomet says to the shiek of Mecca:

> Chargé du soin du monde, environné d'alarmes,
> Je porte l'encensoir, et le sceptre, et les armes.[67]

Zopire, the sheik, challenges Mahomet:

> La discorde civile est partout sur ta trace.
> Assemblage inouï de mensonge et d'audace,
> Tyran de ton pays, est-ce ainsi qu'en ce lieu
> Tu viens donner la paix, et m'annoncer un dieu? [68]

Mahomet replies:

> Si j'avais à répondre à d'autres qu'à Zopire,
> Je ne ferais parler que le dieu qui m'inspire;
> La glaive et l'Alcoran, dans mes sanglantes mains,
> Imposeraient silence au reste des humains;
> Ma voix ferait sur eux les effets du tonnerre,
> Et je verrais leurs fronts attachés à la terre.[69]

The *Correspondance littéraire* held up *Mahomet* as an example of the elevated style fatal to French drama and commented on the "fausseté de l'instrument." [70]

---

[66] *Ibid.,* pp. 237–38.　　　　[67] *Ibid.,* IV, 122, Act II, scene 4.
[68] *Ibid.,* IV, 124, Act II, scene 5.　　　　[69] *Ibid.*
[70] *Correspondance littéraire, philosophique et critique,* VIII, 460.

In the "Dissertation sur la tragédie ancienne et moderne" prefixed to *Sémiramis* Voltaire urges the actors of the Comédie-Française to declaim their verses with the pomp proper to high tragedy.

La plupart de ces pièces ressemblent si fort à des comédies, que les acteurs étaient parvenus, depuis quelque temps, à les réciter du ton dont ils jouent les pièces qu'on appelle du haut comique; ils ont par là contribué à dégrader encore la tragédie: la pompe et la magnificence de la déclamation ont été mises en oubli. On s'est piqué de réciter des vers comme de la prose; on n'a pas considéré qu'un langage au-dessus du langage ordinaire doit être débité d'un ton au-dessus du ton familier.[71]

Sémiramis represents the culmination of Voltaire's efforts to attain the grandiose. The usurper, Assur, makes his way through scene after scene, threatening the queen and her favorite general, vaunting his ambitions in pompous soliloquy. The queen maintains the heroic tone in her replies and in her meditations upon the fate of Babylon. Arzace defies Assur in terms as toplofty as the usurper's.

When he is unable to win from the queen assurance that she will collaborate in his scheme to gain the throne, Assur rants:

> Chagrins toujours cuisants! honte toujours nouvelle!
> Quoi! ma gloire, mon rang, mon destin dépend d'elle!
> Quoi! J'aurais fait mourir et Ninus et son fils,
> Pour ramper le premier devant Sémiramis!
> Pour languir, dans l'éclat d'une illustre disgrâce,
> Près du trône du monde, à la seconde place! [72]

Arzace is without false modesty in talking to his companion in arms.

> Je ne sais en ces lieux quels seront mes destins.
> Aux plaines d'Arbazan quelques succès peut-être,
> Quelques travaux heureux m'ont assez fait connaître;
> Et quand Sémiramis, aux rives de l'Oxus,
> Vint imposer des lois à cent peuples vaincus,
> Elles laissa tomber de son char de victoire
> Sur mon front jeune encore un rayon de sa gloire.[73]

Even Azéma, the princess, talks in epic terms.

> Où donc est Ninias? quel secret? quel mystère
> Le dérobe à ma vue, et le cache à sa mère?

---

[71] *Œuvres*, IV, 498.   [72] Act II, scene 4; *Œuvres*, IV, 526.
[73] Act I, scene 1; *Œuvres*, IV, 510.

Qu'il revienne en un mot; lui, ni Sémiramis,
Ni des mânes sacrés que l'enfer a vomis,
Ni le renversement de toute la nature,
Ne pourront de mon âme arracher un parjure.[74]

The play was produced with lavish settings provided by Louis XV because of the interest the dauphine had taken in the play before her
death, and it met with a certain amount of favor from the public. But
critics were generally unfavorable. Collé, in the *Journal historique,* commented: "Quant à moi, j'ai trouvé la pièce mauvaise; mais *c'est du mauvais de Voltaire."* [75] Raynal, in the *Nouvelles littéraires,* remarked: "Pas
la moindre vraisemblence." [76] Even Frederick II seems to have inserted
praise in his comments only to take the edge from his disapproval. He
said in one letter that he found *Sémiramis* "remplie de grandes beautés
de détail et de superbes tirades," [77] but he confesses later that he would
prefer "moins d'élévation et plus de naturel." Frederick explains:

Le sublime outré donne dans l'extravagance; Charles XII a été le seul
homme de tout ce siècle qui eût ce caractère théâtral; mais, pour le bonheur
du genre humain, les Charles XII sont rares. Il y a une *Mariamne* de Tristan
qui commence par ce vers; "Fantôme injurieux qui trouble mon repos . . ."
Ce n'est pas certainement comme nous parlons; apparemment que c'est
le langage des habitants de la lune. Ce que je dis des vers doit s'entendre
également de l'action. Pour qu'une tragédie me plaise, il faut que les personnages ne montrent les passions que telles qu'elles sont dans les hommes
vifs et dans les hommes vindicatifs. Il ne faut dépeindre les hommes ni
comme de démons ni comme des anges, car ils ne sont ni l'un ni l'autre,
mais puiser leurs traits dans la nature.[78]

The resemblance between the epic manner of Dryden's heroic plays
and the dramatic style of Voltaire has not gone unnoticed. Villemain
thought that Voltaire, in his efforts to raise the style of his tragedies had
Dryden in mind:

Nous croyons cependant que Voltaire, dans son théâtre, a beaucoup profité
de ce brillant poëte. Il y a des ressemblances assez marquées entre la pompe
de son *Alzire* et de sa *Sémiramis,* et ces belles tirades rimées de Dryden,
surchargées d'images élégantes mais un peu communes. Cette fausse magnificence, cette hardiesse, qui n'est que dans le langage, fut pour le poëte
français un modèle qui le trompe peut-être sur l'emploi que son art pouvait

---

[74] Act IV, scene 1; *Œuvres,* IV, 547.   [75] Collé, *Journal et mémoires,* I, 2.
[76] "Nouvelles littérairee," in *Correspondance littéraire, philosophique et critique,* I, 206.
[77] 1747, *Œuvres,* XXXVI, 492–93.   [78] 1749, *Œuvres,* XXXVII, 86–87.

faire des richesses, alors nouvelles, de la scène anglaise. Dans *Zaïre,* dans *la Mort de César,* il cache parfois, en croyant le corriger, le génie de Shakespeare sous les ornements de Dryden.[79]

Likewise Demogeot, in his *Histoire des littératures étrangères,* declares that Voltaire used Dryden as a model. Speaking of Dryden, Demogeot writes:

Il ne sait ni inventer des personnages, ni les ressusciter d'après l'histoire. Il n'a rien de ce don créateur qui fait le génie de Shakespeare. Il ressemble plutôt à Voltaire, qui l'a pris plus d'une fois pour modèle: comme chez notre brillant compatriote, on rencontre dans les tragédies de Dryden la tirade à effet, la sentence ambitieuse, l'image éclatante mais antidramatique. Quel que soit le personnage qu'il mette en scène, Aureng-Zeb, Antoine ou Montézuma, c'est toujours le même luxe de langage, le même éclat de fausses couleurs.[80]

A similar opinion is held by Edouard Sonet in his study of the influence of English literature upon Voltaire. After mentioning the opinion of Villemain, Sonet observes:

Voltaire emprunta à Dryden une certaine élégance, un certain luxe de langage, certains détails brillants, mais tout ce que le théâtre anglais lui fournit d'idées nouvelles, il la doit à Shakespeare. Cela ne l'empêcha pas de placer Dryden au-dessus de tous les écrivains qui l'avaient précédé.[81]

Sonet is particularly impressed by Voltaire's eulogy of Dryden's style in the *Siècle de Louis XIV,* where Voltaire says:

Dans le grand nombre des poëtes agréables qui décorèrent le règne de Charles II, comme les Waller, les comtes de Dorset et de Rochester, le duc de Buckingham, etc., on distingue le célèbre Dryden, qui s'est signalé dans tous les genres de poésie: ses ouvrages sont pleins de détails naturels à la fois et brillants, animés, vigoureux, hardis, passionés, mérite qu'aucun poëte de sa nation n'égale, et qu'aucun ancien n'a surpassé. Si Pope, qui est venu après lui, n'avait pas, sur la fin de sa vie, fait son *Essai sur l'homme,* il ne serait pas comparable à Dryden.[82]

The *Siècle de Louis XIV* was published in 1751, which means that the above passage was written probably during the period of *Mahomet* and *Sémiramis.* A decade later, when Voltaire, under the pressure of the

[79] Villemain, *Cours de littérature française, tableau de la littérature au XVIIIe siècle,* I, 96.

[80] Demogeot, *Histoire des littératures étrangères considérées dans leurs rapports avec le développement de la littérature française,* p. 119.

[81] Sonet, *Voltaire et l'influence anglaise,* p. 42.   [82] *Œuvres,* XIV, 560.

disapproval of exalted diction which was growing steadily greater, shifted his position as to the desirability of an epic style, he accused Dryden of straining his poetic figures.[83]

But Voltaire actually seemed less critical of Dryden in after years than of Corneille. In 1771, in the article "Enthousiasme" in the *Dictionnaire philosophique,* he turned with high praise to Dryden's last and perhaps most famous poem, *Alexander's Feast,* and acquitted Dryden of the charge of inflated rhetoric.

De toutes les odes modernes, celle où il règne le plus grand enthousiasme qui ne s'affaiblit jamais, et qui ne tombe ni dans le faux ni dans l'ampoulé, est le *Timothée,* ou la fête d'Alexandre, par Dryden: elle est encore regardée en Angleterre comme un chef-d'œuvre inimitable, dont Pope n'a pu approcher quand il a voulu s'exercer dans le même genre. Cette ode fut chantée; et si on avait eu un musicien digne du poëte, ce serait le chef-d'œuvre de la poésie lyrique.

Ce qui est toujours fort à craindre dans l'enthousiasme, c'est de se livrer à l'ampoulé, au gigantesque, au galimatias.[84]

And a year later, in writing to Chabanon, who published a *Discours sur Pindare* in 1769, Voltaire spoke in a tone of authority in placing Dryden above Cowley.

Vous appelez Cowley le Pindare anglais; vous lui faites bien de l'honneur: c'était un poëte sans harmonie, qui cherchait à mettre de l'esprit partout. Le vrai Pindare est Dryden, auteur de cette belle ode intitulée *la Fete d'Alexandre, ou Alexandre et Timothée.* Cette ode, mise en musique par Purcelle (si je ne me trompe), passe en Angleterre pour le chef-d'œuvre de la poésie la plus sublime et la plus variée; et je vous avoue que, comme je sais mieux l'anglais que le grec, j'aime cent fois mieux cette ode que tout Pindare.[85]

There are few indications that Voltaire borrowed lines or figures from Dryden, but his Alexandrines often leap up into extravagant thoughts and forced images in a manner which recalls Dryden's heroic couplets in iambic pentameter. The resemblance is most apparent in passages in which the heroes of Voltaire and Dryden indulge in haughty self-appraisal and attach universal significance to their actions and thoughts. Almanzor, Dryden's grandiloquent chevalier, when he vaunts the integrity of his given word in *The Conquest of Granada,* recalls, for example, Azéma in *Sémiramis.* Almanzor cries:

[83] *Œuvres,* XXXI, 186.   [84] *Œuvres,* XVIII, 555–56.   [85] *Ibid.,* XLVIII, 42.

He break my promise and absolve my vow!
'Tis more than *Mahomet* himself can do.
The word which I have giv'n shall stand like Fate;
Not like the King's, that weathercock of State.[86]

Azéma, in lines already quoted, has a similarly sonorous tone.

Qu'il revienne en un mot; lui, ni Sémiramis,
Ni des mânes sacrés que l'enfer a vomis,
Ni le renversement de toute la nature,
Ne pourront de mon âme arracher un parjure.[87]

Dryden's heroes, like Voltaire's, defy man and nature and give global importance to themselves. Abenamar, in Dryden's *The Conquest of Granada*, says of Almanzor:

No haughty boasting; but a manly pride:
A Soul too fiery, and too great to guide:
He moves excentrique, like a wandring star;
Whose Motion's just; though 'tis not regular.[88]

When Zulema, chief of the Zegrys, denies the hand of the queen of Granada to Almanzor and says "she shall not goe," Almanzor answers:

Thou, single, art not worth my answering,
But take what friends, what armyes thou canst bring;
What worlds; and when you are united all,
Then, I will thunder in yours ears,—she shall.[89]

Voltaire never rises quite so high into the false sublime, but there is a similarly exaggerated color to the language of some of his characters. Zamore, in *Alzire*, says that the audacity of his band is "aux mortels peu commune." [90] Sémiramis gives world-wide significance to herself, asserting that her diadem is an object of respect "au monde entier, respectable au ciel même." [91] Assur offers the throne to Azema with the assurance that "L'univers nous appelle, et va nous occuper." [92]

No subsequent play reaches the rhetorical elevation of *Sémiramis*. In 1749, when he was working on *Rome sauvée* and *Oreste*, Voltaire was apparently in an undecided frame of mind. In the preface to *Rome sauvée*

[86] Dryden, *The Conquest of Granada*, The First Part, Act III; Nonesuch ed., III, 45.
[87] Act IV, scene 1; *Œuvres*, IV, 547.   [88] Act V; Nonesuch ed., III, 78.
[89] Act III; Nonesuch ed., III, 57.   [90] Act II, scene 1; *Œuvres*, III, 396.
[91] Act I, scene 5; *Œuvres*, IV, 517.   [92] Act II, scene 3; *Œuvres*, IV, 524.

he said that the play was "beaucoup plus fortement écrite" than *Zaïre*,[93] and while working on *Oreste* he wrote to Frederick that he was meditating on the necessity of giving more force and energy to the language. Yet the variants of *Oreste* reveal that he removed the more declamatory passages,[94] and in a dissertation on tragedy linked by modern editors with the play, Voltaire declares that he who would secure a reputation as a dramatist must accept Racine as a model for style.

The passage in Voltaire's letter to Frederick on the necessity of giving more force to the language reads as follows:

Je roule aussi de petits projets dans ma tête, pour donner plus de force et d'énergie à notre langue, et je pense que si Votre Majesté voulait m'aider, nous pourrions faire l'aumône à cette langue française, à cette gueuse pincée et dédaigneuse qui se complaît dans son indigence. Votre Majesté saura qu'à la dernière séance de notre Académie . . . je proposai cette petite question: "Peut-on dire *un homme soudain dans ses transports, dans ses résolutions, dans sa colère,* comme on dit *un événement soudain?*—Non, répondit-on; car *soudain* n'appartient qu'aux choses inanimées.—Eh, messieurs! l'éloquence ne consiste-t-elle pas à transporter les mots d'une espèce dans une autre? N'est-ce pas à elle d'animer tout? Messieurs, il n'y a rien d'inanimé pour les hommes éloquents." [95]

But in the *Dissertation sur les principales tragédies anciennes et modernes,* published in 1750, Voltaire favors a simple manner and has the following to say of the superiority of Racine's dramatic style:

On peut réussir peut-être mieux que lui dans les catastrophes; on peut produire plus de terreur, approfondir davantage les sentiments, mettre de plus grands mouvements dans les intrigues; mais quiconque ne se formera pas comme lui sur les anciens, quiconque surtout n'imitera pas la pureté de leur style et du sien, n'aura jamais de réputation dans la postérité.[96]

It is clear that Voltaire's use of alternating rhyme in *Tancrède* (1760), giving a more rapid and more conversational effect than was possible in Alexandrines, was impelled by Diderot's charge that verse stood between the spectator and the dramatic action. Voltaire was in continuous correspondence with Diderot during the composition of the play, and Diderot had no complaint except with regard to the fifth act, concerning

---

[93] *Œuvres,* V, 209.
[94] See *ibid.,* pp. 158–61, the opening scenes of Act III.
[95] 1749, *Œuvres,* XXXVII, 56.   [96] *Ibid.,* V, 195.

which he observed: "Le cinquième me paraît traîner. Il y a deux réci-
tatifs. Il faut, je crois, en sacrifier un et marcher plus vite. Ils vous diront
tous comme moi: Supprimez, supprimez, et l'acte sera parfait."[97] If
Voltaire could only see Clairon in the Paris production, he would agree
that the stage profited by less poetry and more pantomime.[98] Yet Voltaire never returned to alternating rhyme, and in his dedicatory letter
to Madame de Pompadour he was apprehensive lest the style of *Tancrède*
was too close to prose. He feared that "il pourrait arriver qu'en voulant
perfectionner la scène française, on l'a gâterait entièrement."[99]

It was during the years 1760–64, when Voltaire was working on the
Commentaire sur Corneille, that he seems definitely to have shifted his
allegiance from Corneille to Racine. Throughout his critical writings
prior to 1760 he had uniformly defended Corneille, and had frequently
praised the last act of *Rodogune.* In 1743, for instance, he had written
the following to Vauvenargues, who had stated his preference for the
noble and simple style of Racine.

La belle scène d'Horace et de Curiace, les deux charmantes scènes du *Cid,*
une grande partie de *Cinna,* le rôle de Sévère, presque tout celui de Pauline,
la moitié du dernier acte de *Rodogune,* se soutiendraient à côté d'*Athalie,*
quand même ces morceaux seraient faits aujourd'hui. De quel œil devons-
nous donc les regarder quand nous songeons au temps où Corneille a écrit![100]

Later in his letter Voltaire admits that at times Corneille's style is inflated, but he protests that "Ce sont des tableaux de Léonard de Vinci
qu'on aime encore à voir à côté des Paul Véronèse et des Titien."[101]

Voltaire's praise of Corneille during these years is characterized by an
apologetic tone, and adverse comment gradually becomes more frequent.
In 1761 he wrote to D'Argental that in his *Commentaire* he would treat

[97] 1760, *Œuvres,* XLI, 78.   [98] *Ibid.,* p. 77.
[99] *Œuvres,* V, 498.
[100] *Ibid.,* XXXVI, 203–4. Cf. Vial, "Vauvenargues and Voltaire," *Romanic Review,*
XXXIII (1942), 41–57. Vial shows that Vauvenargues's preference for Racine was probably instrumental in turning Voltaire from his preference for Corneille. Vial quotes
a letter which Voltaire wrote to Blin de Sainmor in which he says: "L'obligation
où je suis de commenter Corneille, ne sert qu'à me faire admirer davantage Racine" as
an indication that it was during the composition of the *Commentaire sur Corneille* that
Voltaire's change in attitude was made. Vial concludes that "l'attitude généralement
sévère de Voltaire pour Corneille, et qui contraste si étrangement avec les indulgences
du *Temple du Goût,* et des diverses préfaces, est probablement due, dans une mesure
difficile à déterminer, à l'autorité que Voltaire accordait au jugement de Vauvenargues"
(p. 57).
[101] *Ibid.,* p. 204.

Corneille "tantôt comme un dieu, tantôt comme un cheval de carrosse." [102] In the *Remarques sur Médée* he says that Corneille often spoiled his lines by strained and artificial metaphor. He cites two verses.

> Et j'ai trouvé l'adresse, en lui faisant la cour,
> De relever mon sort sur les ailes d'Amour. [103]

But Corneille's faults were the faults of the age throughout Europe, says Voltaire, [104] and cites an example from Dryden's *All for Love* to prove it.

Les métaphores outrées, les comparaisons fausses, étaient les seuls ornements qu'on employât; on croyait avoir surpassé Virgile et le Tasse quand on faisait voler un sort sur les ailes de l'Amour. Dryden comparait Antoine à un aigle qui portait sur ses ailes un roitelet, lequel alors s'élevait au-dessus de l'aigle; et ce roitelet, c'était l'empereur Auguste. Les beautés vraies étaient partout ignorées. [105]

In the same year he wrote to the Abbé d'Olivet that Corneille had produced some works "absolument indignes du théâtre." [106] In 1762 Voltaire continued to praise Corneille in a rather negative fashion, writing on one occasion: "Ce qui est important, c'est de faire connaître combien Corneille, malgré tous ses défauts, était sublime et sage dans le temps qu'on ne représentait sur les autres théâtres de l'Europe que des rêves extravagants." [107]

The shift in allegiance seems to have been definitely made by 1763, when Voltaire wrote to the Abbé Voisenon:

C'est Racine, qui est véritablement grand, et d'autant plus grand qu'il ne paraît jamais chercher à l'être; c'est l'auteur d'*Athalie* qui est l'homme parfait. Je vous confie qu'en commentant Corneille je deviens idolâtre de Racine. Je ne peux plus souffrir le boursouflé et une grandeur hors de nature. [108]

Later in 1763 he conceded that La Harpe's preference for Racine was well justified.

Racine, qui fut le premier qui eut du goût, comme Corneille fut le premier qui eut du génie; l'admirable Racine, non assez admiré, pensait comme vous. La pompe du spectacle n'est une beauté que quand elle fait une partie nécessaire du sujet; autrement ce n'est qu'une décoration. Les incidents ne

[102] *Ibid.*, XLI, 426.
[104] *Ibid.*
[106] *Ibid.*, XLI, 353.
[108] *Ibid.*, 406.

[103] *Ibid.*, XXXI, 186.
[105] *Ibid.*
[107] *Ibid.*, XLII, 130.

sont un mérite que quand ils sont naturels, et les déclamations sont toujours puériles, surtout quand elles sont remplies d'enflure.[109]

References in his correspondence after 1763 show that Voltaire did not turn back from his new position. In 1767 he wrote:

Je sais bien que Racine est rarement assez tragique; mais il est si intéressant, si adroit, si pur, si élégant, si harmonieux; il a tant adouci et embelli notre langue, rendue barbare par Corneille, que notre passion pour lui est bien excusable. M. de la Harpe est tout aussi passionné que nous; il s'indigne avec moi qu'on ose comparer le minerai brut de Corneille à l'or pur de Racine.[110]

In 1769, in a letter to the Russian poet Soumarokof, Voltaire considered Racine the best of French tragic poets, the only one to speak to both heart and mind, the only one who was "véritablement sublime sans aucune enflure, et qui a mis dans la diction un charme inconnu jusqu'à lui."[111] In 1773 he wrote to La Harpe, whose comparison of Racine and Corneille had just been published, that he agreed with those who had said that "Corneille tomberait de jour en jour, et que Racine s'élèverait,[112] and that it was due to the fact that "Racine est toujours dans la nature, et que Corneille n'y est presque jamais." In 1775 there is no praise at all for Corneille in Voltaire's remarks in a letter to La Harpe. He says: "Pour Corneille, il récitait ses vers comme il les faisait: tantôt ampoulé, tantôt à faire rire."[113]

In a letter to D'Argental in 1776 Voltaire's appreciation of *Rodogune* reaches a record low but the last scene is still admirable.[114] Shortly after, in a letter also written to D'Argental, even the last scene is abandoned.

Je suis de votre avis sur *Rodogune*. Il n'y a pas de sens commun dans toute cette pièce, qu'on a regardée comme le chef-d'œuvre de Corneille. La dernière scène même, qui semble demander grâce pour le reste, n'est nullement vraisemblable; mais il y a tant d'illusion théâtrale d'un bout à l'autre, que le public a été séduit.[115]

Voltaire now recognized that the trend toward a pompous style had been exaggerated and that his own plays were not without fault in this respect. In 1769 he wrote to D'Argental that as for imitation of the English he had asked for water, not for a tempest, and that at present "nous allons tomber en tout dans l'outré et dans le gigantesque; adieu les beaux

[109] *Ibid.*, XLIII, 56. [110] *Ibid.*, XLV, 172. [111] *Ibid.*, XLVI, 264.
[112] *Ibid.*, XLVIII, 284. [113] *Ibid.*, XLIX, 265.
[114] *Ibid.*, L, 141. [115] *Ibid.*, p. 156.

vers, adieu les sentiments du cœur, adieu tout." [116] Like Dryden in his latter years, Voltaire regrets the swollen rhetoric of his earlier style. "Que dites-vous des fureurs d'Oreste?" he asks D'Argental, "déclamation, et puis, c'est tout." [117] *Tancrède,* he implies, is in a more suitable dramatic style with poetry subordinated to pantomime and spectacle.

Voltaire appears increasingly conscious of the necessity of avoiding too brilliant a style. Just as he removed the more elevated passages from *Oreste,* he removed them from *Le Triumvirat* (1764), and he wrote to D'Argental: "J'ai ôté toutes les dissertations cornéliennes qui anéantissent l'intérêt. Je respecte fort ce Corneille; mais on est sûr d'une lourde chute quand on l'imite." [118] Grimm was satisfied with the style of *Le Triumvirat* and wrote in the *Correspondance littéraire* (1764) that the style "quoique inégal et souvent faible, m'a pourtant paru le véritable style de la tragédie, aussi longtemps qu'on fera en vers alexandrins." [119]

Voltaire's dramatic criticism ends with a eulogy of Racine's style in the prefatory letter to *Irène* in 1777.

C'est lui qui a proscrit chez tous les gens de goût, et malheureusement chez eux seuls, ces idées gigantesques et vides de sens, ces apostrophes continuelles aux dieux, quand on ne sait pas faire parler les hommes; ces lieux communs d'une politique ridiculement atroce, débités dans un style sauvage; ces épithètes fausses et inutiles; ces idées obscures, plus obscurément rendues; ce style aussi dur que négligé, incorrect et barbare; enfin tout ce que j'ai vu applaudi par un parterre composé alors de jeunes gens dont le goût n'était pas encore formé. [120]

Racine's style is a model for prose as well as for poetry; for sermons and orations as well as for tragedy. Fénelon and Bossuet, not having the genius for verse, imitated Racine in prose and "les ouvrages de prose dans lesquels on a le mieux imité le style de Racine sont ce que nous avons de meilleur dans notre langue." [121] Voltaire has this final advice for writers:

Point de vrai succès aujourd'hui sans cette correction, sans cette pureté qui seule met le génie dans tout son jour, et sans laquelle ce génie ne déploierait qu'une force monstrueuse, tombant à chaque pas dans une faiblesse plus monstrueuse encore, et du haut des nues dans la fange. [122]

---

[116] *Ibid.,* XLVI, 473.   [117] *Ibid.,* XL, 389.   [118] *Ibid.,* XLIII, 325.
[119] *Correspondance littéraire philosophique et critique,* VI, 33.
[120] *Œuvres,* VII, 326.   [121] *Ibid.,* p. 329.
[122] *Ibid.*

Voltaire thus strove to raise the style of tragedy to a grandeur and dignity which he and his fellow critics recognized specifically as epic. He had not only Corneille and Greek tragedy in mind but English example as well, and among English writers Dryden especially. But the current of the century was moving in the opposite direction toward tragedy in prose. Voltaire followed the precepts of Rapin and Dacier until well after the middle of the century, declaring again and again that Racine had lowered tragedy to the level of comedy by an exaggerated purity of style—while his opponents came to believe that even the style of Racine was too elevated and that French tragedy could be saved only by abandoning verse. There was, however, no worthy rival of Voltaire to champion prose tragedy, and he dominated the theater until his death. But he was well aware of the trend of the times and sought to compromise. His stylistic range is consequently a series of shifts back and forth between a grandiose manner and a more simple and easy style. In *Tancrède,* under the spur of Diderot, he abandoned Alexandrines, but this was his only departure from heroic verse. His best plays, *Zaïre, Mérope,* and *Tancrède,* are in a comparatively simple style, and he gradually came to accept Racine as the model not only for poetry but for prose also. There are, however, traces of rhetorical pomp even in his late tragedies, a fact which indicates that he could never be completely won away from his love of the grand manner.

CHAPTER IX   CONCLUSION

THE EPIC POEM was in the air of the neoclassic community which France
and England formed from 1650 to 1750. Tragedy was closely identified
with the epic poem and Hobbes's assertion in 1650, in his prefatory letter
to Davenant's *Gondibert,* that epic and tragedy were the narrative and
dramatic forms of heroic poetry, was a statement based logically on the
critical doctrines of the age. Epic didacticism and the identity of epic
poem and tragedy were fundamental principles in the treatises of Rapin,
Le Bossu, and Dacier, principles which formed the basis of their charge
that French tragedy lacked dignity and elevation. Dryden, in his critical
essays and by his heroic plays, became the outstanding exponent of the
ideal of heroic tragedy. Formal Augustan tragedy maintained the heroic
tradition in England by its elevation of diction and by its embodiment
of the epical conception of poetry as a moral lesson. In France epic
tragedy continued to be largely a critical ideal until Voltaire, whose
approach to the drama, like that of Dryden, was first of all critical, sought
to carry out the recommendations of the neoclassic critics.

The conception of the poet as a moral philosopher was an integral
part of Renaissance epic theory, and Le Bossu had long precedent for
declaring that the epic poem, and consequently tragedy, were fundamentally moral fables in the manner of Aesop and that the poet, before
planning his poem, should pick a maxim useful to the state. Dr. Johnson, in *The Lives of the Poets,* said that in his opinion Milton was the
only poet who had composed an epic poem according to Le Bossu's
precept, but in one sense it would seem that Dr. Johnson was in error,
for Milton, in abandoning his idea of composing an *Arthuriad* because
he became convinced that the Arthur legends were romantic fictions, and
in turning instead to a subject which he valued for its truth, would
seem to have stepped out of the neoclassic frame.

It was on the basis of the epic doctrine of poetry as a moral lesson and
of the poet as the preceptor of the king and gentry that English tragedians
during the period of 1660–1725 and Voltaire, in his turn, seem to have
justified the introduction of religious and political arguments into the
theater. Voltaire's Roman tragedies, like Addison's *Cato,* glorified stoical
patriotism, and in his tragedies based on the heroic romances Voltaire,
as had Dryden in *The Indian Emperour,* stressed the deistic principle

that all men who worship God have a basis for agreement. The late seventeenth and early eighteenth centuries were still in the shadow of the religious wars, and it is not surprising that superstition and fanaticism were considered to be the most dangerous perils to the state. Like Hobbes and Dryden, Voltaire used the League and the assassination of Henry IV as symbols of the evil results of religious bigotry. Dryden's first plan for a tragedy had been based on a plot about the League, but he did not bring out *The Duke of Guise* until 1682, when it was useful as a parallel to the attempt to exclude the Duke of York from the succession. To justify the parallel Dryden added a *Defense of the Duke of Guise* and translated Maimbourg's history of the League. The League was the subject of the *Henriade,* and Voltaire had the assassination of Henry IV in mind when he wrote *Mahomet* and in attacking fanaticism in other plays. Voltaire's tragedies come nearer than Dryden's to fulfilling Le Bossu's precept that a play should be a moral fable, for the lesson is carried by the plots themselves. The only sense in which Dryden's plays approach allegory is in the extreme heightening of the characters, which he carried at times to such lengths that they nearly became abstractions. Voltaire stated frequently that what he valued most in English literature was its capacity for expressing philosophical thought, and there are many indications that he valued Dryden especially for his ability to ratiocinate in heroic verse. He was interested chiefly in Dryden's skeptical reasoning, and he borrowed lines from *The Medal* for *Zaïre,* without caring that Dryden was expressing a deistic sentiment with the specific purpose of quarreling with it. It is evident that Voltaire thought of Dryden, as he did of English literature in general, in terms of drama, and it is in Dryden's plays that his skepticism is most pronounced. Voltaire showed an especially intimate knowledge of *The Indian Emperour,* not only basing his *Alzire* on it but also reverting to it to illustrate an argument in the *Dictionnaire philosophique* and using the torture scene in a passage in the *Essai sur les mœurs.*

In choice of subject matter and in style, as well as in fundamental conception of the aim of tragedy, Voltaire was guided by epic doctrine. He began by taking literally Dacier's advice and going to the Greek theater for elevated subjects. Lessing's observation that *Sémiramis* was written around a maxim applies to Voltaire's Greek tragedies in general, for they prove that there is a "diu vengeur" who punishes secret crimes, a favorite idea of Voltaire's. Voltaire tried several Roman tragedies, embodying in them the conception of the stoic Roman hero offered originally in Lucan's *Pharsalia,* which both Addison and Corneille had consulted. In turning finally to heroic romance subjects there is evidence that Voltaire had Dryden in mind, for his first play of this type, *Zaïre,* is preceded by a preface which Voltaire devotes largely to Dryden, in so far as the English theater is concerned, and the play itself is built around a deistic passage to the effect that religion is a matter of education, which Voltaire had taken from Dryden. Voltaire's most important innovation in tragedy in respect to subject was his introduction of what has been called national history. But Voltaire's tragedies are historical in much the same sense that Dryden's heroic plays are historical, the historical element consisting in the use of chivalric atmosphere and incident from the heroic romances. The introduction of the names of French chevaliers was a daring innovation in Paris, but the evidence points to Dryden's heroic plays as the possible English source rather than to Shakespeare's historical tragedies, as has so often been claimed.

That Voltaire conceived heroic poetry to be fundamentally in the nature of an apologue is evident in the article "Fable" in the *Dictionnaire philosophique* and in the twelfth conversation of the satirical *L'A, B, C.* In the article "Fable" he explains that history is material for artistic use only when it is rewritten, for, he says, it portrays "ce que sont les humains," while the duty of the poet is to teach "ce qu'ils doivent être." In using historical themes for his tragedies Voltaire changed the facts so that his characters should portray to the spectators "ce qu'ils doivent être," a point of view which is basically epic, as neoclassic critics employed the term. In the twelfth conversation of *L'A, B, C* Voltaire returns to the same point of view with regard to heroic romances, this time preferring Fénelon's *Télémaque* to the *Iliad,* because it was more moral. This attitude is important for the understanding of Voltaire's use of heroic romance material in his plays.

In the chapters demonstrating the underlying epical basis of Voltaire's conception of the purpose of tragedy and his closely related conception of the subject matter proper to tragedy it was necessary to depend on evidence that was often inferential. But in discussing Voltaire's efforts to raise the style of tragedy this was unnecessary, for Voltaire and his contemporaries recognized his ambitions explicitly as "epic." "On a beau dire que ces beautés de diction sont des beautés épiques; ceux qui parlent ainsi ne savent pas que Sophocle et Euripide ont imité le style d'Homère," wrote Voltaire on one occasion, and the comments of his contemporaries were no less explicit. Until well after 1750 Voltaire believed that Rapin and Dacier and their followers were justified in charging that the simple purity of Racine's style had robbed the language of its capacity for sublime expression. He had heard the same criticism made again and again in England, and he strove to elevate the style of tragedy in France to an epic grandeur and dignity. He had not only Corneille in mind but English example as well and Dryden especially. The trend of the century was directly against him, however, and his plays give evidence of several determined efforts toward an epic style and as many retreats to a more fluent and easy manner. He was gradually won away from his grandiose ideal, and his final critical position is that the noble simplicity of Racine should be the model not only for poetry but for prose as well. His own verse, however, never completely lost the elevation which had gone out of fashion by the middle of the century.

After Voltaire the neoclassic ideal of epic-tragedy passed into Germany along with neoclassic criticism. Gottsched made the categorical assertion that the author of tragedy should first conceive a general moral principle and then assemble plot and characters to fit. In 1732 he brought out a *Cato* based on the plays of Addison and Deschamps and in the preface he says he picked his hero because he was a pattern of stoical resolution and a thorough patriot. Gottsched mentions Dacier and other neoclassic critics, including Voltaire.

Le Bossu was translated into German in 1753, and shortly thereafter Lessing was translating Dryden's *An Essay of Dramatick Poesie*. The correspondence between Lessing, Mendelssohn, and Nicolai in 1756 and 1757, which constitutes the celebrated *Briefwechsel,* that has been a traditional source of interest to Lessing students developed into an elaborate discussion of the nature of tragedy, Lessing trying to limit tragedy to pity and epic poetry to admiration. His definition of pity is similar to that of Voltaire, being essentially compassion for the unfortunate. Lessing's later and celebrated *Nathan the Wise* is a play on the familiar Voltairian formula. Once more we see an intolerant Christian knight converted by the "grandeur d'âme" of the infidel he is persecuting. The play was among the books burned in 1933 by the Nazis, as were numerous works of Voltaire.

The relation of arts and morals is an ever-recurring problem in the history of literary criticism. Fifty years after Lessing's death Goethe, in a brief commentary on Aristotle's *Poetics,* took issue with the neoclassic point of view and declared that the arts have little power to influence morality and that it is always wrong to demand such results from them. In the twelfth book of the *Dichtung und Wahrheit* he observed further that great art will always have a moral effect, but that the moral effect must not be held to have been the purpose of the artist.

APPENDIX

EXCERPTS FROM *THE INDIAN EMPEROUR*

When Montezuma with his eldest son, Odmar, first encounters Cortez, Vasquez and Pizarro, he demands to know from whence the Spaniards derive their authority, and the following conversation ensues (Act I, scene 2, Nonesuch ed., I, 285–86):

Cort. From *Charles* the Fifth, the Worlds most Potent King.

Mont. Some petty Prince, and one of little fame,
For to this hour I never heard his name:
The two great Empires of the World I know,
That of *Peru,* and this of *Mexico;*
And since the earth none larger does afford,
This *Charles* is some poor Tributary Lord.

Cort. You speak of that small part of earth you know.
But betwixt us and you wide Oceans flow,
And watry desarts of so vast extent,
That passing hither, four Full Moons we spent.

Mont. But say, what news, what offers dost thou bring
From so remote, and so unknown a King?

Vasq. Spain's mighty Monarch, to whom Heaven thinks fit
That all the Nations of the Earth submit,
In gracious clemency, does condescend
On these conditions to become your Friend.
First, that of him you shall your Scepter hold,
Next, you present him with your useless Gold:
Last, that you leave those Idols you implore,
And one true Deity with him adore.

Mont. You speak your Prince a mighty Emperour,
But his demands have spoke him Proud, and Poor;
He proudly at my free-born Scepter flies,
Yet poorly begs a mettal I despise.
Gold thou may'st take, what-ever thou canst find,
Save what for sacred uses is design'd:
But, by what right pretends your King to be
The Soveraign Lord of all the World, and me?

Piz. The Soveraign Priest,—

Who represents on Earth the pow'r of Heaven,
Has this your Empire to our Monarch given.
Mont. Ill does he represent the Powers above,
Who nourishes debate, not Preaches love;
Besides, what greater folly can be shown?
He gives another what is not his own.

Vasq. His pow'r must needs unquestion'd be below,
For he in Heaven an Empire can bestow.

Mont. Empires in Heaven he with more ease may give,
And you perhaps would with less thanks receive;
But Heaven has need of no such Vice-roy here,
It self bestows the Crowns that Monarchs wear.
Piz. You wrong his power as you mistake our end,
Who came thus far Religion to extend.

Mont. He who Religion truely understands,
Knows its extent must be in Men, not Lands.

Odm. But who are those that truth must propagate
Within the confines of my Fathers state?

Vasq. Religious Men, who hither must be sent
As awful Guides of Heavenly Government;
To teach you Penance, Fasts, and Abstinence,
To punish Bodies for the Souls offence.

Mont. Cheaply you sin, and punish crimes with ease,
Not as th' offended, but th' offenders please.
First injure Heaven, and when its wrath is due,
Your selves prescribe it how to punish you.

.   .   .

Mont. Those ghostly Kings would parcel out my pow'r,
And all the fatness of my Land devour;
That Monarch sits not safely on his Throne,
Who bears, within, a power that shocks his own.
They teach obedience to Imperial sway,
But think it sin if they themselves obey.

The Second Scene of Act V (Nonesuch ed., I, 327 ff.) shows a prison
with Montezuma and his Indian High Priest on the torture rack, a scene
which Voltaire used in his *Essai sur les mœurs*. Pizarro and a Christian Priest
direct the drawing of the cords:

Piz. Thou hast not yet discover'd all thy store.

Mont. I neither can nor will discover more:
The gods will Punish you, if they be Just;

The gods will Plague your Sacrilegious Lust.

Chr. Priest. Mark how this impious Heathen justifies
His own false gods, and our true God denies:
How wickedly he has refus'd his wealth,
And hid his Gold, from Christian hands, by stealth:
Down with him, Kill him, merit Heaven thereby.

The Spaniards wind the cords tighter and the Indian High Priest begs
to die. Montezuma shows fortitude and shames him with his courage. Before ordering further torture the Christian Priest tries again to convert the
Emperour:

> *Chr. Pr.* Those Pains, O Prince, thou sufferest now, are light,
> Compar'd to those, which when thy Soul takes flight,
> Immortal, endless, thou must then endure,
> Which Death begins, and Time can never cure.
>
> *Mont.* Thou are deceiv'd: for whensoe're I Dye,
> The Sun my Father bears my Soul on high:
> He lets me down a Beam, and mounted there,
> He draws it back, and pulls me through the Air:
> I in the Eastern Parts, and rising Sky,
> You in Heaven's downfal, and the West must lye.
>
> *Chr. Pr.* Fond Man, by Heathen Ignorance misled,
> Thy Soul destroying when thy Body's Dead:
> Change yet thy Faith, and buy Eternal Rest.
> *Ind. High Pr.* Dye in your own, for our Belief is best.
>
> *Mont.* In seeking happiness you both agree,
> But in the search, the paths so different be,
> That all Religions with each other Fight,
> While only one can lead us in the Right,
> But till that one hath some more certain Mark,
> Poor humane kind must wander in the dark;
> And suffer pains, eternally below,
> For that, which here, we cannot come to know.
>
> *Chr. Pr.* That which we worship, and which you believe,
> From Natures common hand we both receive:
> All under various names, Adore and Love
> One power Immense, which ever rules above.
> Vice to abhor, and Virtue to pursue,
> Is both believ'd and taught by us and you:
> But here our Worship takes another way.
>
> *Mont.* Where both agree 'tis there most safe to stay:

For what's more vain than Publick Light to shun,
And set up Tapers while we see the Sun?

Chr. Pr. Though Nature teaches whom we should Adore,
By Heavenly Beams we still discover more.

Mont. Or this must be enough, or to Mankind
One equal way to Bliss is not design'd.
For though some more may know, and some know less,
Yet all must know enough for happiness.

Chr. Pr. If in this middle way you still pretend
To stay, your Journey never will have end.

Mont. Howe're 'tis better in the midst to stay,
Then wander farther in uncertain way.

Chr. Pr. But we by Martyrdom our Faith avow.

Mont. You do no more than I for ours do now,
To prove Religion true—
If either Wit or Suff'rings would suffice,
All Faiths afford the Constant and the Wise:
And yet ev'n they, by Education sway'd
In Age defend what Infancy obey'd.

Chr. Pr. Since Age by erring Child-hood is misled,
Refer your self to our Un-erring Head.

Mont. Man and not erre? What reason can you give?

Chr. Pr. Renounce that carnal reason, and believe.

Mont. The Light of Nature should I thus betray,
'Twere to wink hard that I might see the day.

Chr. Pr. Condemn not yet the way you do not know;
I'le make your reason judge what way to go.

Mont. 'Tis much too late for me new ways to take,
Who have but one short step of life to make.

Piz. Increase their Pains, the Cords are yet too slack.

Chr. Pr. I must by force, convert him on the Rack.

Ind. High Pr. I faint away, and find I can no more:
Give leave, O King, I may reveal thy store,
And free my self from pains I cannot bear.

Mont. Think'st thou I lye on Beds of Roses, here,
Or in a Wanton Bath stretch'd at my ease?
Dye, Slave, and with thee dye such thoughts as these.

(High Priest turns aside and dyes.)

Cortez rushes into the prison at this moment, stops the torture and orders the release of Montezuma. He exclaims:

Ha—
What dismal sight is this which takes from me
All the delight that waits on Victory! (*Runs to take him off the rack.*)
Make haste: how now, Religion, do you Frown?
Haste holy Avarice, and help him down!
Ah, Father, Father, what do I endure, (*Embracing Montezuma.*)
To see these Wounds my pity cannot cure!

Cortez threatens Pizarro with court martial and then turns to the priest:

And you,
Who sawcily, teach Monarchs to obey,
And the wide World in narrow Cloysters sway;
Set up by Kings as humble aids of Power,
You that which bred you, Viper-like, devour,
You Enemies of Crowns.
Chr. Pr.—Come, let's away
We but provoke his fury by our stay.
Cort. If this go free, farewel that Discipline,
Which did in Spanish Camps severely shine:
Accursed Gold, 'tis thou hast caus'd these crimes;
Thou turn'st our Steel against thy Parent Climes!
And into *Spain* wilt fatally be brought,
Since with the price of Blood thou here art bought.

BIBLIOGRAPHY

Addison, Joseph. The Miscellaneous Works. London, 1914.
—— The Spectator. Cincinnati, 1860.
Aristotle, Poetics, in S. H. Butcher, Aristotle's Theory of Poetry and Fine Art. 4th ed. London, New York, 1911.
Athenian Mercury. 20 vols., London, 1690–97.
Baldensperger, Fernand. "Esquisse d'une Histoire de Shakespeare en France," in Etudes d'histoire littéraire. 2d ser. Paris, 1910, 155–216.
—— "Voltaire anglophile avant son séjour d'Angleterre," *Revue de littérature comparée,* IX (1929), 25–61.
Beaune, Henri. Voltaire au collège. Paris, 1897.
Beljame, Alexandre. Le Public et les hommes de lettres en Angleterre. Paris, 1897.
Bellessort, André. Essai sur Voltaire, Paris, 1925.
Bibliothèque françoise. 18 vols. Paris, 1741–56.
Boileau-Despréaux, Nicolas, Œuvres complètes, 3 vols., Paris, 1819.
Borgerhoff, E. B. O. The Evolution of Liberal Theory and Practice in the French Theatre, 1680–1757. Princeton, 1936.
Boswell, James. The Life of Samuel Johnson, LL.D.; ed. by Percy Fitzgerald. 3 vols. Philadelphia, 1889.
Bradley, Cecil. Shakespearean Tragedy. London, New York, 1904.
Bray, René. La Formation de la doctrine classique en France. Paris, 1927.
—— La Tragédie cornélienne devant la critique classique, Paris, 1927.
Bredvold, Louis I. The Intellectual Milieu of John Dryden. Ann Arbor, 1934.
—— "Dryden, Hobbes and the Royal Society," *Modern Philology,* XXV (May, 1928), 417–38.
Brenner, Clarence D. L'Histoire nationale dans la tragédie française du dix-huitième siècle. University of California Publications in Modern Philology, Vol. XIV, No. 3, 1929.
Breval, John D. An Epistle to the Right Honourable Joseph Addison Esquire. London, 1717.
Brower, Reuben Arthur. "Dryden's Epic Manner and Virgil," PMLA, IV (No. 1, March, 1940), 119–38.
Brumoy, Pierre. Le Théâtre des Grecs, 16 vols. Paris, 1820–25.
Brunetière, Ferdinand. Conférences de l'Odéon; les époques du théâtre français. Paris, 1893.
—— L'Evolution des genres dans l'histoire de la littérature. Paris, 1931.
—— "Le Théâtre de Voltaire, par M. Emile Deschanel," *Revue des deux mondes,* CLXXXIX (Sept. 1, 1886), 213–25.
Burlingame, Anne Elizabeth. The Battle of the Books in Its Historical Setting. New York, 1920.

Butcher, S. H. Aristotle's Theory of Poetry and Fine Art. London, 4th ed., 1911.

Bysshe, Edward. The Art of English Poetry. 3 vols. London, 1718.

Charlanne, Louis. L'Influence française en Angleterre au dix-septième siècle Paris, 1906.

Charlton, H. B. Castelvetro's Theory of Poetry. Manchester, 1913.

Chase, Lewis N. The English Heroic Play. New York, 1903.

Cherel, Albert. Fénelon au dix-huitième siècle en France, 1715–1820. Paris, 1917.

Clark, A. F. B. Boileau and the French Classical Critics in England, 1660–1830. Paris, 1925.

Clark, Barrett Harper. European Theories of the Drama. New York, 1930.

Clark, Cumberland. Shakespeare and the Supernatural. London, 1931.

Clark, William Smith. "Definition of the Heroic Play in the Restoration Period," *Review of English Studies*, VIII (1932), 437–44.

—— The Dramatic Works of Roger Boyle. Cambridge, Mass., 1937.

—— "The Sources of the Restoration Heroic Play," *Review of English Studies*, IV (Jan., 1928), 49–63.

Collé, Charles. Journal et mémoires. 3 vols. Paris, 1868.

Collier, Jeremy. A Short View of the Immorality and Profaneness of the English Stage. London, 1698.

Collins, John Churton. Bolingbroke, a Historical Study; and Voltaire in England. London, 1886.

Corneille, Pierre. Œuvres. 12 vols., Paris, 1862–68.

Correspondance littéraire, philosophique et critique, par Grimm, Diderot, Raynal, Meister, etc. 16 vols., Paris, 1877–82.

Courtin, Nicolas. Charlemagne pénitent. Paris, 1687.

Crane, T. F. Critical edition of Boileau's Les Héros de roman. Boston, 1902.

Croce, Benedetto. Ariosto, Shakespeare and Corneille, translated by Douglas Ainslie. New York, 1920.

Dacier, André. La Poëtique d'Aristote, traduite avec des remarques, Paris, 1692.

Dacier, Anne Lefèvre. L'Iliade d'Homère; traduite en françois avec des remarques. 3 vols. Paris, 1711.

Daniels, Walter Melville. Saint-Evremond en Angleterre. Versailles, 1907.

Deane, Cecil V. Dramatic Theory and the Rhymed Heroic Play, London, 1931.

Demogeot, Jacques. Histoire de la littérature française. Paris, 1884.

—— Histoire des littératures étrangères considérées dans leurs rapports avec le développement de la littérature française. Paris, 1880.

Dennis, John. The Critical Works, ed. by Edward Niles Hooker. 2 vols. Baltimore, 1939–43.

—— Remarks upon Cato, London, 1713.

—— Remarks on Pope's Homer. London, 1717.

Deschamps, François-Michel-Chrétien. Cato, a tragedy as it is acted in the Theatre in Lincolns-Inn-Fields, Written in French by Monsieur Des Champs, Done into English by Mr. Ozell. To which is added a Parallel between this play and that written by Mr. Addison. London, 1716.

Desnoiresterres, A. Gustave. Voltaire et la société française au XVIIIe siècle. 8 vols. Paris, 1871–76.

Diderot, Denis. Œuvres Complètes. 20 vols. Paris, 1875–77.

Dobrée, Bonamy. Restoration Tragedy, 1660–1720. Oxford, 1929.

Dowlin, Cornell March. Sir William Davenant's Gondibert, Its Preface and Hobbes's Answer; a Study in English Neo-Classicism. Philadelphia, 1934.

Dryden, John. The Works of John Dryden; illustrated with notes, historical, critical and explanatory, and a life of the author by Walter Scott. 18 vols. London, 1808.

—— The Works of John Dryden; illustrated with notes, historical, critical, and explanatory, and a life of the author by Sir Walter Scott, bart.; revised and corrected by George Saintsbury. 18 vols. 1882–93.

—— The Dramatic Works of Dryden; ed. by Montague Summers. Nonesuch Press, 6 vols. London, 1931–32.

Du Bos, Jean Baptiste. Critical Reflections on Poetry, Painting and Music; tr. by Thomas Nugent. 3 vols. London, 1748.

Duchesne, Julien. Histoire des poëmes épiques français du XVIIe siècle, Paris, 1870.

Egger, Emile. Essai sur l'histoire de la critique chez les Grecs. Paris, 1886.

Faguet, Emile. "Jugements particuliers de Voltaire," *Revue des cours et conférences*, IX, 1st ser. (November 29, 1900), 7–106.

—— "Voltaire—ses idées sur les genres épique et dramatique," *Revue des cours et conférences*, VIII, 2d ser. (May 31, 1900), 481–91.

—— "Comment Voltaire a conçu l'épopée," *Revue des cours et conférences*, IX, 1st ser. (January 24, 1901), 481–89.

Fénelon, François de Salignac de la Mothe. Les Aventures de Télémaque. London, 1798.

—— Œuvres. 3 vols. Paris, 1835.

Fidao-Justiniani, J. E. L'Esprit classique et la préciosité au dix-septième siècle, Paris, 1914.

—— Qu'est-ce qu'un classique? Paris, 1930.

Foulet, Lucien. Correspondance de Voltaire (1726–1729). Paris, 1913.

Gildon, Charles. Complete Art of Poetry, in Durham, Willard H. Critical Essays of the Eighteenth Century. New Haven, 1915.

Green, F. C. Minuet. London, 1935.

Gros, Etienne. Philippe Quinault. Paris, 1926.

Harbage, Alfred. Cavalier Drama. New York, 1936.

Hartsock, Mildred E. Dryden's Plays; a Study in Ideas, in Seventeenth Century Studies, 2d ser., Princeton, N.J., 1937.

Harvey-Jellie, W. Les Sources du théâtre anglais à l'époque de la Restauration. Paris, 1906.

—— Le Théâtre classique en Angleterre. Montreal, 1932.

Hassall, Arthur. Life of Viscount Bolingbroke. London, 1889.

Hathaway, Baxter. "John Dryden and the Function of Tragedy," PMLA, LVIII, No. 3 (September, 1943), 665–73.

Havens, George R. "The Abbé Le Blanc and English Literature," Modern Philology, XVIII, No. 8 (December, 1920), 79–97.

—— "The Abbé Prévost and Shakespeare," Modern Philology, XVII, No. 4 (August, 1919), 1–22.

—— The Abbé Prévost and English Literature. Princeton, 1921. Elliott Monographs 9.

Hill, Herbert W. La Calprenède's Romances and the Restoration Drama. Reno, Nevada, 1910–11.

Homer: an Introduction to the Iliad and Odyssey. Boston, 1887.

Huet, Pierre-Daniel. De l'origine des romans, in Jean Renaud de Segrais, Zayde, histoire espagnole, 2 vols., Paris, 1674.

Hughes, Merritt Y. "Dryden as a Statist," Philological Quarterly, VI, No. 4 (October, 1927), 335–50.

Johnson, Samuel. The Works of Samuel Johnson. 16 vols. Troy, N.Y., 1903.

Journal littéraire. 23 vols. The Hague, 1713–36.

Jusserand, J. J. Shakespeare en France sous l'ancien régime. Paris, 1898.

Kames, Henry Home. Elements of Criticism. London, New York, 1859.

Ker, W. P. Epic and Romance. London, 1931.

—— The Essays of John Dryden. Oxford, 1899.

—— Form and Style in Poetry. London, 1928.

Krutch, Joseph Wood. Comedy and Conscience after the Restoration. New York, 1924.

—— The Modern Temper. New York, 1929.

Lacroix, Albert. Histoire de l'influence de Shakespeare sur le théâtre français jusqu'à nos jours. Brussels, 1856.

Lancaster, Henry Carrington. A History of French Dramatic Literature in the Seventeenth Century. 9 vols. Baltimore, 1929–42.

Langbaine, Gerard. An Account of the English dramatick poets. Oxford, 1691.

Lanson, Gustave. Esquisse d'une histoire de la tragédie française. Columbia University Press, 1920.

—— "Voltaire," in Les Grands écrivains français, Paris, 1906.

—— Histoire de la littérature française. Paris, 1898.

Larroumet, Gustave. Etudes d'histoire et de critique dramatique. Paris, 1892.

—— "Shakespeare en France à l'époque de Voltaire," Revue des cours et conférences, VIII (May 17, 1900), 463–71.

Le Blanc, Jean Bernard. Letters on the English and French Nations, 2 vols., London, 1747.

Le Bossu, René. Traité du poëme épique, Paris, 1675.

Legouis, Pierre. "Corneille and Dryden as Dramatic Critics," in Seventeenth Century Studies, Oxford, 1938.

Lessing, Gotthold Ephraïm. Hamburgische Dramaturgie, in Sämmtliche Schriften, 13 vols., Berlin, 1838–40.

Lion, Henri. Les Tragédies et les théories dramatiques de Voltaire. Paris, 1895.

Lounsbury, Thomas R. Shakespeare and Voltaire. New York, 1902.

Lovering, Stella. L'Activité intellectuelle de l'Angleterre d'après l'ancien "Mercure de France," Paris, 1930.

Lowenstein, Robert. Voltaire as an Historian of Seventeenth Century French Drama. Baltimore, 1935. Johns Hopkins Studies in Romance Languages and Literatures, XXV.

McKnight, Thomas. The Life of Henry St. John, Viscount Bolingbroke. London, 1863.

McManaway, James G. "Philip Massinger and the Restoration Drama," E L H; a Journal of English Literary History, I (Dec., 1934), 276–304.

Maillet, Albert. "Dryden et Voltaire," Revue de littérature Comparée, XVIII (1938), 272–86.

Marni, Archimede. Allegory in the French Heroic Poem of the Seventeenth Century. Princeton University Press for the University of Cincinnati. 1936.

Mélèse, Pierre. Le Théâtre et le public sous Louis XIV, 1659–1713. Paris, 1934.

Miller, John R. Boileau en France au dix-huitième siècle. Baltimore, 1942.

Monod-Cassidy, Hélène. Un Voyageur-philosophe au XVIIIe siècle. Cambridge, Mass., 1941. Harvard Studies in Comparative Literature, Vol. XVII.

Morand, Pierre de. Théâtre et œuvers diverses. 3 vols. Paris, 1751.

Muralt, Béat Louis de. Lettres sur les Anglois et les François et sur les voiages, 1728; ed. by Charles Gould. Paris, 1933.

Murray, Gilbert. The Rise of the Greek Epic. Oxford, 1911.

Nadal, Augustin. Les Parodies du nouveau théâtre italien, 4 vols. Paris, 1738.

Naves, Raymond. Le Goût de Voltaire. Paris, 1938.

Nethercot, Arthur H. Sir William D'Avenant. Chicago, 1938.

Nicoll, Allardyce. A History of Restoration Drama, 1660–1700. Cambridge, Eng., 1923.

—— Dryden and His Poetry. London, 1923.

—— "Political Plays of the Restoration," Modern Language Review, XVI Nos. 3–4 (July–October, 1921), 224–42.

Nouvelliste du Parnasse, ou Réflexions sur les ouvrages nouveaux, by P.-F. Guyot Desfontaines and François Granet, 2 vols., Paris, 1734.

Observations sur les écrits modernes. ed. by P.-F. Desfontaines, François Granet, A. M. de Mairault, Jacques Destrées and E. C. Fréron. 25 vols. Paris, 1735–41.

Parsons, A. E. "The English Heroic Play," *The Modern Language Review,* XXXIII, No. 1 (January, 1938), 1–14.

Pemberton, John. Cato Examined. London, 1713.

Pendlebury, B. J. Dryden's Heroic Plays. London, 1923.

Peyre, Henri M. Le Classicisme français. New York, 1942.

Porée, Charles. An Oration in Which an Enquiry Is Made Whether the Stage Is, or Can Be Made a School for Forming the Mind to Virtue: and Proving the Superiority of Theatric Instruction over Those of History and Moral Philosophy; tr. by J. Lockman. London, 1734.

Prévost, Antoine François. Le Pour et contre. 20 vols. Paris, 1733–40.

Racine, Louis. "Réflexions sur l'Andromaque d'Euripide et sur l'Andromaque de Racine," in Mémoires de littérature, tirez des régistres de l'Académie Royale des inscriptions et Belles Lettres, X (1736), 311–22.

—— Remarques sur les tragédies de Jean Racine suivies d'un traité sur la poësie dramatique ancienne & moderne. 3 vols. Amsterdam and Paris, 1752.

Rapin, René. Les Œuvres du P. Rapin. 3 vols. Amsterdam, 1709.

—— Reflections on Aristotle's Treatise of Poesie: tr. with a preface by Thomas Rymer. London, 1674.

Ressler, Kathleen. "Jeremy Collier's Essays," Seventeenth Century Studies, second series, Princeton, 1937.

Riccoboni, Luigi. Historical and Critical Account of the Theatres in Europe. London, 1741.

Rigault, Hippolyte. Œuvres complètes. Vol. I. Paris, 1859.

Routh, Bernard. Lettres critiques sur le Paradis Perdu de Milton. Paris, 1731.

Rowe, Nicholas. Three Plays; ed. by J. R. Sutherland. London, 1929.

Rymer, Thomas. Edgar or the English Monarch. London, 1678.

—— A Short View of Tragedy. London, 1693.

—— The Tragedies of the Last Age. London, 1678.

Saint-Evremond, Charles de Marguetel de Saint-Denis, seigneur de. Saint-Evremond critique littéraire. Collection des chefs-d'œuvre méconnus, 44 vols. Vol. XXII. Paris, 1920–25.

Saintsbury, George. A History of English Criticism. Edinburgh and London, 1911.

—— Miscellaneous Essays. New York, 1892.

Sewell, George. Observations upon Cato. London, 1713.

Sheffield, John. The Works. London, 1726.

Sherwood, Merriam. Dryden's Dramatic Theory and Practice. Boston, 1899.

Smith, D. Nichol. Eighteenth Century Essays on Shakespeare. Glasgow, 1903.

Sonet, Edouard. Voltaire et l'influence anglaise. Rennes, 1926.

Spingarn, Joel E. Critical Essays of the Seventeenth Century. Oxford, 3 vols., 1908–9.

—— A History of Literary Criticism in the Renaissance. New York, 1899.

Steele, Richard. The Lucubrations of Isaac Bickerstaff, Esq. 4 vols. London, 1713.

Stephen, Leslie. Hobbes. New York, 1904.

—— English Literature and Society in the Eighteenth Century. London, 1904.

Swedenberg, Hugh Thomas. The Theory of the Epic in England, 1650–1800. University of California Press, 1944.

Taine, Hippolyte A. Histoire de la littérature anglaise. 5 vols. Paris, 1905.

Teeter, Louis. Political Themes in Restoration Comedy. 1936. Unpublished Johns Hopkins dissertation.

—— "The Dramatic Use of Hobbes's Political Ideas," *E L H; a Journal of English Literary History*, III, No. 2 (June, 1936), 140–69.

Telleen, John Martin. Milton dans la littérature française. Paris, 1904.

Texte, Joseph. "Béat Louis de Muralt et les origines du cosmopolitisme littéraire au dix-huitième siècle," *Revue d'histoire littéraire de la France*, I (1894), 8–26.

—— Jean-Jacques Rousseau et les origines du cosmopolitisme littéraire. Paris, 1895.

Throop, George R. "Epic and Dramatic as Revealed in Aristotle's Poetics," *Washington University Studies*, V (October, 1917), 1–32.

Tillyard, E. M. W. The Miltonic Setting. Cambridge, Eng., 1938.

Toinet, Raymond. Quelques recherches autour des poèmes héroïques-épiques français du dix-septième siècle. 2 vols. Tulle, 1899–1907.

Torrey, Norman L. Voltaire and the English Deists. New Haven, 1930.

—— The Spirit of Voltaire. New York, 1938.

—— Voltaire and the Enlightenment. New York, 1931.

—— "Voltaire's English Notebook," *Modern Philology*, XXVI, No. 3 (February, 1929), 307–25.

Torrey, Norman L., and George R. Havens. "Voltaire's Books: a Selected List," *Modern Philology*, XXVII, No. 1 (August, 1929), 1–22.

Van Doren, Mark. The Poetry of John Dryden. New York, 1920.

Van Tiegham, Paul. Outline of the Literary History of Europe since the Renaissance. New York, 1930.

Vaughan, Charles Edwyn. Types of Tragic Drama. London, 1908.

Vernier, Léon. Etude sur Voltaire grammairien et la grammaire au dix-huitième siècle. Paris, 1888.

Vial, Fernand. "Vauvenargues and Voltaire," *Romanic Review*, XXXIII, No. 1 (1942), 41–57.

Villemain, François. "Voltaire et la littérature anglaise de la Reine Anne," *Revue des deux mondes*, 4th ser. X (April, 1837), 59–93.

Villemain, François. Cours de littérature française; tableau de la littérature au XVIIᵉ siècle. 4 vols. Paris, 1859.

Vines, Sherard. The Course of English Classicism. New York, 1930.

Voltaire, François Marie Arouet de. Œuvres; ed. by Beuchot. 72 vols. Paris, Garnier, 1834–40.

—— Œuvres; 52 vols., ed. by Louis Moland. Garnier, Paris, 1877–85.

—— Candide; critical ed. by André Morize. Paris, 1931.

—— Voltaire's Essay on Epic Poetry; a Study and an Edition, by Florence D. White. Albany, 1915.

—— Lettres philosophiques; ed. by Gustave Lanson. 2 vols. Paris, 1917.

—— Sottisier, No. 183 in Library of Congress, Reproductions of Manuscript and Rare Printed Books, under the title Leningrad Publichnaia Biblioteca, Voltaire Manuscript 240, Vol. IX: Sottisier, with Various Manuscript Notes and Comments. 137 sheets.

Wade, Ira O. Voltaire and Madame du Châtelet. Princeton, 1941.

Ward, A. W. A History of English Dramatic Literature to the death of Queen Anne. 3 vols. London, New York, 1899.

Ward, Charles E. "Massinger and Dryden," E L H; a Journal of English Literary History, II, No. 3 (Nov., 1935), 263–66.

Wilcox, John. The Relation of Molière to Restoration Comedy. New York, 1938.

Wilmotte, Maurice. Le Français a la tête épique. Paris, 1917.

Wilson, John Harold. The Influence of Beaumont and Fletcher on Restoration Drama. Columbus, 1928. Ohio State University Studies.

Wollstein, Rose Heylbut. English Opinions of French Poetry, 1660–1750. New York, 1923.

Wood, Frederick T. "The Supernatural in Shakespearean Drama," Revue Anglo-Américaine, IX, No. 3 (February, 1932), 200–17.

Yart, Antoine. Idée de la poésie anglaise. 8 vols. Paris, 1749–71.

Yvon, Paul. Traits d'union normands avec l'Angleterre. Caen. 1919.

INDEX